Foreign
Correspondences

Foreign Correspondences

A TRAVELER'S TALES

Lesley Krueger

KEY PORTER BOOKS

Canadian Cataloguing in Publication Data

Krueger, Lesley
        Foreign correspondences : a traveler's tales

ISBN 1-55263-181-8

1. Krueger, Lesley – Journeys. 2. Krueger, Lesley – Family. 3. Authors, Canadian (English) – 20th century – Biography.* I. Title.

PS8571.R786Z53 2000   C813'.54   C00-931527-6
PR9199.3.K78Z47 2000

THE CANADA COUNCIL LE CONSEIL DES ARTS
    FOR THE ARTS   DU CANADA
    SINCE 1957   DEPUIS 1957

The publisher gratefully acknowledges the support of the Canada Council for the Arts and the Ontario Arts Council for its publishing program.

We acknowledge the financial support of the Government of Canada through the Book Publishing Industry Development Program (BPIDP) for our publishing activities.

Key Porter Books Limited
70 The Esplanade
Toronto, Ontario
Canada M5E 1R2

www.keyporter.com

Design: Peter Maher

Electronic formatting: Heidi Palfrey

Printed and bound in Canada

00 01 02 03 04 6 5 4 3 2 1

"He, who would bring home the wealth of the Indies,
must carry the wealth of the Indies with him."

——SPANISH PROVERB

For Paul and Gabe Knox

T R A V E L / T R A V A I L

THE FREAK BUS COURSED DOWN THE HIMALAYAS ON THE road out of Nepal. Inside we were swathed in the heaviest of air, dust blowing through the windows from the runneled brown mountains, smoke rising to the ceiling like desiccated mist. Weed smoke, cigarette smoke. This was supposed to be a four-day run from Kathmandu to New Delhi, overnight stops only, sold out from the start. But on the second morning, as we were about to leave the Nepali town of Pokhara, the freak bus manager wedged kitchen chairs in a line down the center aisle.

"It is all a mistake," he caroled. "Tickets have been sold unfortunately. Please to take your seats and we will proceed religiously on schedule."

A glassy-eyed stubborn scuffle for space broke out between the established travelers and Pokhara arrivals. I was already on board and guarded my window seat with the baleful tenacity of the mildly ill, sniffing from the remains of bronchitis and the start of another bout with dysentery. I'd celebrated my twenty-second birthday three months earlier during an ice fog in Sarajevo, migrating from café to café in the old Turkish quarter, drinking lemon tea in a diuretic effort to get warm. A ticket to Asia had taken care of the warmth. Breathing, however, was becoming a problem.

I shifted uncomfortably in my seat, burrowing my head in my shoulder to escape the smoke. At least it was a familiar species of discomfort. I'd been on the road for six months by then, traveling as cheaply as I could to stretch my savings around the globe. Lumpy bus seats, humid jitneys, hard train benches: I'd ridden them all, bumping along as if the ancient trains were horses.

My grandmother had ended one epic journey on horses, hitching a ride on the mailman's team and democrat when she'd arrived on the Prairies, a Swedish teenager immigrating to Canada. I was increasingly conscious that I came from generations of migrants and wanderers, not all of them willing. All four of my grandparents had immigrated to Canada before the First World War, and almost all of the members of my father's generation had battered around the globe in the Canadian Forces during the Second. Or at least, they'd been battered by it. My father, the busted-down sergeant, came home traumatized and limping, while one of my uncles was liberated from Thailand, where he'd been a prisoner of war.

What made us travel? It wasn't just an idle freak bus question—what the hell am I doing here?—although I began asking myself that, as well. My temperature was rising and my innards churned as we switchbacked down the Himalayas. But I also wondered what had made me cast myself away from home on such an immensely long trip. I'd traveled before, heading down to Mexico a couple of times on my own, a teenager on the loose from her parents. The Maritimes, the Prairies: I'd taken off whenever I could. Now I had an inkling that I'd keep doing this, that people kept doing this, moving restlessly and passionately toward something, or away from it, and for the first time, I alighted feverishly on the puzzle that soon preoccupied me, the question of why.

One of the passengers on the freak bus was a teacher, a Tibetan lama. He was a middle-aged man surrounded by acolytes, one of whom spoke excellent English and told me about the teacher's powers. They sat a bit behind me, the five young men in saffron robes and the teacher in muted scarlet. He was everything that I believed a Tibetan lama should be, alert and limber, wearing horn-rimmed glasses and bald as a speckled brown egg. He giggled like a boy at every adventure—the chairs in the aisle, another flat tire. When a Stones song thumped over the speakers, he played an air guitar, yodeling "ya, ya, ya" until he was bent double laughing. The teacher seemed so simple that I thought he must be infinitely complex, and wondered if he might have an answer to my question. He was astute, reflective: a living Zen koan, peeling an orange in an overloaded freak bus rocking down the Himalayas toward the Indian plains.

Yet there was no opportunity to talk to him in the noisy crowd. The bus was bursting with a miscellaneous collection of travelers, backpackers, kids from all over, Europe and Australia and the US, many of them students, others drugged-out hippies, their faces wiped clean of everything but dust. Myself, I was a backpacker, traveling the region with Canadian journalist friends who were half working, half on vacation, and stretching their budgets by taking the bus. One of them was chatting with a blond Australian woman across the aisle, and I began to eavesdrop when she said that she'd just graduated from medical school. Given my fever, which was getting worse, I leaned over and tried to cadge some free advice.

"Stop eating," she said. The freak bus ethos had been quickly established as anti-corporeal, modulating at times into self-disgust. There was also a Swiss woman with rebarbative elbows grumbling from her chair in the aisle, a doleful engineering student from California who kept pestering the driver—"Can't we hear some American music?"—and a tall, weedy, brackish drink of water named John in an outback hat and Mexican serape who sometimes said he was English, sometimes Australian. He made a point of sleeping on the bus, conserving his dollar-a-day budget and sneering at those of us who'd shared a hotel room for forty-seven cents each in Pokhara.

"Was the experience relaxing?" he asked the next morning. "Were the servants obedient and suitably obsequious?"

The Tibetan monks were a quieter bunch, and I could see that part of their dignity came from the unassuming purpose of their trip. They had to get from one place to another and the freak bus was the best way to do it. Other people's motives were much more complex, at least the ones I heard about. One of my friends was trying to write about India, filing reports to his Canadian newspaper about the national election campaign, in which Indira Gandhi was seeking reelection as prime minister. Many other passengers said that they were on a spiritual pilgrimage, visiting babas and yogic masters and retreats to find peace, sometimes testing themselves through great hardship, spending weeks, even months in silent meditation, or maybe tending the terminally ill at Mother Teresa's hospice in Calcutta. But I was just tagging along with my friends, saying that I wanted to *see*, even if I didn't know what or why.

On our second night, we stayed at the Hotel Yark in Gorakhpur, across the border in India. Some of us rented rooms, others shared the empty cafeteria for two rupees each, about eighteen cents the night. John slept in the bus again, but not before telling us that he rode the trains. He'd done the TransSiberian twice, ridden China top to bottom. India, he said, had the fourth largest train system in the world, and since the Emergency—then in force—the trains had run on time. It was hard to tell if this pleased him or he spoke ironically. Probably both.

"The point is to be a traveler," he said. "This way I experience the real India. You're just tourists."

Outside the Hotel Yark was a sign:

Philosophy on Life

Life is a challenge meet it. Life is a struggle accept it.
Life is a tragedy face it. Life is an adventure dare it.
Life is a fraud beware of it. Life is a duty perform it.
Life is a game play it. Life is a song sing it.
Life is a love enjoy it. Life is a beauty worship it.
Life is a journey complete it.

Remember in your life
Hotel Yark
Sapna Restaurant

The next day we rattled across the grain fields of northern India. By this time, the countryside seemed dismally crowded. Listless people streamed over the highway. They hunkered in the doorways of inadequate huts—the walls of mud and roofs of straw like hovels in some punitive fairy tale. We chuffed past a cyclist in a diesel cloud clinging to the back of a speeding truck, past a funeral cortège carrying a young man's corpse on a bamboo platform, his poor toes splayed. Not enough food, I thought, feeling morally and physically ill. Soon I was battling a high fever and felt as if the sun was beating down on the back of my neck no matter which direction I turned. As beggars reached up to the bus windows, I tossed around uncomfortably, sweating, parched, growing frantic with diarrhea.

"Bathroom break!" someone called, and I jostled between the kitchen chairs in a confused rush for the door. Stepping unsteadily onto the ground, I found myself part of a group of ill foreigners milling around outside. With no latrines in sight, three or four of us finally spaced ourselves behind the roadside bushes. At the next stop there were more of us; next time, even more. Finally I had to scuttle far up the road before I was able to squat, shaking with relief, only to see the village children filtering out of the fields. They hunkered down to watch a short distance away, pointing at me and conferring. I gave in to India and shat.

"Let's have some American music!"

The bus blew another tire. Slowly, we tilted westward.

That afternoon we reached Lucknow, part of Indira Gandhi's home riding. My head was aching by this time, and the waves of hot air coming off the parched earth seemed to splinter and pierce my eyes. At sunset we passed an industrial town with a blank-faced munitions factory that unreeled endlessly along the highway, menacing and barred. Soon afterward we had a rest stop, pulling up at a roadside stall where they served cinnamon tea in rough clay cups. Drinking that tea meant grit chafing lips and the suave flow of water. When you finished, you threw the cup onto the ground so it broke with a mutter. Usually I loved that tea, loved even the joke of symbolic sanitation. Breaking the cups guaranteed you'd never drink from a used cup, but I'd got my dysentery from something like the water they used. Shifting feverishly in my seat, I didn't find the joke all that funny any more.

The bus emptied out around me. I stayed inside, too sick to move, sprawling across the empty seat beside me, sweating, clammy, feeling as if the sun still burned into the back of my neck long past dark. I couldn't remember when I'd been so ill, and I felt thankful at least to be alone. Then I realized that I wasn't alone. The teacher was sitting across the aisle in the row behind me. Turning around, I met his eye, and made what I hoped was a wry face at my own illness and absurdity. He stared at me and through me, and I fell immediately asleep.

When I awoke an hour later, I was well, and the monks were gone.

A little unfair that this happened to me, isn't it? I wasn't one of the spiritual seekers on a quest for revelation or redemption. At least, I don't think I was. I don't think that's why I was traveling, or why I've kept traveling. I took off to so many places after that trip—to Japan and Brazil, to Rigolet, up the Labrador coast, to Trochu, Alberta, where my Swedish great-grandparents homesteaded when they first got to Canada.

Maybe it really is time to figure out why.

2

SOME PEOPLE SAY THAT WE DISPLACE OURSELVES NOT TO find what we're looking for, but to find out what we're looking for. Whatever the reason, it's clearly visceral. We say that we push off, hit the road, pull up roots, take off. Hit, pull, take, push— potent verbs, gut expressions.

Birth is like that, a push from the gut. Fascinating, when you consider the New World obsession with being born again.

There's also a German expression I've been thinking about lately, *ein bewegtes Leben*, a hard-traveled life, which I've seen beautifully translated as a life of both travel and travail.

3

I DIDN'T TRAVEL MUCH AS A CHILD. MY FATHER WAS A machinist and had only two weeks' holiday a year. We lived in suburban Vancouver and sometimes strapped a roof rack on the car to go camping in the Interior of BC. I especially remember the time when we spent a week in a family motel on Osoyoos Lake. The lake was shallow, with minnows darting like freed shadows above the golden ridges of sand. I spent my days catching minnows in an empty mayonnaise jar and letting them go, murmuring stories about their adventures and singing breathy little songs.

One morning my father made toast, something that he never did at home. The motel room kitchen had an old drop-sided toaster, filigreed steel with glowing elements inside. My father wedged thick slices of bread against the elements, toasting them until they were slightly charred before laying on thick slabs of butter straight from the fridge. When he handed me a slice, biting into hot and cold was like eating the summer breeze.

My father was a tall man, but stooped and brooding after five years overseas as a Canadian soldier during the Second World War. This was a person who always said that he never slept well outside his own bed, and in retrospect, I can't help noticing that the only trips he really liked to take were to the Interior. He said that he wanted to retire to the Interior. Such an inward-looking man. I hardly knew him, in the way that you hardly know your father, but when I look back on my travels, he's everywhere, both motivation and mystery. I have to get away from him, I'd think. Get away from what?

I never did. I look in the mirror and there he is. I have his hazel eyes exactly, and so does my son. Which is a hell of a thing to look down on when you're breast-feeding.

One year, my father drove us across the Rockies in a pink Cadillac, a chromium-plated beast borrowed from my aunt, who owned The House of Beauty. My brother and I were in the back seat, leaning against pillows. We could roll the windows up and down with automatic buttons, although not too often or we'd be told to stop. The first night we made it to the foothills and stayed in a room with knotty-pine walls and a fireplace made of river stones.

I awoke very early the next morning and went outside to walk in a mountain meadow. Just inside the nearby forest, a pale slash interrupted the trees. It was a doe, watching me as I watched her. I raised my hand slowly, and even more slowly walked toward her, trying to flow across the meadow like a cat hunting birds. The doe hunched her shoulders, inclining away from me. But she didn't run, and when I'd almost reached her, knock-kneed she moved toward me, nostrils wide. For an instant she nuzzled my palm, breathing cool humidity. Then she kicked her legs and was gone.

"Guess what I saw?" I cried, running into the motel room.

"Did you?" my father asked, and I still remember the rich doubt in his voice as clearly as I remember the doe, so that I don't really know any more whether I'd been telling the truth or not.

We were on our way to Edmonton that time, planning to visit my father's mother, my Swedish Granny. She had a smoker's harshly lined face and a slow deep laugh that ended in a cough.

Her hair was pulled into a scant charcoal-colored bun, and she wore an old lady's flowered dresses, the back zippers forced out in a taut arc by her painful spinal curvature. We went there fairly often, and a couple of times when we were walking down the street some neighborhood children threw stones at us.

"Dirty Swedes! Dirty Swedes!"

But I liked going there because my Granny was indulgent and gambled. We'd sit at the kitchen table while she shuffled an old deck of cards with her nicotine-ripened fingers. Usually we played gin rummy for pennies, her pennies kept in a brown cup without a handle and thrown good-humoredly across the table. Sometimes we went to the races and she put two bucks on a horse for me, cigarette stuck in the corner of her mouth, racing form held in one armpit. I breathed quickly, pumped by the acrid stench of sawdust, horse piss and adrenaline. My knees felt itchy as the horses thudded down the track, sounding like a landslide in a forest.

My poor Granny. I learned later that she was a reluctant immigrant, one of the many travelers in my family who would have preferred to stay home. There was also my mother's mother, my Scottish grandmother. We visited her one summer, too, driving all the way to Ontario, putting in sixteen-hour days on the road so we could make it there and back in a couple of weeks.

My grandmother still lived in the town where her husband had been bank manager, although as a widow she often returned to the Old Country to nurse her maiden sisters, sometimes for a year at a time. Her Ontario town was built on rolling granite hills: the Canadian Shield surfacing like a pod of whales. When we finally drove in, I felt seasick riding up and down, and left the car staggering on a sailor's legs.

We didn't stay with my grandmother but with my mother's brother, the former prisoner of war. He'd been an air force officer shot down over Thailand during the Second World War, and when he returned home, they gave him a parade. At least, that's what I thought someone said, although I was more interested in raiding the raspberry canes in my uncle's big backyard than in listening to family history. Or maybe I was trying to hide from family history between the rows of canes.

It didn't work. My grandmother's lectures carried into the yard, especially after she and my father started fighting, as they always did. Her back had never touched the back of a chair. They'd had sixteen servants in the big house near Oldmeldrum. The servants never had names, but the house did. Coutens.

Look what it had come to. A generation later, my mother had married a man so far beneath her that she shouldn't even have been able to see him.

"What am I doing here?" my grandmother cried. "Oh me, I should never have left home."

But we all kept doing that, again and again and again.

4

NOT LONG AGO, I WAS TALKING ALL THIS OVER WITH A friend. We were sitting outdoors at a Greek restaurant on the Danforth in Toronto. Children at school, *melitzanosalata* on the table. We were left to womantalk, personal and spiraling.

Enjoying the scene, the noise, the plate of dip, we ended up cheerfully agreeing that I was pretty ordinary. Everyone eventually grapples with the realization that they've spent most of their adult lives repeating themselves, circling around the same subjects, the same obsessions, the same type of people—friends—men—and decides that the time has come to figure out why.

I told my friend about my journals, the fact I'd been rereading them, often for the first time. In some cases, I didn't have any memory at all of doing the things I wrote about or meeting the people I described. That kind man who helped me find a hotel in Sarajevo? I can't picture him at all, although I still remember the stinging hot tea and the cold sheath of fog that I was escaping. At other times, whole days come back—a long walk through apricot incense at temples in Japan, the purple welts of skin disease on children's arms at a shantytown in Rio.

"You were educating your senses," my friend replied.

Travel as education. The school of travel. (Schools of minnows flashing through the water of Osoyoos Lake, gliding, diving, twisting back.) That felt right, fitting people who didn't write, as well. It also fit rather nicely into the North American obsession with self-improvement, self-education, self-creation—although it left me considering the much more difficult question of what I'd learned, not to mention how.

5

THAT FIRST ASIAN TRIP STARTED WHEN I FLEW INTO THAILAND to visit some expatriate friends. Sherry and Paul were journalists who had worked in England and Australia before trying their luck in Bangkok. Now they were moving on, and I was planning to join their farewell wander through Asia. Sherry had promised trains, planes and riverboats, freak buses and inner tubes. One of their foreign friends ran a model farm bordering a river, and he'd drive us upstream with an inner tube we could throw in and use to ride the current back down. This was the River Kwai where, I seemed to remember, my uncle had been a prisoner of war.

I bought my ticket having only the haziest ideas about my uncle's imprisonment, or for that matter, Thailand. It was a three-month return ticket, London-Bangkok, Sherry's letter of invitation having reached me as I was backpacking around Europe a bit more than a year after university. Thailand sounded pretty good after the ice fogs of Sarajevo, if somewhat less worthy than the Israeli kibbutz I could have visited with some people I'd met. We were all out on our Grand Tour, our *Wanderjahr*—a real disjunction for the daughter of a machinist who didn't like to sleep outside his own bed.

Stepping off the airplane in Bangkok, I got my heat, so dense with diesel and humidity it almost pushed me back on the plane. But I knew Sherry and Paul would be waiting outside customs, and got my passport stamped, shouldered my one small bag. When the customs doors opened, it was hard to miss Sherry, with the nimbus of wiry red hair that gave her a Thai nickname, Mee Grob, after a kind of spicy noodle. Paul stood behind her, smiling, rocking on his heels.

"Front seat or back?" Sherry asked. "It depends on whether you can take the traffic."

I was too jet-lagged to care, hoping only to get a breath of air. But that didn't take account of the trucks or the canals, dark ditches of weedy-looking water we ran past on narrow, potholed, fast-paced roads. The miasma made me cough—stinking sewage and rotten greens and billows of evil-looking gritty black fumes from the trucks that were chasing us, none of which showed any signs of having brakes. With the trucks bearing down in the rear-view mirror, Paul wove around overloaded buses and bicyclists and bullock carts. There was no air and the damp fumes congealed on my arms. Sherry gave me a shrewd glance.

"In any case," she said, "we have to go up north. I have to do a magazine piece." After that, she said we'd visit Nepal and India before circling back to Bangkok. Sherry had an itinerary already planned, a schedule cooked up from our wish lists. We'd visit the River Kwai after returning to Bangkok, she said.

Feeling that I had to say something, I asked whether anyone had put a marker where the Allied prisoners of war had blown up the famous bridge, the one they'd constructed as slave laborers for the Japanese army. I'd seen the movie on late-night TV, *The Bridge on the River Kwai*. Paul giggled.

"There's a bridge where they take tourists," he said, "a railway bridge near Kanchanaburi. The guides call it a reconstruction. But the movie is based on a novel. The prisoners built plenty of bridges, but they never had a chance to blow up anything."

"The suffering was real enough," Sherry said. "You could say that they're honoring that."

"Or you could look at it this way. The bridge isn't a reconstruction of something that no one ever blew up, but it might be one of the bridges the prisoners actually built. The tourists could be honoring an authentic monument under the impression that it's fake. They think it's a metaphor, but it's real." Paul giggled again. He was a Buddhist and liked muddles.

"Water buffalo," Sherry told me, pointing out the window at the humped back.

Years later, I learned that my uncle had never been held at any of the prisoner-of-war camps along the Kwai River. His story was singular and strange. Well, so is everybody's. But already in that weaving car I felt unmoored, and between that and heat and jet lag, I couldn't bring the landscape into focus. You seemed to need a bridge into it. Lacking one, I kept failing to connect with anything in Bangkok, tripping on cracks in the sidewalk, biting into chilies so fiery I couldn't taste the rest of the meal, finding I was so much taller than almost every living Thai that I was given a street nickname.

"Elephant. Come and see the elephant," children cried. By the time we boarded the train to Chiang Mai for Sherry's assignment, I stowed my bag praying that in a smaller place, I would find some way to connect.

Yet the north left me feeling even more vulnerable and porous, pierced by light so clear it vibrated. We were high in the mountains. Waist-deep in a drowsy field of poppies, opium poppies, their flowers crinkled like crepe paper, like old skin, pastel-colored, cupped like hands, nodding toward the light as I shrank from it. Sherry crouched nearby, photographing the opium sap as it eased out of a poppy hip cut open by a farmer. The farmer mimed for us how he cut the ripe hips three times with his three-bladed knife, collecting the sap a few hours later in a leather pouch, which he would sell to an itinerant buyer. Sherry was doing a magazine piece about a United Nations attempt to persuade farmers to join a crop replacement program. We'd hitched a ride on a UN jeep a couple of hours after reaching Chiang Mai, jouncing up into the mountains to visit fields like this one, some still growing poppies, others producing replacement crops, lentils and plums.

Away from the capital, I'd been expecting to see a stable, rooted society. But I grew increasingly confused as we met expatriates from a different set of places. Or from no-places. The opium farmer turned out to be ethnically Meo, a member of a formerly migratory group now resettled into sketchy villages like the one behind us. People there still dressed as colorfully as cardinals, flitting between bamboo houses raised on stilts. The children in the one-room school had a hard time chanting the unfamiliar Thai intonations and seemed uncertain as I did when they filed past us at recess, the girls holding their hands in front of their faces while the little boys bowed.

Later, back in Chiang Mai, we lunched on a type of sweet white fish native to Japan that had been introduced locally through the crop replacement program. As we ate, our guide pushed his fish around his plate and told us that he'd originally held Taiwanese and Laotian passports, but he'd had to renounce his Taiwanese citizenship when going to work for the UN, and had subsequently lost his Laotian passport during the communist takeover. When his Thai work permit expired, he said, touching my heart, he would officially come from nowhere and have no place to go.

Over the next week, we visited many hill tribes, temples and villages of Chinese Kuomintang supporters, exiles from Mao's China. We took riverboats, as Sherry had promised: dugout canoes powered by smelly outboards. Quite often, they leaked. Yet one ended up taking us to the village of Ban Mai, which impressed me so profoundly with its well-rooted dislocation that only a day after arriving, I climbed the ladder into our raised bamboo house and started writing a short story, imposing an elaborate plot on the napping community.

Ban Mai was a village of Shan exiles from Burma, four miles away, where Shan State Army was fighting a guerrilla war against the military government, trying to regain control of its traditional territory, and meanwhile taxing caravans of heroin traders passing by. It was laid out in a neat military grid, its dirt pathways kept swept, the houses bare and clean. Chickens pecked underneath our house, and there was a winsome smell of cooking pumpkin and tropical fruit, which the headman's wife was preparing, kneeling, across the way. We were in town for the Shan national day celebrations, and as I wrote, a helicopter stuttered closer. Sherry put her head inside and told me a Thai prince was arriving for the celebrations, the same prince we had met earlier at the royal agricultural station, a sinuous man, great-grandson of the revered King Mongkut—the one from *The King and I*—who wore five knotted threads of rank around one wrist.

We walked out to meet the prince, who was getting out of the helicopter as we arrived. With him this time was a young man he introduced as his nephew, a beautiful Eurasian named Arthur who looked as if he'd wandered out of one of Gauguin's Tahitian paintings. The town headman said something lengthy to the prince, who answered with a quick upward movement of one hand. He looked bored and invited us back to the headman's house, where he would wait for the celebrations to start. The prince settled onto the floor, his eyes very dark, and answered Paul's polite questions about Southeast Asian politics. His English was a fluid march of well-rehearsed aphorisms.

"The Shans are Buddhist and will stay so, they say, until the Buddha returns as a Burmese."

"Democracy is a French concept and travels no better than their best wines."

Behind his back, Arthur held up a large bag of dope and gestured for us to join him outside.

Soon it was dark, and we walked with the prince up to the temple on the hill, which seemed to be the social center of the village. Inside, people gossiped and ate, while monks sat on pallets along the wall. Outside, the national celebration was getting casually underway. Women danced like stylized birds, the men like warriors, as meanwhile a technician tried to hook up a loudspeaker which sometimes blared snatches of static. An impromptu cinema set up nearby played a black-and-white American film from the fifties, the reels out of order. Occasionally the film was interrupted by a Thai anti-drug commercial, during which the prince stood beside the screen with his arms crossed. A man sang onstage, reedy notes rising through the cooling air. Then the loudspeaker caught and we were listening to the Doobie Brothers.

What am I doing here?

My grandmother's question. Sitting there, I felt lost and stupid, nothing but a clumsy foreigner. I didn't know where *here* was, or even who *I* was. I'd always thought I was a bit brighter than this, a bit more intuitive. But even though I hated seeing myself in this light, I didn't want to leave. Unlike my grandmother, I didn't want to go home, and I sat on the hillside, chilly and misplaced and mesmerized, until everyone suddenly left.

6

I'D WORKED AS AN EDUCATION REPORTER AT *THE VANCOUVER Sun* for a year before taking off on my backpacking trip. That's what financed my travels. Writing about education often did. I'm not sure why most journalists don't like the education beat, but it was lucky for me that they didn't, since I could get back from a trip and pick up work quite easily. I also thought that it was a crucial area, even before I had my son.

Maybe that's why I was so quick to accept my friend's theory that day on the Danforth about the educational slant of travel. It was an echo, a repetition of something that I'd often thought about, and repetition is so comforting, so musical; music itself both deliberately made and meaningful. It would be a comfort to think that I'd found some meaning in my travels, that I'd managed to learn something. But of course, you can easily impose a pattern on random events. A Tibetan lama happens to look in your direction just before you fall asleep. In sleeping, you recover from a minor illness. I didn't like to think so. But.

7

ONE THING I LEARNED ON THAT BACKPACKING TRIP WAS THE first part of my Swedish Granny's story. Between Sarajevo and Thailand, I spent three weeks in Sweden with my Sten relatives, starting with my father's cousin Edit and her husband Eric in the southern city of Lund. Edit and Eric were jolly hospitable people, two broad short fireplugs who seemed to like to see me eat. "All this is for you," they said, pointing to a table lavish with smoked salmon, ham and *lutefisk*, with pancakes and lingonberries. It took me far too long to learn they would always ask three times if I wanted an extra helping, and it wasn't rude to turn them down all three times. In Canada, I realized, we can only turn food down twice. By that time I was a balloon, rolling through the cousins' flats, through living rooms cheery with pine and books. Lamps were lit, candles burning. Winter light fell as dim as rain through the clean square windows.

One day Edit sat me down at the kitchen table and brought out an old tin biscuit box bound by a red elastic band. The first thing she pulled out was a bill of sale from a shipping agent for passage on the *Titanic*. This didn't register at first. How could we be connected to anything so dramatic? Yet there it was: Her mother, my grandmother's sister Hilda, was booked to sail from Malmö to Southampton with her brother Johan, and after that, they were scheduled to board the *Titanic*. Edit told me that Hilda was being sent to the United States to marry my grandfather, her first cousin.

"She wouldn't go," Edit said. Her English was prim and halting, my Swedish out of a phrase book. We added nuance to our conversations through shrugs, grimaces, eye-rolls. She said that Hilda had agreed to the marriage at first but changed her mind, putting up a stubborn fight to stay and marry the man she wanted. Finally the family decided that my grandmother, Ida, would go instead, although by then she and Johan had missed the *Titanic*. Edit let me touch the creamy bill of sale, then folded it neatly along the old creases and put it back in the biscuit box. If my grandmother had sailed, she would have gone steerage and likely never have arrived.

On the wall behind the door were several rows of family pictures. We got up to look at an old portrait photograph of Hilda. Years before, I'd found a photo in my father's trunk of my grandmother as an exquisite young girl. Her thick hair and lips were lush against her narrowed eyes. Hilda was recognizably Ida's sister but somewhat blunter in the face, and apparently quite watchful. As I tried to read her, Edit told me that her daughter had said that if she was going to hang the pictures, she shouldn't put them behind a door. "But I said they're mostly dead now, so what does it matter?"

She sat me back down and brought out a bundle of letters written on thin blue paper. To my surprise, Edit said they were letters my grandmother had written to her sisters up to the time of her death a year before. My grandmother's English was so rudimentary that I had thought of her as barely literate, yet the letters were in a beautiful hand, and Edit said that they were fluidly written. "I only have time to write a few lines today," my grandmother said, "but send my love to you all." After describing a birthday party, she added, "You still think of me as the girl who left, but I'm far from a girl now." In one letter, written in the early fifties, after a gap, she said that her three sons had settled down well after the Second World War. The oldest was a barber married to a smart ladies' hairdresser, the second a university-educated chemist who had recently bought and renovated a large old house. The youngest, my father, was building his house himself. "I don't know the cost, although it must be about 10,000 *kroner*. Things are going well for all three of them. I'm so glad my boys don't have to work as hard as we did."

Running through all the letters we read, starting from her first, in 1916, was her wish to return home for a visit. It was always "home," and there was always a problem. "Rune isn't very well," she wrote of her husband. "It's something in his chest. He doesn't remember the old language, but he wants to come for a visit too, when his chest is better." My grandfather died broke in his late sixties, and after that there were other difficulties, mainly financial. Finally we reached the longest letter, written not to one of my grandmother's sisters, but to Edit's daughter, Ingrid. Ingrid was thinking of emigrating to Canada and wanted my grandmother's advice.

"Don't come," my Granny said. "It's terrible for women here. The men have jobs, taking them out into the community. Even the ones who don't speak much English when they arrive can learn it pretty quickly. But women are trapped in the house all day with the children. No one to talk to, especially in one's own language. You think you'll be independent, get a job, but you'll end up married and trapped in the house. The isolation is terrible. Don't leave your own country. Stay home."

I didn't have a chance to tell my parents about the letters until a few years later. By the time I did, I'd been on my own for long enough to be a guest in their house, and my mother served a roast beef dinner formally in the dining room. As I talked, my father looked down at the good china, and afterward he stayed silent for a long time.

"They made her go," he said finally. "She'd never told anyone, but I had to look at some papers for her. She said, 'Clarence, you'll find that Walter isn't Poppy's.'" My oldest uncle was not my grandfather's son.

"This isn't very nice," my mother said.

"She was raped," my father told me. "She was raped and got pregnant, back in the Old Country, and they made her go. She was sixteen."

"I always liked Pops," my mother said. "He was a good man. And he worshipped Granny."

What you learned, I thought, and the indirection you learned it from. No wonder the best trips were the ones that didn't go as planned.

8

WE GOT OFF THE FREAK BUS EARLY, IN AGRA, PLANNING TO visit the Taj Mahal and catch a speech by Indira Gandhi. Two monuments, both female. My guidebook told me that "Taj Mahal"

means "crown of the palace," title of the favorite wife of Shah Jahan, whose tomb it is. As for Gandhi, she was fighting a federal election after ten years in office. For the past two years, she'd exercised dictatorial powers during the Emergency, which she'd declared a couple of weeks after she was convicted of electoral malpractices and banned from politics for seven years. Now she and her Congress Party were being challenged by a coalition, the Janata Party. We heard she was holding an election rally in Agra and decided to go.

By this time we'd been joined by a friend from Canada who was filing reports on the election for his Vancouver newspaper. Rod had arrived in Bangkok a few days after we'd returned from the north, and we flew out to Calcutta not long after, making our way up the Himalayas to Darjeeling, crossing into Nepal, and taking the freak bus back toward New Delhi. It was all very complicated and sometimes fraught, trying to get at least four or five people organized and on time, but Rod kept his wallet crammed with cut-out newspaper headlines, absurdities he could produce at unfortunate moments. "Dead boy ate bark, leaves." "Cancer kills Mr. Funny."

After days on that suffocating freak bus—and far too many headlines—I felt glad to walk through a passageway into the grounds of the Taj Mahal. From the end of the passage, I could see women in saris of all colors calling to each other in bright high voices across the formal gardens. They glittered and pattered on their high heels, making the grounds seem blithe and, in the old-fashioned sense, sweetly gay. The famous reflecting pool shimmered at their busy feet, catching an oblong of pure blue sky, while the monument itself glowed like a billowing cloud in summer. It was pristine, transcendent; as limpid as the wrist of a Michelangelo Pietà. As I moved closer, I saw the tomb was twined with floral inlays, while the marble burned with the translucence of eyes. Such depth! I sat inside the vaulted chamber for as long as they'd let me, listening to the tour guides crying, showing the echo, their dire wails magnified before ebbing and flowing peacefully away.

Indira Gandhi's rally was held at sunset outside Agra's Red Fort. It was a common tourist destination, yet when we hailed a bicycle rickshaw, we were surprised to find that the driver wouldn't take us.

"Indira Gandhi," he said, and spat in the dust. Other drivers set absurdly high prices; it was clear that they didn't want to go, either. The one who finally took us said, "Dangerous, dangerous," as he let us off at the top of a hill and quickly pedaled away.

Sherry wasn't with us. I was the only woman in sight, although there was an unimaginable number of men cresting the darkening hills and flowing onto the measureless field below. Tens, even hundreds of thousands of them. It was a wide-screen extravaganza, a raucous battle scene out of some great thumping Hollywood epic—classic era, over budget, historical importance guaranteed. The organizers had erected bamboo barriers to channel people into sections, each divided from the other, all overseen by soldiers standing on raised platforms, shouting and waving sticks. We joined a stream of people pouring down the hill, jostling forward until we reached a barrier a soldier wouldn't let us past. Near there we found a mat to sit on and were immediately surrounded by men, staring and pointing. One wanted to talk. This was Indira Gandhi, this was Congress Party. A cross old man leaned in front of him and bellowed something our talkative friend translated as an indictment of our powers of distraction. Our friend laughed too loudly and told us he was with a bank. Mrs. Gandhi was a nice lady, he insisted, her son Sanjay a very good man. The Emergency was also good. It gave land to the farmers, and India was ninety percent farmers.

Paul did most of the talking. I only listened. Then Paul made a mistake. I wasn't his wife, he said, only a friend. Men giggled.

From then on, they giggled every time I stirred. It was an odd sound, high-pitched. I wasn't used to it. Soon Paul was called away to the edge of the crowd and came back looking firm.

"We have been advised to leave and we are leaving, now."

As we walked away, he told me that the man who'd spoken to him wasn't threatening, but panicked about my presence there. "It is dangerous. It is the lady. You don't know people in Agra. Please, *please* leave." We pushed back between the bamboo railings against the tide, and this time I was grabbed and fondled as we moved along. The mood was gross, the men exhilarated, titillated, as if they were fearful of what they might be forced to do to me.

We retreated, bruised, to stand among the bicyclists and rick-shaw drivers at the top of a hill, looking down at the restless mass below. From there it seemed immeasurable and it was still grow-ing. People streamed past us down every possible path. Lightbulbs blinked on above them, but even when it got very dark they only glowed faintly, obscured by a haze that seemed to rise from the thousands upon thousands of shifting humid bodies. In the back-ground, we could see a faint lit outline of the Red Fort, and even-tually a man's exhortations rose from a stage in front of it.

"Indira Gandhi. Nehru. Mahatma Gandhi," he repeated in crescendo. Finally there was a huge muted roar. But it trailed off raggedly as a woman started speaking. This was an anticlimax. The crowd buzzed restively, and people around me gossiped and fixed their bicycles, paying little attention. I thought the woman onstage must be a local candidate preparing the way for Mrs. Gandhi. But she went on too long, and finally I asked a boy beside me if the tiny figure we could barely see below might be the prime minister. He said it was.

"She will lecture for thirty minutes," he told me. But before she had got fifteen minutes into her speech, the crowd that was flowing ceaselessly onto the field reversed itself and started flowing off. There was no discernible break, and no foreseeable end to it. From the stage I heard one clear word, "Unity." The rest was an undifferentiated female murmur above the inattentive crowd.

I wasn't really scared that evening. Maybe I should have been. Maybe I was becoming inured. By that time I'd learned that being a woman traveling in India—a young woman traveling almost any-where—meant becoming not quite a sex symbol, but at least a symbol of sex. Female prime minister or no, I was sniggered over, pawed at and propositioned before and after Agra, running the gauntlet as we made a great looping journey around the subconti-nent, traveling back and forth to New Delhi, down to Bombay, cross-country to Varanasi and back to Calcutta for a final plane east.

Mainly I had a lucky, happy and privileged time. Sherry's grandfather was an English peer with investments in India, and she'd sometimes gone with him on business trips. Many of the friends she'd made invited us into their homes and offices, or took us to restaurants that we'd never have found ourselves. We talked election with superbly educated, influential women, socialist socialites, Fabians luxuriant with jewels. We found our way into Janata Party headquarters: a few small rooms with sluggish Teletypes. And we made it to the tourist spots, riding an elephant for a day through Corbett National Park, the sun shining through the pink freckled edges of her ears as she trod down herbs in the forest, raising a smell like basil as she moved each great foot inde-pendently forward, and we rolled one-two-three-four, one-two-three-four as if held in a conductor's hand.

But there was also the night we stayed in Jhansi, a clean town near a military base. I read late but finally turned out the light in my hotel room, and someone started scratching at the door.

"Madam, madam, let me in."

"Who is it?"

"It is I, madam. Let me in. I want to spend the night with you."

"No. Go away."

"But madam, why can't we spend the night together? No one would have to know. Let's spend the night together. Remember, we met at the desk this afternoon? I am the one in the white and brown shoes."

Wrong to laugh. He turned threatening, pushing against the tenuous door until I had to call in Rod and Paul.

And what about the man on the overnight train from Varanasi to Calcutta, booked into a four-berth compartment with the three of us then traveling? The man protested that he was Muslim, a state counselor, and didn't wish to share a compartment with women. The conductor explained that he could change to second class, but the man refused. In the middle of the night I heard him clear his throat and looked across at the other upper berth to see him masturbating.

The joke was, most of the young women traveling as I was then were really quite chaste. It would eventually come out in conversation that they, we, were tied up with someone at home, and most of the ones I kept up with married not long after they returned. A few women were much bolder, profligate with themselves—and good for them. I don't think the way they behaved, or misbehaved, had much to do with the way the rest of us were treated. Much more important, at least to the men, was the fact we were unsupervised. Our jeans and cotton dresses were unreadable and unsettling, and from a local perspective, we were gallingly spendthrift. We got what we wanted when we wanted it, and our self-indulgence resonated with sex. At least it seemed to in men's minds, given the way they defined "indulgence." And so we became symbols of sex. My life as a sex symbol. What a laugh. It had so little to do with reality that I couldn't take it seriously, which was probably the reason men's behavior didn't usually frighten me. It was too impersonal, too reflexive. We were symbols, and the response, ritual.

Ritual can incite, of course, and symbolic thinking be used to depersonalize victims. This gave traveling an edge. You never knew what could happen. What a kick: *Anything* could happen. No wonder I loved to travel.

"You were educating your senses," my friend said.

"But there's still the question of what happened," I said. "Whether I actually learned anything."

"You tell me," she replied.

9

WHAT HAPPENED IN INDIA, THAT TIME, IS THAT INDIRA Gandhi lost the election. We were back in New Delhi while the counting was finished and spent an odd splintered night roaming the city. We went first to the big notice board off Connaught Circus, where results were slipped into appropriate slots by men climbing ladders at the back of the board. It was clear very quickly that the Janata Party was winning, so we went to the Janata offices, the tiny rooms with three ringing telephones, where tired-looking people told us the national outcomes. Afterward we decided to go stand outside the house of Jagjivan Ram, who might have been named prime minister, but wasn't.

It was a squat building with white porticoes like an abbreviated Southern mansion and a row of mother-in-law's tongues in clay pots, some toppled, placed along the front. Supporters gathered there chanting, "Janata, Janata." A freelance journalist from Berkeley turned on his tape recorder to catch the ambient sound, and a man told him, "The things I have seen, I don't have the courage to describe." Soon afterward, a car pulled up, the door opened, and a beautifully groomed collie emerged, to be led by a servant into the house. Finally an opposition tactician came outside, said he had no comment and advised us to get some sleep. Eventually we did.

The next day, as I wandered through the stunned city, a man put his hand gently on my arm.

"Please."

I steeled myself.

"Today we have defeated a tyrant. Thank you very much."

He touched a telephone pole as he passed me, as if trying to keep his balance. I can still see the tilt of him, outlined by the sun.

THE

ANCESTRAL

HOME OF

COUTENS

THE SUBURB WHERE I GREW UP WAS CARRIED ON THE HIP OF Grouse Mountain, across the inlet from downtown Vancouver. My parents bought their lot in the district of North Vancouver in the early fifties, building the house so close to the edge of development that deer ate their fledgling garden, and sometimes they glimpsed cougar and bear. They lived in the house before it was completed, so that my mother had to fetch buckets of drinking water from a communal pump. Luckily, the pump was uphill, and she could carry the full buckets back down.

I realize now that most of the stories I was brought up with were stories of breaking new ground. From my father, I heard about the sod hut on the prairie where his grandparents lived when they first moved to Canada, huddling out the winter near Trochu, a town founded by well-born Frenchmen that once seemed to be the next big thing. My mother told me about the camp where her Scottish family spent their Canadian summers, beating back the bush in search of lawns and graciousness. The women and children from their small town moved to a northern lake in June, while the men chuffed up on weekends on a railroad trunk line. These days, it's a moneyed retreat. When we tried to get close to it on a recent family trip, we found the nearby shoreline closed off by a yacht club. But when my mother was growing up, drinking water was carried from the lake in buckets, and my grandmother ran around the yard chasing chickens for dinner, first to cut off their heads, then to catch them again once she had.

I felt closest to the prairie stories, not just because they were the most picturesque and harshest, the most romantic, but because I seemed to be more a product of the Swedish side of the family, the Stens. My father and his brothers were tall men with strong genes. I got my height from the Stens, and my brother is

taller than our uncles, almost all of my female cousins on that side
of the family are tall, and most of us look Nordic. When I was
backpacking around Stockholm one day, a woman said something
to me in Swedish that I couldn't understand.

"I'm sorry, I thought you were a student at the school here,"
she said, switching to English.

We've got the nose, the shoulders, the hips, the coloring.
Children in our family are very blond, although our hair darkens
as we get older. For as long as I can remember, my father's dark
hair receded at his temple to form two deep bays, and it stayed
that way until he died. Below were narrow, watchful, hazel eyes.
My eyes, and my son's.

Yet there was often something extra in my father's eyes: the
Second World War. That's what our other family stories were
about, the war. It brought my parents together, even though they
met a couple of years after it ended. My father was demobilized
by then and visiting a friend who was still being treated at
Shaughnessy Veterans' Hospital in Vancouver. My father's name
was Clarence, but like every Clarence I've ever heard of, he used
a nickname that wasn't much like the original, in his case, Ron.
Ron Krueger—it takes another story to explain why a Swede was
named Krueger. My father walked into the hospital that day with
the slight limp the war had left him. My mother was one of the
nurses, the girls, the kids, they called themselves, and they all
noticed the new visitor. At the time, my mother says, limps on
men of her age seemed eloquent.

And my father was handsome. Oh, he was so handsome, my
mother says. Didn't he look like a movie star? Like Gary Cooper.
No, like Leslie Howard in *Gone with the Wind*. He was so jaunty;
he wore such beautiful clothes. A fedora, a suit, a watch chain
stretched across his waistcoat. My mother liked good clothes too,
although of course she wore her uniform that day, and a stiffly

starched cap. She had to hold back her hair with bobby pins, the curls of strawberry blond. But my father must have noticed that she was a pretty lassie, with great legs, enveloping freckles and big blue baby-doll eyes. "Brucie" Bruce. Vivacious, my youngest uncle says, yet by her own account, she was nervous and painfully self-conscious, especially as her thirtieth birthday approached. She'd transferred to Shaughnessy three years earlier from the maternity ward at Grace Hospital in Winnipeg, saying that she'd helped deliver far too many other women's babies. Afterward, she ended up tending men so badly injured that many would never leave the hospital. My father had come to visit one of these men, an old army friend, but seized his chance and asked my mother out to dinner. They were married three months later.

Yet every fairy story has its test, its trial. Throughout their married lives, my parents wrangled about my Bruce grandmother, who disapproved of my father before they even met. He was an apprentice machinist at the time, learning how to fix the clanking, glowering old Linotypes at Vancouver's *Province* newspaper: someone, it turned out, who lost his early jauntiness to hard work and bad luck, at least as he saw it, pushing an endless series of boulders uphill only to watch them roll back down on him again. But my grandmother wouldn't even meet him. She refused to attend the wedding, although her kindly, bookish husband took the train out from Ontario. Maybe my grandfather would have smoothed things over eventually. But he died not long after my parents married, following an operation for ulcers, and my grandmother was left to her own devices. She sold the camp on the lake she'd always hated and started her restless journeys home, heading east, in the opposite direction to objectionable marriages, visiting her maiden sisters for as long as both her money and the sisters held out.

The problem was, my mother worshipped her mother. As my grandmother crisscrossed the Atlantic, she was trailed by a stream of my mother's letters, detailing the way my mother and father worked extra shifts, saved every penny, bought the lot on Grouse Mountain and, as the years passed, sadly concluded that they wouldn't have children. My grandmother answered with glossier news, saying that she'd inherited one sister's house in London, other sisters' jewelry. She took ocean liners, she even flew, and she often wrote about her favorite sister, Lesley, who had been invested with the OBE for wartime services by King George VI. Seven and a half years after their marriage, my parents finally had a daughter. I've come to think of my given name as something of a plea.

It wasn't particularly successful. By the time my parents built their house, my grandmother had begun to visit, but these weren't happy occasions. I turned out to be an unsatisfactory grandchild, always puddling in the mud outside and coming home damp and grubby. My brother, born almost three years later, was far more successful, having been blessed with a sweet temperament, our mother's big blue eyes and a pair of robust ears that our grandmother, Nannie, called his Scottish lugs. Whenever Nannie was in town, I hid out in the ravine at the end of the road, which fell toward a fast-moving mountain creek. Once I came home very late, filthy, happily unconscious of the time, and found my mother crying. The kids who'd come back earlier had told her that I'd fallen in the creek, and she was beginning to think I'd drowned. My grandmother scolded me, her accent whistling, her back held fiercely away from the sofa, her arm crooked stiffly around her weeping daughter.

"You miserable geddle," she said. "Look what you've done to your mother. You're nothing but a Krueger." I have no memory of her ever calling me by my given name, although I can still recall the fern pattern on the slipcovers, the brown shadows on the walls and the cold clean throb behind my nails, put there by the numbing waters of the creek that I loved.

When I think about where I'm from, my start, my roots, I think of my family first and then of that creek. Our street was called Edgewood Road and this was Mosquito Creek. We moved to a bigger house when I was eight, but we were still only a block from the creek, to my mother's horror, and I spent the best part of my childhood down there.

The ravine that fell toward the creek was superbly wet in the spring, the ground springy to walk on and fragrant with sweet vegetable rot. The humid, chocolate-colored earth was made up of disintegrating logs and fallen leaves. Vancouver's incessant rain dripped down on the leaves, seeping into the porous soil and draining downhill, leaving the slopes damp but not muddy. To find mud, you had to slide down to the hollows at the bottom of the ravine. It was slippery around the hollows and you could be silly, go for falls, although the tea-colored water was filled with thread-like squirming that older kids said would grow into mosquitoes. I liked to crouch at the slippery edge to watch the squirming, the way the threads touched one end to the other, then contorted backward to touch their ends again.

Big trees—cedar and Douglas fir—towered above. At ground level we found more delicate prizes. Flowers were modest and usually white. In spring, the three-leafed star flowers each sent up a single stalk, a growing eyelash that put out two tiny blossoms. The banks of salal flowers were waxy, while the huckleberry bushes had rounded blooms with frills at the edge. I had an idea that salal was bad to eat, but I tried the huckleberry flowers once to see if they tasted like the fruit, and found them far less sweet than the honey from the scarlet salvia bracts that I sucked on in our garden.

In spring, I usually went down the creek alone, but in summer more kids were interested, and sometimes we tried to dam the creek to make a swimming hole. The water ran over a bed of tumbled stones, and we figured all we had to do was rearrange the stones, making a jigsaw wall that slowed down the creek enough to pool it. We took off our shoes and rolled up our pants to wade in. It looked funny as we stood there, the water foaming against us in a way that seemed to break the line of our legs, so our feet looked to be in a slightly different place than where they ought to have been.

It felt good, though, to stand on the smooth stones curving under our arches like the curve of the world. We found two stones the right distance apart and planted ourselves there, lifting another rock from between our legs and setting it down to teeter on the top of the sketchy wall, holding it for a while to steady it, then letting go to watch it sometimes stay and sometimes fall, pushed downstream by a steady run of water that didn't seem so strong against our legs. It didn't matter. We'd put another rock up, grunting, then another and another. Smooth rocks, cold in our hands, that slowly got heavier, too heavy, much too heavy to lift.

The other kids gave up and I was left to work on my own, a dogged and solitary girl, not popular with other children, but not minding it, usually, when I was down the creek. Immersed in my plans, my work, in the foaming water, I'd be looking at each smooth stone in my hands and the finished dam in my head. My job was to connect the two, present and future, and I never figured out that there was a fracture between them, like the break the running water made in the line of my unbroken legs. Everyday truths were beyond me, although I learned some of them from other girls who caught me on my way home.

"Look at how you've scraped your knee," they said, and it began to throb as they pointed.

"You've lost your socks again, haven't you?"

"Torn a button off your blouse."

"Just look at her hair!" Which I'd pushed off my face with muddy hands and left to dry straight up.

Eventually, I learned to head off on my own even when the other kids wanted to play. I picked huckleberries in empty ice-cream pails, collected toadstools and shelf fungus for school projects and chose autumn leaves to dip in wax, or iron between sheets of waxed paper after my mother grew frightened of paraffin fires. The creek furnished me with everything I needed. It was where I really lived, a concrete place, minutely noted, that nevertheless let me dwell in my imagination, making up stories, possibilities, lies as the need arose. I won't stay long. I didn't eat any. Promise.

Good training for a traveler, wasn't it? I grew independent there—a forager—observant, introspective, maybe a little cranky, and in my constant push to move beyond my mother's reach, far more like my hard-headed, restless Nannie than I care to acknowledge even now.

11

ALL FOUR OF MY GRANDPARENTS HAD ARRIVED IN CANADA by the beginning of the First World War. The men came first. In 1913, my Bruce grandfather moved from Oldmeldrum to Winnipeg, where he got a job in a bank. Once he was established, he sent for Nannie and their older son, David, who was not quite two years old. My mother and her twin sister were born in Winnipeg, then my grandfather was sent to a bank in small-town Ontario. My youngest uncle was born there seventeen years after his sisters.

With the Swedes it was a little more complicated. My father told me that my great-grandfather was a bishop in the Swedish Lutheran Church. His name was Haughlund, and he disgraced himself over drink sometime in the late 1880s. This meant he was defrocked, and his scandalized family shipped him off to North Dakota. He was a remittance man, receiving payouts from home to stay away. Haughlund had brought along his wife, Maria, but he had a hard time supporting her, regularly losing the remittance payments in an unsuccessful cartage business. A horse kicked him in the head and his partner ran off with the profits. The only thing Haughlund seemed to get right was producing an heir. My grandfather Rune was born in Ray, North Dakota, in 1890.

Whatever hope that was kindled in Haughlund by the birth of his son didn't last. When Rune was four years old, Haughlund went to work in a mine and soon got killed in an explosion. My father usually said that it happened four days into the job, although his repetition of Rune's four years and Haughlund's four days always sounded a bit bardic to me. The bardic bishop, a remittance man. If nothing else, he was a useful ancestor. You could be anything you wanted to be in a family that was one part myth. No one remembered Haughlund's given name, and even the family name was erased a couple of years after he died, when my great-grandmother Maria married a Pennsylvania Dutch blacksmith, Michael Krueger, who was so good to my grandfather that he became Rune Krueger, later Henry Krueger, an assimilated American.

Poor feckless Haughlund. When I was backpacking around Sweden, people told me stories that rubbed the last of the luster off his single name. Sitting in her apartment kitchen, hands clasped and reclasping over her tin box of documents, my father's cousin Edit told me that Haughlund wasn't a bishop. It was Maria's father who was the bishop. Haughlund was a young minister caught up in a reform movement within the Lutheran Church, a drinker and a gambler, another unsatisfactory son-in-law. Edit told me that marital disappointments had been common on that side of the family, as well. In the stories she'd heard around the kitchen table, the women usually came off as stronger than the men. They were also longer-lived, which probably had something to do with their reputation for strength, not to mention the slant of the stories.

Maria was one of the strongest. My father knew his grandmother and always spoke of her as an educated woman, sober-minded and genteel. She made a point of being well dressed, he said. Presumably even in Ray, North Dakota, where the cartage business finally failed and where, to support her, poor mythic Haughlund underwent one last transformation, becoming a miner, the last of the Swedish trolls heading into the earth. A boulder rolled down, a tunnel closed, and the poor soul was lost there forever, everyone forgetting the name that might otherwise call him back out.

It was Maria who eventually sent to Sweden for a wife for her son, paying for the ticket on the *Titanic*. After the first niece changed her mind, Maria asked for my grandmother. She apparently knew about the rape and had made up her mind to offer the pregnant teenager a home, understanding that my grandmother was disgraced in Sweden. It didn't matter that she'd been raped, the goods were soiled. She had no future there, so Maria brought her to a place where she would have no past.

The thing is, no one seems to have asked my grandmother whether she wanted to go. Or at least, they didn't care about her answer. Once Edit had read me the letter she'd written to my cousin Ingrid, telling her not to emigrate, I went back to the earlier letters. My Granny told family stories and kept her sisters up to date on her moves, but at the same time, so many of the letters hummed with regret. She wished that she'd never left. She'd been too young and had aged so much they wouldn't recognize her even if she could find her way home. You could see how she resented them, how she missed them, how she longed for her mother's care.

It was 1912 when she headed to a new home, one in Alberta. At some point, the Krueger family had left North Dakota and crossed the porous border into Canada, taking up a land grant two miles south of Trochu. This means the former Rune must have been the first of my grandparents to arrive in Canada, although no one knows any longer when this happened, or why. But we know that sixteen-year-old Ida Olivia Sten sailed out of the port of Malmö that spring, getting her last glimpse of Sweden as the seacoast fell below the horizon. At her side was her seventeen-year-old brother, Johan, a lean young man with a long face that often dropped into a roguish smile. No one I talked to knew whether Ida had a babe-in-arms or was still pregnant, and it was not the sort of thing that ever got written down.

They landed at Quebec, clearing customs before taking the train across the country to Calgary, where they caught a CPR local to Olds. In Olds, they hitched a ride back south with the mailman, who drove his team and democrat through a driving rainstorm that turned the rutted roads into a quagmire. When they finally reached their aunt's farm, two miles beyond Trochu, Maria was waiting with a hot dinner. Also a new name. My great-grandmother Maria Nilson Haughlund had become Mary Krueger. My great-uncle Johan Magni Sten soon became John Steen. And with her marriage, my grandmother took on the respectable identity of Ida Krueger, wife and mother, even if it didn't happen in exactly that order.

When I was growing up, I was told that my grandparents married soon after my grandmother's arrival and homesteaded on their own farm near Trochu. But Rune Henry was a restless man, short but wide in the shoulders, with a quick temper, a hearty laugh and an overload of ambition. He sold that farm to buy another, then sold the second one to set himself up as a mechanic. At different times, he owned a gas station, a used-car lot and property in what is now downtown Calgary that he sold before it was worth anything. For a while, he and Ida worked as superintendents in an apartment building in Edmonton. He also got his tickets as a plumber and a welder. Once, working up a telegraph pole,

Rune killed himself with a powerful shock, although his heart restarted almost immediately when he fell onto the frozen ground. Along the way, he and Ida had two sons and a daughter, while Mary Krueger looked after Ida's oldest boy, Walter. My father was the youngest son, named Clarence by the midwife. On our trips back to Alberta when I was a kid, my father drove circuitous routes to visit all the places he'd lived—not just Trochu and Calgary and Edmonton, but Grande Prairie, Olds, Rumsey and Rowley, some of them sad grassed-up towns where only a few retired farmers lived in houses that badly needed a coat of paint.

Behind all their moves was the fact that Rune was a spiritualist. The spirits told him to buy this and sell that, my father said years later. He was disgusted when he said it; my father had no religion himself. When my mother brought us home from Sunday school, he'd ask, "You planning on letting them fool you?" My mother explained that he'd been disillusioned by the war, or rather by the behavior of chaplains during the war. But Rune, the defrocked minister's son, had joined a group of spiritualists. According to my mother, he went to weekly meetings where they tried to communicate with the dead, using Ouija boards and rapping on tables. Rune claimed to be a seer. Shortly after my parents got married, they took the train out to Alberta. My mother said Rune had a vision of their journey. "He told me, 'I could see you. You were in an upper berth.' I said, 'No, we were in a lower berth, Pops.' But usually I didn't say anything, just nodded my head."

I never met my grandfather, who died from cirrhosis of the liver when I was two years old, even though he didn't drink. But I knew something about spiritualism because Rune had passed it on to Walter, whom I thought to be his oldest son. Uncle Walter was a sweet, vague presence in my childhood. He had gone overseas with the Royal Canadian Navy during the Second World War and met his future wife in England. Walter was another handsome

Sten, although when I was growing up I heard him compared to different movie stars than my father. With his broad accommodating face and sleepy wide-set eyes, Walter was supposed to look like Michael Caine, especially when he wore his commodore's cap from the West Vancouver Yacht Club. Auntie Ann came out from England after the war to marry him in Edmonton, although they didn't last long on the prairies before moving to Vancouver, where she opened The House of Beauty.

They were my rich uncle and aunt, although everyone knew that Auntie Ann was the one with the money. Also the brains. She turned The House of Beauty into a chain while buying up real estate in West Vancouver. Walter puttered away his days as a hairdresser in the downtown store, which had bubble-headed dryers and long mirrors and low tables covered with hairstyle magazines that I often had a chance to read, since my parents sometimes worked there nights as cleaners. Auntie Ann and Uncle Walter lived in the British Properties, in a big house with thick white wall-to-wall carpeting, two layers of swag drapes and toy poodles allowed on the sofa, yappy things that looked less like small dogs than particularly vicious cushions. We would go there for tea, although my brother and I were happiest outside, burrowing into the hammock that was slung in a corner of the yard.

Since this was Vancouver, the hammock stank of mildew and the walls on either side of us were furry with moss. Yet we preferred being there to staying inside and puffed out deep hollow melodies on our soft-drink bottles. Uncle Walter had an idea that children liked ginger beer, so he always kept a case in the garage and handed us each a bottle when we went outside. He'd also registered the fact that I liked flowers and often gave me a bouquet of the sweet peas he liked to grow in his garden, wrapped first in dampened paper towels and afterward in tinfoil. And then there were the tracts—a word I learned from my mother. These were his wallet-sized booklets of eight or twelve pages printed on such cheap paper you could see woodchips, pinkish-beige paper with a drawing of a rocketship blasting off from the top of the first page and banks of italicized headlines beneath. Uncle Walter always bent down to give me a copy, looking at me, unblinking, with his wide pale eyes, innocent as eggs.

"Look at this," he told me once. "The Venusians have landed."

Auntie Ann called from upstairs. "Wol-tah! Wol-*tah*!"

"Coming, dearie."

The way I saw it, I was descended from a long line of strong women and wacky fictions. Not that I ever took my background very seriously, planning as I was to leave it all behind.

1 2

THINGS I LEARNED ABOUT MY SCOTTISH NANNIE WHEN sitting with my mother and aunts at the kitchen table:

That during the Depression, when my grandfather always had a job, she kept a pot of soup simmering on the back of the stove for tramps, hobos, the unemployed, so the tramps put a mark on their house—she was literally a mark, known for her charity;

That she was very popular in her small Ontario town, an upright woman with many friends who nursed the sick, cooked for the bereaved and made bracing visits to the unlucky;

That her kind and bookish husband was a drinker whom my mother had to fetch home from the bar, saying as her mother had told her, "Your children are hungry and waiting for their tea";

That when she first moved to Canada, she and my grandfather had a house on the last street in Winnipeg, and my grandmother would sit on the back stoop shooting gophers straight through the eye, or bottles off the fence posts, being a crack shot;

That in her later years she asked to be driven to the cemetery, where she knelt at the grave of her elder son, the former prisoner of war, crying for an hour at a time as my mother shifted from one cold foot to the other;

That her prisoner-of-war son had been a drinker;

That her favorite sister was actually called Jem, Jemina being her middle name, although her given name was Lesley, thank god;

That despite her relentless nostalgia for the Old Country, when some relatives finally paid a visit to Canada, some cousins who'd immigrated to the States, she couldn't wait to get rid of them;

That one day an envelope arrived in the mail from a certain Mr. Ogg, which she opened and put away without comment, and which after her death was found to contain a family tree showing that she was descended not from a distinguished family of county gentry, as she'd always implied, but from centuries of crofters, one of whom had enough brains or luck at the beginning of the nineteenth century to become an overseer to a real member of the gentry, and whose son became a prosperous estate agent, and whose grandson—my Nannie's father, Adam Birnie—was purchased a place in the merchant marine and went to Peru, where he disembarked and spent nine years in the 1850s manufacturing concrete blocks for the expansion of the port of Callao, earning the small fortune that eventually landed him and his consumptive wife and their large family of unmarriageable daughters in the "ancestral" home of Coutens.

There's something else I understood quite recently. It started at a dinner party in the Forest Hill neighborhood of Toronto. The guest of honor was introduced as the former deputy director of the Sarajevo office of a large international aid agency. The tragic siege of Sarajevo was not long over, and it was whispered that the stocky Bosnian had done honorable work throughout. Now, in the well-proportioned living room, the deputy director seemed melancholy and displaced, on the whole rather unreachable. Yet I had made some close friends in the growing Bosnian community in Toronto and I thought I might mention their names. Did he know my friends Goran and Amela?

"Yes," he said, although he seemed startled and displeased. "I know them, certainly." I was confused, since I'd found my friends to be generally well-liked, even esteemed for their own work distributing aid during the siege, which they lived through with their two children in an apartment in the old Turkish section of Sarajevo. Yet I also knew something about the splits and dissension within the former Yugoslavia, and wondered whether my friends and this man might have had a political disagreement. It seemed wise to let it pass. The melancholy former deputy director nodded absently and walked over to the baby grand piano at the far end of the room, where he began to play a Chopin nocturne while the other guests stopped talking for a moment, meeting their neighbors' glances and pursing their lips in sympathy.

When I saw Amela, I asked her about this man.

"Deputy director?" she replied. "He was never deputy director, never anything like it. He worked in the office, it's true, although I believe he left before the war."

I thought of my grandmother and began to laugh. We really *were* alike, at least in our preferred forms of art. Travel was a form of writing. Or at least, rewriting, even for people who weren't writers.

Good on them, I thought, laughing and laughing, laughing so long that Amela looked puzzled, being a person who made a point of telling the truth herself.

1 3

I BEGAN TRAVELING ON MY OWN A FEW MONTHS AFTER I started university, figuring that I'd earned my independence along with my high-school diploma, even though I was only sixteen. Of course, I didn't put it so clearly at first. Traveling was just an urge, although one legitimized before my seventeenth birthday by a sandal-footed poet, who told me, "Write about what you know." I realized soon afterward that this was just a line, but at the time I was impressed. Contemplating the poet's furry toes, I decided that I would seize any opportunities that arose. That way, I'd have something to write about. And if my writing never went anywhere, at least I'd have led a full life, wouldn't I?

Amazing how most of the truly important decisions in your life are taken before you're twenty, and how often they're based on mistaken information. Which doesn't mean they're wrong.

It also strikes me how selectively I listened to my family's stories. Ignoring all warnings, implicit and otherwise, I took off for San Francisco, for the Yukon and the Prairies, getting in trouble all over the map. It started with a trip to the Maritimes right after first-year university. My gap-toothed friend Marina and I arrived in Charlottetown and went looking for a room in what our guidebook told us was the cheapest hotel in town. Stepping off the bus—two innocents in duffle coats with pale round faces— we found a white clapboard box with a vacancy sign swinging from a wooden post. Inside was flaccid brown felt carpet and a waist-high counter of the same fake paneling as the walls. An unshaven man stood behind the counter, his belly bulging out of his undershirt.

It was puzzling; he didn't want us to stay there. When we showed him our guidebook, he agreed that the hotel was cheap and that there was a vacancy, but he still didn't want us. "We get to pick our clientele," he said. It was dusk. We were tired; we wanted to eat the shrink-wrapped sandwiches we'd brought from the ferry. We showed him his listing in our guidebook again, and he told us to go away.

When we didn't leave, a chunky middle-aged woman came out from behind a curtained doorway, took our money and handed us a key. As we walked upstairs, we heard a short indecipherable argument. We didn't care. We had our room, our sandwiches and an early night.

Then it got noisy. First it started on one side, the sound of huffing and puffing from the room next door and soon the rhythmic rattling of a bed, as if someone was striking a clacker faster and faster. Faster and faster and faster and faster until it stopped. It stopped so abruptly we giggled, and stifled our giggles with our hands. Soon the room on the other side of us was occupied, bump bump *bump* of the creaky old bed, while the door on the first side opened and footsteps descended the stairs. Soon enough, other footsteps came up and entered the original room.

"We're staying in a *hooo-er* house," I said, and we broke down helplessly in giggles. When we could control ourselves, Marina got the idea of using one of the water tumblers on the dresser to try to hear what the prostitutes were charging. She showed me how to put the open end of the glass against the wall and my ear on the closed end as if it were a stethoscope. But we were giggling too much, and the Charlottetown prostitutes turned out to be laconic; we didn't hear a thing.

It was still an adventure, we decided. Isn't that what we'd been looking for? Except that the rooms were used so often that it finally stopped being funny. We couldn't sleep and the halls were getting rowdy. Men were falling down outside, stumping into walls, slamming into doors, yelling and slurring their words. We got a little nervous and shoved the dresser in front of the door, telling each other that we were safe, no one knew we were there.

It must have been the middle of the night when someone started calling, "Gu-ruls. Guuuu-ruls," in a high-pitched, servile, suggestive voice right outside our door. He rattled the knob and pushed against the door, yawped a little and pushed harder.

"Guuuuuu-ruls," he whinnied. We huddled inside, frightened and not knowing what to do. Outside the yawping and grunting got louder, the door thumping heavily against its lock, thumping rhythmically, when suddenly there was such a heavy whack it seemed as if *two* men were shoving, scuffling, even fighting, until the high-pitched voice yelled, "Fock!" and went slamming down the stairs.

The hotel went quiet after that, although we couldn't sleep. After it had been calm for a long time, I slid back the dresser as noiselessly as possible and took a look outside. Seated on a kitchen chair across from our door was the fat hairy man in the undershirt. He gave me an exasperated look from his bloodshot eyes, making me close the door quickly. But we were able to get to sleep after that and crept out early the next morning before anyone else was awake.

My parents would have died if they'd known half the things I got up to. Or maybe not. Maybe they thought it was time I grew up, and they didn't want to know how. In any case, as I continued my travels for the next decade, I was often taken care of by people like the man in Charlottetown. By other people's families, I now realize. The well-paying jobs so readily available at the time meant I could save up and take off for places all over the world. I learned a great deal, usually inadvertently. But when you get right down to it—at least according to my friend John on the freak bus—I spent my teens and twenties being a tourist. I was dabbling. A week here, ten days there, get back on the bus/train/plane.

As if John couldn't have left any time he'd wanted to. As if that isn't the real definition of tourists—people who can leave any time they really want to.

Yet one of these early trips took me to a place I had trouble leaving. I went to Mexico with my friend Sue when I was nineteen and she was a year younger, using cheap triangle-fare tickets that let us fly into Puerto Vallarta, Guadalajara and Mexico City. We had three weeks, some traveler's checks, no Spanish and a guide-book. We thought we were pretty tough, although in the fading color pictures of the trip Sue sent me recently, we look so mal-leable and young. After her letter arrived, I hauled more pictures out of storage and spread them on the floor. Sue's small smile and enormous blue eyes give her the look of a silent film star. I loom above her, ducking my head shyly. The succession of pictures shows the way our long brown hair streaks lighter throughout the trip and our bare arms tan deeply.

We landed in Puerto Vallarta. I'd never smelled anything like coastal Mexico before, so heated and fruity and damp. Walking away from the airplane, breathing in the warm, saturated air, I had a sense that things were brilliantly out of order. In Vancouver, the chilly air of winter made your lungs feel this heavy, while on the best days of summer, the hot wind was so light you scarcely seemed to breathe it. To meet heat and weight together in the early tropical darkness was new to me and I loved it, rocketing toward our hotel in a taxi with no springs and an empty blue Noxema face-cream jar covering a light on the floor. Dogs scat-tered on the road outside as we bumped over potholes and onto cobbles, passed burros, stinking diesel trucks and overcrowded buses; passed women turning their broad faces toward us.

Our hotel was by a seawall in the middle of the town, a low-rise newly rebuilt and whitewashed inside and out, with terra-cotta-tile floors and large pots of rather dusty tropical plants in the lobby and on the stairs. Opening the heavy door to our room, we found acidic pink and green cotton bedspreads vibrating under the artificial light. A small balcony outside double doors looked down on the thundering sea. We threw it open and sat there a while, then slept in the damp noisy disorder until the vivid light woke us at dawn.

Walking out after breakfast, we found a small town built around a curving seawall. Beyond that was a rocky cove where fishermen stood casting nets into the water. The houses there were whitewashed adobe with palm trees towering above them. Beyond even that, further down the coast, was a wide beach where we found other foreigners sunning themselves. It wasn't crowded; Puerto Vallarta was pretty much undeveloped then. We were able to lay out our towels on a hot expanse of sand before running down to the ocean, where powerful turquoise waves broke against our legs, pushing us back to the beach. It became a game, to wade and swim out into the resistant water before letting go, giving ourselves over to the water and bodysurfing back to shore. The water was salty in our mouths and roaring, and at times we swam beyond the surf, treading water or doing a slow crawl below the turquoise sky, the colors so much deeper than the Canadian winter we had left behind that we wanted to burrow in there and never leave.

Unfortunately, sunburn. Having broiled ourselves that first day, we had to come up with something more than the beach to occupy our time. So we started walking, which is what we ended up doing in Mexico. We poked around Puerto Vallarta, spending most of our time in the covered market between flapping serapes, breathing in the funk of humid wool and charcoal fires heating tamales we weren't supposed to eat. In Guadalajara we walked all over the solid provincial downtown and took a bus out to Tlaquepaque, which was then a separate village and not the contiguous suburb it is now, visiting artisans in their open-air studios shaded by blooming poinsettia trees and fenced at the side with cactus. In Mexico City, guidebook in hand, we walked through the Zócalo and down the Alameda, staring at Diego Rivera's murals and the cathedrals and Sanborn's House of Tiles, taking the subway out to Tlatelolco where students our age had been massacred only a few years before. Afterward, we took the subway back at rush hour, so we were packed in tight by whispering, leering young men, one of whom rubbed himself against me as I tried helplessly to push him away, so that when we got off at the next stop, I found my jeans wet at the hip.

That was the soundtrack to our wanderings, men hooting and imploring and whimpering, "*Chica, chica, hola mamacita, como estás güerita, ven para acá chiquitita, ándale mamacita, chica, chica, chíngame güerita*, will you marry me, bay-bee?"

We hated it but refused to back down, marching like a pair of suffragettes down the dusty pathways of Chapultepec Park, through the Museum of Modern Art and into the splendid Museum of Anthropology, keeping off the subway at rush hour but still taking the crowded buses. And, of course, that's when it happened. In a shoving match to get onto a bus, someone cut the cord of the pouch I wore around my neck, which held the last of our money. I knew right away that someone had got it and was running away with it, but we were hemmed in, maybe by accomplices, and I could only shriek incomprehensibly in English.

I don't remember whose idea it was to go to the police. Our guidebook gave directions to police headquarters along with a warning about corruption that we chose to ignore. If I was stubborn, Sue was determined and persistent. Later on, she would be a union organizer in the mill towns of British Columbia. Stealing wasn't right, we agreed. Also, we had an idea that whoever took the pouch might pocket the cash and drop the pouch itself, which had a couple of mementoes inside that we thought might be turned in to the police. So with our stray change we made our way to police headquarters, which I remember as a closed-looking building with soiled linoleum on the floor. Someone behind a desk shuffled papers and smirked, then called for the *jefe*, a small man in a spiffy uniform who spoke English and listened gravely to our complaint.

"There are problems," the *jefe* told us. Then he brightened and proposed taking us on a tour of police headquarters. Sue and I exchanged a glance, deciding that we were game. So the *jefe* clicked us through the heavy security door and we entered the official side, which felt much different than the public area, more crowded and bustling and everyday, but also rather muffled and antique, like the covered markets we'd been visiting. The *jefe* led us through a maze of corridors, a labyrinth of cubicles and little rooms that were often too brightly lit and overloaded with policemen who made kissing noises behind us.

"*Ándale*," they told the *jefe*, who showed us binders of mug shots taken from creaking filing cabinets, roughed-up faces that made us want to leave even before he took us into a room where they were getting together a lineup. Knackered-looking men of all sizes were being pushed up against a wall. For once, the room was dim, a shadowed sick sepia color, but I could still see the dried blood matted on one man's hair, and others who appeared bruised and beaten. The policemen made jokes with the *jefe*, who seemed imperturbable. I badly wanted to leave by then, having an idea what the policemen were saying to the *jefe* without understanding more than a few words of Spanish. But we were trapped, and I felt increasingly claustrophobic as we followed the *jefe* deeper and deeper into the building, past handcuffed criminals and murmuring policemen—"*chica, chica*," and to the *jefe*, admiringly, "*chingón*"—wondering whether we'd ever get out of there, and in what shape, until we turned down a final corridor and with bewildering suddenness were on the public side of the security door, standing on soiled linoleum again.

The amiable *jefe* didn't turn flinty-eyed and dismiss us with a cinematic warning. No, "Don't ever come back here." No, "Yankee go home." He just waved good-bye. Maybe he hadn't even meant to warn us. Maybe he'd just been touched by our stupidity. Yet we still got away from there as quickly as possible, heading to the telegraph office to wire our parents for money that never arrived, eating all our meals in the hotel, on a tab, as the staff grew increasingly suspicious, and finally throwing ourselves on the mercy of the Canadian embassy, where they lectured us, took our passports in return for a cash loan and, worst of all, phoned our parents with the whole story, which surprised them, since they hadn't received our wires and had no idea what was going on, although they sent money fast enough once they did, and we got our passports back. By the time we flew home, watching Mexico scroll away behind us, I was amazed that we'd managed to leave.

Ten years later, my husband, Paul, applied for a job at one of his newspaper's bureaus outside Toronto, where we'd been living off and on for several years. This wasn't Paul from India, but another Paul, Paul Knox. He was a reporter on *The Globe and Mail*, and we heard that his editors were going to offer him a job in Ottawa. Instead, they asked us to move to Mexico City. It was a big surprise, and we were worried about the pollution, the effect it might have on our two-year-old son, Gabriel.

But people told us how to cope, and we agreed to go. It was a big chance for Paul, and I was too restless not to give it a try, fully molded by then by whatever it is that molds you—my family, their example and a gap-toothed selection of their advice and stories, even the ones that weren't true. I guess luck might also have made me brave. Other people's relatives don't always protect you, and not all policemen in Latin America let the innocent go free.

In any case, I moved south, learned Spanish and finally understood what had happened to me, and hadn't, on that first trip to Mexico. It's just as well that I'm a slow learner, or I might never have left home.

FAULTLINES

THE EARTHQUAKE WOKE US AT WHAT WE LATER LEARNED was 7:19 in the morning of September 19, 1985. We were in a hotel at the western edge of the dried-up lake bed on which downtown Mexico City is built. As I opened my eyes, the stucco room was sunny, and the hanging lamp with its rococo crystals was swinging on its three-foot chain in an increasingly energetic arc until it was brushing the ceiling at each end of its glittering trajectory. The beds started walking across the floor, lurching from side to side toward the window wall as if a giant ship in which we were riding had hit high swells and was rising and falling, rising and falling, though listing more and more to port. The feeling of rolling power was extraordinary. Exhilarating, too. It was quiet and sunny, and the huge roll of the landlocked ship was one of the most delightful things I have ever felt. I sat up in bed, loving the power, the fun house bucking, not even worried as it went on and on and on and on until, with a silent thud of settling, the movement finally stopped.

Ten thousand people were dying all around me in one of the worst earthquakes of the century, but I didn't know that. I knew it was strong but didn't know how strong. I didn't know anything. We'd been in Mexico City for two days, after spending about a month at a language school in nearby Cuernavaca. Moving to the capital meant that Paul was officially taking up his post as the *Globe*'s Latin America correspondent. The paper's length of posting for its foreign correspondents varied, and it seemed like such a big thing to move countries, cultures—really, identities—that I was still telling myself if it didn't work we could bail out after a couple of years. As it happened, we lived in Mexico for three years and in Brazil for three after that. We got to do more traveling and explored something a little different, something that my grandparents knew: what it was like to live in a foreign country.

It wasn't easy. In fact, what ended up fascinating me was the layers of knowing and not knowing a place, layers that shift as time passes in slow upheaval, like the pressure on sedimentary rock that can eventually turn the horizontal layers vertical. This happens through earthquakes, of course. Also through continuous pressure exerted by the weight of years.

After returning from the backpacking trip to Europe and Asia, I'd worked as a journalist in Toronto while trying to write fiction. I loved them both, but learning two professions at once was almost impossibly hard, especially with the fiction relegated to the off hours. An editor I was hoping to impress once told me that a short story I'd shown him sounded as if the poor thing was dragging around a ball and chain. But slowly I began to publish stories in literary magazines, meanwhile finding ways to work part-time and keep on traveling, which by this time I did with Paul.

We'd met on the student paper at university and even lived in the same crappy communal house for a while, calling the place "Likely" after a town in BC, so that if people from, say, the food co-op phoned, they'd have to ask, "Is this Likely?" Paul was one of six or seven of us in the house; it was hard to keep track. Eventually there were even a couple of babies. Also three cats, including Iichiro, a jet-black tom that one of the women had brought back from Nagasaki, a post-post-nuke cat missing several body parts, including his eyelids, with a very loud lovesick yowl that made him sound like a country singer in pain. We rotated the cooking, mainly doing stove-top dishes, stews and pastas, no one caring what they ate. Ill feelings were more likely to arise out of hygiene issues, beer stains on the kitchen floor two weeks after a party, and we often had lengthy household discussions about cleanliness as bourgeois analism, Jainist preservation of all life forms, germs, bacteria, etc., men just trying to get out of doing any work.

Paul had been thinking of studying law but found journalism much more immediate and fun. Like all the rest of us, he got a part-time job on *The Vancouver Sun* during the school year, covering municipal council meetings one night a week to pay the ridiculously tiny expenses of student life, forty dollars a month for a room in the house and maybe a hundred more for food. He also owned a series of tiny cars, finally taking off in the latest model a couple of years after graduate school, camping around the US before backpacking in Europe. We ran into each other again in London, a surprise, since we'd lost touch. Both of us subsequently moved to Toronto, where Paul joined the *Globe* and I worked for the CBC. We got married a couple of years later and Gabriel was born.

Having a baby put an end to my hopes of combining fiction and journalism, at least for a while. Fortunately, Paul got a fellowship in the States when Gabriel was seven weeks old, and following that, the job in Latin America. None of the foreign governments would give me a working visa, and I more or less forgot about journalism for the better part of eight years to stay at home with Gabriel and write.

When we got to Mexico, I also had that other project, to find out what it was like to be a foreigner. When I was a child, I'd never really thought of my grandmothers as either immigrants or foreigners. They both had accents and talked about the Old Country, but that was just the way they were. It never even occurred to me to ask them what it felt like to uproot yourself. Of course it didn't. In our family, children didn't have the confidential relationships with adults that parents seem to strive for lately. The fact is, no one ever told us anything. We were expected to have our wits about us and pick it up.

For all its faults and frustrations, I suppose it's a manner of child-rearing that twigs curiosity rather than the world-weary knowingness you find too often in kids these days. When we moved to Mexico, I was curious for all sorts of reasons to find out what it felt like to be displaced. I had a sense of family tradition; I was following in footsteps. I felt nervy and alert, sensing that this was somehow crucial. Packing up, I could hardly wait to find out what it felt like to actually live abroad. Not just find out; I wanted to plumb the experience, to learn from it, to understand the lives my grandparents had led, wondering all the while if this might be something I could write about.

As it turned out, I couldn't—can't—write about anything else.

1 5

THE CUERNAVACA WHERE WE STUDIED SPANISH DIDN'T look anything like the edgy and fetid village described by Malcolm Lowry in *Under the Volcano*. Maybe it never has. It's over the mountains from Mexico City, and after leaving the airport, and heading up a long steep toll road, we turned a corner and saw Cuernavaca as a big urban center spread out across the valley below us. As we descended the switchback passes and arrived on the outskirts of the city, smog from local industries was thick enough to obscure the distant mountains we'd left behind. I never figured out if Malcolm Lowry had been able to see Popocatépetl from Cuernavaca in cleaner (if more fetid) times. I never caught a glimpse. Instead, we found miles of pleasant suburbs with winding, cobbled streets and comfortable houses behind high walls. The two dozen language schools and rich escapees from the capital buoyed the local economy, so it made for a soft landing in Mexico.

Even so, the whole time we were there I felt elated, delirious, writing down everything I heard and saw each night in my journal. Walking the streets each afternoon after class, poking into gardens and markets, I thought again that Mexico looked so much more vital than Canada, exotic and hotter in every sense. The inner fire of bougainvillea so bright you could cut off a branch and use it to light a castle. The sunset on a rough wall giving the plaster the glow of a young girl's skin. They say if you're really going to see a place, you should stay either three weeks or three years, and my feverish descriptions in those first weeks make the next year of my journal look pallid.

Just as we were about to leave Cuernavaca for Mexico City, one of my teachers told me a story. Her two sisters had been shopping in a two-story market, one of them holding her very blond son. The mother put the boy down for an instant, and he was snatched by a market woman, a vendor. The aproned vendors began passing the child from hand to hand, from one stall to another, over oranges, behind melons, kidnapping him for sale, probably in Europe or north of the border, as the frantic mother screamed and screamed. Fortunately the sister, who was on the second floor, heard the poor mother. As the baby was handed upstairs, the sister somehow snatched him back, while the market women scattered.

"*Cuidado con el güerito.*" Be careful with your little blondie, the teacher told me, meaning Gabriel, who was two years old. I believed her: This had happened to her sisters, after all. I left Cuernavaca feeling wary and mistrustful, and spent my first weeks in the capital shrinking away from jolly vendors in the *tianguis*, while preferring the wilted and unthreatening vegetables in my local supermarket.

We got through the days after the earthquake and moved into our house once the power and water had been restored. The first people we met were foreign journalists and diplomats, and at their parties I realized the blond-baby-snatching story was a staple of foreigners' lore in Mexico. You heard it most frequently from embassy wives, although no one seemed to know anyone whose baby had actually been stolen. A light went on. I realized the story was a prime example of foreigners' fatuous distrust of Mexicans and decided that by repeating it, the teacher in Cuernavaca had been making fun of me. She was laughing at the credulous *gringa*, secretly despising me for my protected, prosperous life, getting her jollies from scaring me. You didn't need to be in Mexico for very long to learn that underlying the great national politeness and reserve was a streak of hatred for foreigners. It wasn't just "Yankee go home." There was also the time, shortly after we arrived, when we got a wrong-number call. Instead of being apologetic, the man called back several times, insisting that he speak to someone named Maru. My Spanish-language skills were still shaky and deteriorated with each call. Finally, I repeated in a bad accent, "We have no, there is no, I don't know. . . ."

The man cut me off, asking in perfect, scornful, American-accented English, "Why don't you go back to school and learn proper Spanish?"

So I decided my teacher had been making fun of me and resented her for it. I never saw her after leaving Cuernavaca, and my memory of her face was fading. Certainly I was unable to remember her expression as she told me the story. But it was hard not to imagine that the corners of her lipsticked mouth had twitched faintly with malice.

A while later, Gabriel and I joined Paul on a trip to Nicaragua. The Sandinista government was in power and fighting American-funded Contras in the countryside, but Managua was peaceful and I felt safe taking my son there. We stayed in a crumbling bungalow with a six-foot iguana rattling around on its corrugated roof. Paul rented the place along with three other journalists, since they were all in Nicaragua often enough that it was cheaper to rent a house than stay in a hotel. Wilting from the heat, I sank into one of Nicaragua's famous rocking chairs, called an *abuela*, or grandmother.

Odd to think of rocking in my grandmother's lap, feeling displaced yet curious as I read my way through a pile of newspapers.

Barricada reported that an anthropologist had been forced to leave her work in a Managua neighborhood because a local woman spread stories that she was a witch. Another *Barricada* story said that residents in a different *barrio* had recently stormed the local precinct to demand that police arrest a bag lady who wandered through the area wearing four skirts. The Contra radio station had broadcast stories that the Sandinistas were stealing little kids from the *barrios*, butchering them, and shipping the meat to soldiers at the front. The story got around that the bag lady supplied the Sandinistas by hiding babies under her skirts. I thought of other stories I'd heard, tales of foreign-aid workers chased from Guatemalan slums because of rumors they were stealing babies. It finally hit me that stories involving strangers/babies/stealing were all over northern Latin America, and rather than being lies—or as well as being lies—they were urban myths that said something central about local fears and preoccupations.

After a year and a half in Mexico, I'd finally made some Mexican friends, mostly professionals from well-educated families. When I got back and asked them about the baby-stealing myth, they became embarrassed and waved me off, apparently reluctant to talk about the backwardness of their fellow countrymen. By this time I'd realized that my teachers in Cuernavaca did not belong to the same social class as my friends. They didn't have university degrees, the *licenciaturas* that mean so much in Mexico, but were clever people rising from the lower middle class. While some were just as skeptical and sophisticated as my friends, in retrospect others seemed far more self-conscious, unworldly and often under social strain. Thinking back on the teacher who'd told the story, I began to wonder whether she'd sincerely believed what she'd said. I didn't think the attempted kidnapping had actually happened, or at least that it had happened to her sisters. But maybe her sisters had told her the story, and since she'd believed it, the teacher had simplified the details to make the story's message so clear it would impress even a foreigner.

I remembered how she'd emphasized the baby's blondness. I knew by then that being blond and European-looking is a sign of high status in Mexico, just as being Indian is almost a guarantee of being poor. The president's cabinet always looks like a group of Goya's pale Spaniards, and from there down the social ladder, people's complexions get darker. Maybe the teacher had wanted to assert her social status by claiming close connection to a blond, kidnap-able child. If so, it had passed right over my head at the time, and almost two years later, I remembered her so vaguely that I couldn't picture what she looked like, much less how she'd looked when telling the story. Yet one thing seemed clear: The significant Mexican variation on the baby-stealing story was its emphasis on male blondness. The myth showed how European males were so prized and hated by the lower classes that women like the ones in the market longed to snatch them up and cradle them and ship them back to where they came from. Or so the men appeared to fear.

Six years later, when I arrived back in Canada, I felt as elated and displaced as when I'd arrived in Mexico, and my eyeballs were peeled just as raw. Everything looked so plush, so protected. There was an almost pestilent amount of choice. I sympathized with some Mexican acquaintances who had stayed with a friend of mine in Miami on their first trip north. Just before going home, they had taken their two daughters to a huge Toys "R" Us so they could each pick a present. One girl was fine. The other sat down on the floor and started crying in confusion. They had to take her back to my friend's place, where the father drew a map of the store with the approximate locations of the types of toys displayed there. Aisle by aisle, they went over the map, crossing out toys she didn't care for until they zeroed in on a particular section. Then they went back to the store, and the girl closed her eyes as her father led her to the chosen aisle. When she opened her eyes, she grabbed something quickly and they left.

I felt that way in Canadian supermarkets, trying to choose between two dozen types of olive oil. Virgin or extra-virgin? In Brazil and Mexico, there were one or two brands of cooking oil, which were either available or out of stock, and if there was a shortage, you wouldn't find any for weeks. People seemed pretty effete in Canada, reduced to worrying about meaningless distinctions, and their children struck me as overprotected and spoiled.

I'd never picked up on Canadians' protectiveness toward their children before. Of course, that's partly generational. When we'd left home, hardly anyone we knew had kids. Now friends told me that when their son or daughter went two doors away to play with buddies, they stood on their porches to make sure the kid got there. It wasn't like when we were kids and played in the streets. Children shouldn't play outdoors except when supervised, and I had to be especially careful not to let Gabriel walk in the alley behind our house. The police said it was a prime snatching area. Excuse me? They seemed embarrassed that I hadn't noticed all the headlines, or embarrassed that I was making them say it. Well, they told me, the pedophiles.

So we have our child-snatching myth in Canada, too. I don't mean to say that it never happens. It's possible that my teacher's nephew *was* almost kidnapped. Yet knowing what I now know about Mexico, I would guess that if someone had tried to grab him, the market ladies weren't behind it. A gang would have been trying to extort a ransom from his family. Still, it's not very likely. Violent crime has become a major problem in Mexico lately, but children still aren't kidnapped very often, and they certainly weren't when I lived there.

Yet there's another part to this. My friends in Mexico wrapped their kids in just as much cotton wool as my friends in Canada, even when abduction rates were minuscule. Especially in Mexico City, the few percent of children from professional class and rich families never left their houses unescorted. They were taken to and from school, wouldn't have dreamed of playing in the street and didn't trot off on their own to the corner store. Part of this was social convention, a show of being gently bred.

But I also came to realize that my friends in Mexico looked hesitant when I mentioned kidnapping not because they were embarrassed at coming from a "backward" country—or not only that—but because kidnapping is a raw subject for parents every-where in every class, who are terrified that something will happen to their children. People just *are*. I ended up thinking there were probably child-snatching myths in Africa and Asia too, although it occurs to me that local variations on the myth say something cru-cial about cultural preoccupations. It strikes me as powerfully sig-nificant that Mexican parents fear their children will be taken for money, while Canadians fear they will be taken for sex.

So, years after hearing the story, I come to the point of saying, We're more alike than different, God help us. My foreign-looking grandmothers, walking down Canadian streets. Me living in Mexico.

Yet before I reread my Cuernavaca journal for the first time in ages, I had completely forgotten about my teacher and her story. I didn't remember that she was the one who had started me thinking about kidnapping. Try as I might, I can now barely remember her, although I have a mental picture of a pretty young face turned half away from me. Much clearer is the room behind her. It's a class-room with a greenish-colored chalkboard held on the wall by metal brackets. No, it's the school's outdoor cafeteria with a glass-fronted metal cooler under the palm-frond roof. No, it isn't that either, though I see both places clearly with her shadowed figure placed just off-center. I see both places falsely. Even more important, I have no idea what she was thinking when she told me the story—who she was, what she meant, what she hoped to prove.

All I really have left of that moment is my own response, which I remember very well. The young mother I was then felt a dark and physical need to hug her only, precious, infinitely enviable child as close and tight as she possibly could. Then, and in the weeks that followed, she—I—looked out on the world through narrowed eyes, distrusting the foreign-looking people around me. (Foreign-looking! In their own country!) And even though I don't like to think of myself in these terms, I can see that there's probably a way in which this didn't stop. I was never again trusting enough to take my teacher's story at face value, after all.

So what layer of telling comes nearer to the truth? My intellectualized and optimistic conclusion that we're all in this together? Or my original, naive distrust of foreigners, which keeps us all apart?

16

ONCE WE COULD LEAVE THE HOTEL, AFTER THE EARTHQUAKE, we moved into the house we'd rented in a Mexico City suburb called Lomas de Chapultepec, where we lived for three years. Part Spanish, part Nahuatl, the suburb's name can be approximately translated as Grasshopper Hills. Las Lomas, as it's usually called, rolls up the mountains that rise on the western edge of the downtown plateau, and though after leaving home I'd planned never to live in another suburb, we decided to rent a house there for a couple of pragmatic reasons. People told us that the telephones, electricity and so on were far more reliable there than elsewhere in the city, and reliable services are crucial to a foreign journalist, whose telephone and computer line is an umbilical cord to home office.

Even more important, the pollution was said to be less intense than in the suburbs to the south—Coyoacán, San Angel and Pedregal—which were also supposed to have reasonably dependable services. Even then, Mexico was probably the most polluted city in the world, and parents did everything they could to protect their children. People who could only afford to live downtown kept their kids inside when pollution counts got too bad. Some people tied handkerchief masks across their faces. We tried to choose a place high enough in the hills that it lay above the smog line, although I felt a little isolated and moved in thinking it was going to be harder to connect with people than it would have been in the exhaust-ridden downtown.

Maybe it was, maybe it wasn't, but living in Las Lomas made an important difference in the way people saw us. We soon learned that as far as most Mexicans were concerned, Las Lomas was better translated as Locust Hills. The big industrialists lived there, and high insiders from the governing party—these were often the same thing—as well as ambassadors, retired and foreign, and the plain old rich-for-generations. Nob Hill (Snob Hill), Beverly Hills: We found that the suburb was not just a place, but a symbol. Many of the people who lived in Las Lomas also saw it in symbolic terms, of course—in this case as the only place People really lived.

No big revelation. Places are always more than just geography. He was born in the east end of London, she lives on the Upper West Side, they were from the wrong side of the tracks. But Las Lomas is a particularly powerful symbol known across Mexico, and for us, its power was compounded by the fact that we were looked upon as symbols, too. Not people, but foreigners. Not just foreigners, but *gringos*. I sometimes felt like wearing a sign: I did not steal Texas at the Alamo. In fact, being *gringos* got bloody tiring after a while, although the whole experience was also fascinating. We lived in a state of tension—quite revelatory tension— between being symbols living in a statement and being real people living in a house.

I loved that house. An oval plaque on the front said it was designed by architect Jorge del Rio before the Second World War, and the rooms were very pleasingly proportioned, with carefully rough-hewn beams in the ceiling and thick, cream-colored walls throughout. In a city where the majority of the twenty-five or so million people lived in appalling conditions, crowded together with suspect water to drink, we enjoyed marvelous beauty and comfort. Yet I don't want to give the wrong impression. The house was small for the neighborhood, about the size of houses occupied by reasonably successful journalists in London or Washington or Toronto. This, of course, was the answer to visiting friends who asked us whether we felt guilty living so well when most people lived so abysmally. "Don't you?"

(And yes, yes we did. We did. Children the same age as my son sold Chiclets on the street, filthy and starving and tugging at my leg. *Por favor?* My cat ate meat when those children never did. I got fogged into months-long depressions, got lost in a revolving series of anecdotes about the designer and poet William Morris, about his socialism and his arts-and-crafts workshops, about the contradictions between ideology and practice. Or if you wish, between symbols and reality. How Morris said he felt his inherited wealth to be a burden, yet calculated once that if he distributed his entire fortune among the artisans in his workshops, none of them would receive enough to make a difference in his life, while his own wife and daughters would end up miserable. Yes but. There was something Dante Gabriel Rossetti once said about Morris that casts doubt on his sincerity: "Did you notice that Topsy never has a penny for a beggar?" Yes but. Rossetti was the lover of Morris's wife Jane and didn't speak impartially. Yes but. That doesn't mean he was wrong.)

There's something else. Our house was also about the size of those occupied by the more successful Mexican journalists, writers and intellectuals, although most of them lived in a different part of town, down toward the university in the southern suburbs. Our house wouldn't have looked out of place down south. Most of theirs would have fit fine in Las Lomas. That's why I didn't appreciate the difference between the two areas at first—there isn't one.

Oh, Las Lomas is hilly and the roads are smoothly paved, while Pedregal is built on the flat reaches of a lava flow and the roads are often charmingly cobbled, but both have big, walled houses and gardens flaming with bougainvillea. They have tiled entranceways, maybe fountains, and most importantly, all are tended by the maids and gardeners who provide homeowners—or renters like ourselves—with the trappings of a gentle life.

Yet the cachet is much different. The southern suburbs are the arty ones, the leftist ones, where a degree of solidarity with the poor of Mexico is implied, although not always acted upon. In other words, there's a big symbolic difference between the two areas. That's not surprising, seeing that the southerners control the arts and therefore the symbols. Obviously, they want to live somewhere they find acceptable, so they artfully make it so, in part by comparing it both favorably and unfavorably to more philistine areas, even though the unfavorable comparisons have an unfortunate repercussion on their property values, which are lower than they are in Las Lomas.

It's funny, this cross-continental business of symbols. After living in Mexico for three years, I ended up thinking the telephones in Las Lomas didn't work any better than they did in the south. Just like friends in San Angel or Coyoacán, and about as often, I would have to get in the car and chase *Teléfonos de México* trucks so I could bribe the drivers to come and fix my phone. Yet it was a woman born and bred in Coyoacán, the well-educated daughter of a noted director, who first assured me that everything worked better in Las Lomas.

As for the pollution, I came to feel there was no significant difference anywhere in the city. It's true, friends in Coyoacán lived through a nightmare when their son contracted meningitis, and the doctor said it probably came from breathing the powdered human shit that's blown through the air. Yet friends who lived a few blocks from us in Lomas found that their son had lost twenty-five percent of his hearing in one ear after a series of infections the doctor also ascribed to the fetid smog.

So we lived under a symbol as well as a roof and were looked upon as symbols ourselves. Foreigners, *gringos*, somehow apart. At first, we were very much apart. Of course we were. It takes time to meet local people when you move, whether to a new city or a new country. People are busy. Why should they make room for you in their lives? Instead, we were welcomed most warmly by our fellow foreign journalists, immensely privileged people who formed a distinct society overlaid on their host country or countries with a private pecking order: staff correspondents for the big magazines and newspapers on top, followed by correspondents for the smaller papers, then the contract employees—the stringers—who worked for reputable organizations like the BBC, then photographers and freelancers, and finally the unilingual network cowboys who flew in periodically to shoot themselves some TV. This is not the way TV would put it, but by definition, TV doesn't count.

For three years we partied together. Or six, since roughly the same people kept turning up all over Latin America. It was a footloose, dislocated society, sometimes louche and sometimes fractious, yet we lived very much inside it, especially when we first arrived in Mexico. Collectively, we were indeed exotic outsiders, so it's no wonder the Mexicans saw us in that light. But the point of being a correspondent (or agreeing to move abroad with one) is to get to know something about another country, and like most people in our position, we ended up trying to leave the society of our colleagues in which, frankly, we felt most comfortable.

We cultivated Mexicans—or Brazilians, or Chileans, if that was where we found ourselves. We tried really *really* hard to be friends, exactly like some nerdy kid at school, which many journalists admit to having been. But the thing is, it often worked, because aside from any real qualities we may have had on offer, there was also that symbolic glow. We were foreigners, and even though we were disliked on one level, there was also a deep, itchy curiosity about *gringos* that got us invited places we'd never have got near otherwise. We looked at them while they looked at us, all of which meant we could sometimes feel like a very strange sort of trophy. See, I'm important enough to have a foreigner in my house. Would you like to come over and laugh at her?

Living in Las Lomas meant this curiosity started at the highest reaches of Mexican society. My next-door neighbors were very pleasant people whose families had been rich for generations, and my son and I were always invited to their children's birthdays, and periodically for afternoon coffee. The lady of the house, who spoke perfect English, told me about the days she used to ride her horse down the Paseo de la Reforma, how it used to be warmer in Mexico City before the pollution got so bad, how I was overpaying the servants.

That's the other thing about being in Las Lomas. We also lived in close daily contact with people, servants, who came from the poorest levels of Mexican society. Four of them, actually. It sounds extravagant, but two were gardeners who cultivated our postage stamp of lawn because, for years, they'd done the gardens for all five houses on our street, and if I'd let them go, their income would have been cut by a fifth.

There was also a woman named Delfina who came in three times a week to clean the house, bringing her son, who was about my son's age. I was basically told to hire her by our landlords/neighbors so she could look after their property, for which you couldn't blame them. Finally, there was a family living with us, a married couple who eventually had three children. Maria was the housekeeper while her husband, who worked in construction during the day, was around at night to act as watchman, which made me feel easier with Paul so often gone.

I can't say we ever got to know any of these people very well, either my neighbors or the women who worked in the house. I simply didn't have anything in common with any of the neighbors I met, while Maria and Delfina—who had both worked for foreigners before—made it subtly and wisely clear that if we were all to live and work together in the same small house, a certain distance had better be maintained. Yet things slipped out over the years: how Maria, an indigenous woman from the mountains of Oaxaca, had started working as a servant at age eleven, how one employer had thrown boiling water at her, how she'd tenaciously educated herself at night. She was very smart and self-contained, a brilliant cook who fed us better than the best restaurants in Mexico. In fact, she planned to open her own small restaurant after we left.

Delfina, on the other hand, was pregnant by that time, and wanted nothing more than to quit work and stay home. She was a breezy, happy person, who invited me to her son Hugo's birthday once, at her home in a distant *colonia*. "You drive along Reforma all through the rich section," she said, "until you get to . . . well, I guess you'd call it the poor section." You could have eaten off the floor of Delfina's house, although she wiped the plastic-covered chair she gave me before I was allowed to sit down, then served me the biggest portion of Jello-with-fruit. At my neighbors' parties, they hired magicians to entertain the kids, or rented expensive diversions like pony rides or merry-go-rounds.

"You were Delfina's pony ride," a friend said later. "You were her magician and her merry-go-round."

The gardeners I knew even less well, although it wasn't hard to see that Porfirio was much shrewder than Juan, who drank. One weekend, as Juan and I watched a plane fly over, he told me they'd moved the airport from its old location for a secret reason. There was a hole in the sky and too many planes had fallen into it.

It was a strange life, knocking up against both rich and poor. But of course the richest and poorest live in claustrophobic proximity throughout the Third World, just as they once did in Europe and North America (although that doesn't seem to be how the rich see it). What was different about our experience is that we also, gradually, got to know journalists and intellectuals much more like ourselves. Their preoccupations and recreations were the same as ours, politics and the arts. Many employed a cleaning lady, some a nanny, but they didn't live buffered by servants. Nor did the rich invite them, and they preferred it that way. We knew people who disliked coming out to Locust Hills, including one freelance photographer who hung out just inside the gate at our parties, accepting plastic glasses of beer but refusing to enter the house, and leaving as soon as he considered it polite.

Still, by the time we left, we were being invited to houses all over town, and introduced to all sorts of cousins and uncles, from insurance agents through sculptors and dancers to airline flight attendants. We'd visit high-rises in Condesa, or restored houses in lower-middle-class Colonia Roma, or head outside town to the cleaner exurbs like Tepoztlán. It was the final layer of Mexico we got to know, the middle class. Because obviously the layers I'm now talking about are the social classes, class being something that struck me—struck at my heart—the entire time we lived abroad.

It was my grandmothers who did it. Arriving to drink coffee with my Lomas neighbor, looking at the silver-framed photos of her immaculate children on a table in the entranceway, at the uniformed maid balancing a tray, the Limoges brought back from Europe generations before, at the gracefully crossed ankles of the other, elegant guests, *las señoras de Las Lomas*, I thought how desperately my Scottish Nannie had wanted all of this. If she'd lived to visit us in Mexico, she might finally have approved of me.

I winced at the thought, even though I'd learned more about my Nannie by then, and had come to see her as a disappointed woman. She'd been displaced a second time, in Canada, when her husband had stepped down as manager of the local bank. Two of his employees had been caught embezzling, and although Head Office didn't ask for his resignation, he resigned anyway and took a job as a clerk with the ministry of highways. It had to do with his drinking; he felt he would have caught them if he'd been more alert. He seems to have been an honorable, anguished man. My brother now owns the artists' pencils he used at night to draw detailed models of sailing ships. He'd wanted to be an architect, but instead he'd married early and came out to the colonies, hoping to better his family instead of himself.

My ambitious grandmother had fought his decision to quit banking. When someone told me that, I could almost hear her hectoring voice: Take it as warning. Pull up, man, and get a new bank somewhere else, where they don't encourage your weakness.

I don't think she was wrong. They had four children, after all. But I couldn't help believing that she'd resisted mainly out of horror at the prospect of falling off the top of the small-town social heap, knowing her snobbery as I did. You miserable geddle! You're nothing but a Krueger! I felt uneasy each time I thought of her in those Lomas living rooms, intimations of her posthumous approval making my arms prickle. Nor could I forget that my parents had worked as cleaners, pulling scummy wads of hair from The House of Beauty sinks, scrubbing off the soap film and bending to angle the vacuum cleaner nozzle into corners until they had to straighten up and stretch, arching their spines, hands on their hips, wincing the way Delfina winced while vacuuming our house.

By then I also knew that my Swedish Granny had worked as a chambermaid before leaving the Old Country. She was fourteen or fifteen when the family put her out as a maid, maybe three years older than our housekeeper, Maria, had been. I wondered if anyone had ever thrown boiling water at my Granny, if she'd been raped in the hotel, if the husbands and sons of Las Lomas still carried on the aristocratic tradition of impregnating the maids. At Delfina's party, I couldn't help remembering that the last time I'd eaten Jello-with-fruit was when my mother served it as a side dish to her Sunday roast beef.

Such social dislocation! There I was, surfing the Mexican class system; riding waves of heightened feeling for my grandmothers. The more I learned about the status my Nannie aspired to, the more disgusted I felt. Those Limoges-tasting, porcelain-blond, French-manicured coffee klatches were breathlessly, frantically, teeth-grindingly boring. Mainly the *señoras* complained about their maids. And if the maids' conversation wasn't any more edifying— usually they complained about the *señoras*—at least they had justice on their side. Their stories weren't about spilled food or missing soap, but slaps and hair-pulling and mingily withheld pay. My poor little Granny, raped and displaced. I felt a growing tenderness for her and wondered what you did to help.

Pay people decent wages for eight-hour days: one practical answer. But I also kept trying to understand what my Granny had gone through, uprooting herself, moving countries. I wondered if she'd seen Canada as clearly as I sometimes saw Mexico, and whether she felt as sickened and outraged as I often did at the many layers of injustice an outsider's perspective revealed.

Maybe she just felt neutered. No matter how outraged I felt, I knew I couldn't do anything about it. No one wanted foreigners meddling in Mexican affairs. No one, from any class. Take it from me, that's where the country's cohesive nationalism lies, in the widespread, central agreement that foreigners belong outside. I often felt cruelly squeezed between my real and symbolic roles, between being a person living her life and being a foreigner there to perform a function—the function of observing, and of being observed—in a way that was useful to other people as well as myself. Maybe my Granny found that, too.

Dirty Swede, dirty Swede. Help me elevate myself by putting you down.

And surely that's what class really is. It's the place where the real and symbolic come together to define you, and confine you. Everything you are is real—the way you talk, the color of your skin—but it also symbolizes your position in society, and simultaneously acts to keep you there. Most of us know that, and most of us live our lives without thinking too much about it. We live inside our roles, where we're comfortable. But when you move to another country where you don't fit in, all the different layers become very clear. The class system is revealed as sedimentary rock that's been formed under conditions of great pressure. And you know what? It's awful. It's awful. It's awful.

1 7

AFTER THE LAMP IN OUR HOTEL ROOM STOPPED SWINGING, we got dressed so we could go out and see what the earthquake had done. The television we flipped on wasn't working, and the radio was broadcasting panicky messages about this having been a big one, although no one really knew how big or how bad. We put Gabriel in his red-and-blue-striped stroller and started downstairs. The hallways looked a bit disheveled, littered with overturned plant pots and fallen tables, but the hotel itself seemed largely undamaged. When we got to the lobby, we saw one big jagged crack in the two-story, terra-cotta-colored wall in front and a man in a beige uniform scratching his head underneath it. We walked past him out the big glass front doors, planning to head toward downtown and the Foreign Press Club, where we assumed people might gather.

The sidewalks were uneven outside the hotel and Gabriel got a bumpy ride in his stroller. But some degree of unevenness was normal, and we didn't really see much for a few blocks, when we suddenly came upon a building with the front fallen off and several floors of open offices exposed to view. I took a picture. It looked strange because the buildings on either side were completely undamaged. A few men picked through the fallen concrete on the sidewalk, acting a bit puzzled. There weren't many people around, and it was pretty quiet. This part of town was heavily commercial; in fact Paul would rent an office there not long afterward. We walked on, and saw a few places where the asphalt had split and a few more damaged buildings. There was a growing smell of gas that began to worry me, but we weren't far from the press club by then, and soon began climbing the stairs.

We found three people there, listening to the radio. By this time everyone was saying that the earthquake had hit eight points on the Richter scale. Hundreds were dead, and buildings had fallen down all over the center of the city. There were gas leaks, fires and explosions. You could hear sirens on the radio. The international phone lines were dead, meaning Mexico City was completely cut off from the outside world. The people in the press club looked stunned. After a quick conference, Paul decided he'd better head off toward the damaged area and get to work. He hadn't expected to be working so soon. We'd come to Mexico City from Cuernavaca because our furniture had arrived in the airport, and people said it would take a couple of weeks to steer everything through customs, take delivery and so on. But now he was going to have to prepare a story on the earthquake and somehow send it to Toronto, despite the lack of international communications.

My job was less glorious: to jostle son and stroller back to the hotel. But it was easily accomplished, and I soon saw the man in the beige uniform up on a tall ladder in the lobby, quickly plastering the two-story crack. As a matter of fact, it would be both plastered and painted by 11 A.M., and by the time the paint dried a couple of hours later, you couldn't tell there had ever been anything the matter. In the meantime, I was able to get Gabriel some breakfast and took him swimming not long afterward in the hotel pool. It was a beautiful day, warm and sunny, and the clear blue sky and the turquoise pool and terra-cotta walls of the hotel all seemed so bright they vibrated. Yet what in God's name was I doing, paddling a child in water wings through a swimming pool in the middle of a disaster?

"What can I do?" I'd asked in the press club. "What should I do to help?"

A Mexican woman looked at me as if I was crazy. "Take your baby back to the hotel, *señora*. This has nothing to do with you."

Paul came back late that night, grimy and shaking. Buildings in the garment district had collapsed so concrete floors fell together like layers in a torte, killing hundreds of workers. Fronts had fallen off buildings, or they'd simply tumbled to pieces. A downtown hotel was raging with fire. Everywhere, for miles and miles, they were pulling bodies from the wreckage. Trapped people screamed, relatives screamed, survivors sat dazed on the ruins.

Paul met one woman from Montreal who had walked through a crack in her hotel wall onto the roof of the next building, then watched her hotel fall down behind her. He ran into another foreign journalist and they wandered around together for a while, before losing each other in the noise and confusion.

Yet what had impressed him was the way ordinary people quickly joined together to defeat the confusion. They formed cooperative teams to dig through the wreckage and lift the injured to those who could nurse them. They doused fires by passing bucket after bucket of water along endless, tireless human chains. The authorities were hopeless. They bleated meaningless messages on the radio but couldn't seem to get anything started. People muttered that they were a disgrace and told Paul that this would be a turning point for Mexico. Now Mexicans would finally see they didn't need the smothering, corrupt and insidious Institutional Revolutionary Party, which had won every municipal, state and presidential election in Mexico for more than fifty years (or said it had). The PRI was hollow; the PRI was finally proved useless. Now the people would break out and run a cleaner, more efficient Mexico on their own.

How to turn disaster into a symbol. How to take hope from a tragedy. Maybe they were even right, since fifteen years after the earthquake, the PRI is crumbling. In 1997, as soon as Mexico City residents were allowed to elect their own civic government, they returned an opposition mayor and council. Unfortunately, there's also an increase in drug running in Mexico, cartels are emerging and—as in most countries these days—the economy is in a mess.

For both these reasons, violence is growing. When I lived there, Mexico City was remarkably safe. I walked everywhere. But on a recent trip back, Paul was robbed at gunpoint in a taxi, and friends are putting barbed wire on top of the walls surrounding their houses. "This year wasn't as bad as last year," one friend wrote recently, "when the watchman was killed in front of his children and C's brother was kidnapped. But they shot the accountant at the factory and made off with the payroll. Our car was stolen and the house broken into twice." Things have changed, and the earthquake now looks like a neat symbolic breaking point between past and future, a marker of social as well as physical upheaval. Though, God help us, it felt real enough at the time.

The morning after, a Friday, Paul grabbed a taxi very early to the airport. He planned to catch the first available plane to a city with operating telephones, file his story, then turn around and come back. I caught a taxi in the other direction to meet the moving van at our house. The movers had called the previous night saying that the government had told them to clear everything out of their warehouse and prepare to receive foreign aid. So much for the ponderous Mexican bureaucracy. Now I too would see the other side of the coin: people working with backbreaking efficiency.

And in fact the van pulled up at our house precisely at 7 A.M. A team of men much smaller and stronger than I jumped out and began humping box after box into the house, working without pause as I ran around telling them this goes here and that goes there. I kept asking myself what any of this mattered, and imagined the men must have wondered that, too. How were their families, what had they been through, what were they going through; were they afraid not to show up for work no matter how much they wanted to stay home, if they had homes left standing? This goes here and that goes there. It was all very practical and very mysterious—especially at that point in the early afternoon when they decided silently and implacably to abandon the remaining boxes in the yard, get in their truck and leave.

I don't know how I got everything inside. I remember carrying a floppy double mattress upstairs, though I don't remember how I managed, or what Gabriel was doing at the time. What I next remember is being back at the hotel and giving Gabriel a bath, kneeling on the floor and suddenly feeling very dizzy. I was obviously overtired and felt as if the room had started revolving around me. Then I noticed that the few inches of water in the deep tub were slapping up the sides, slapping first on one side, then the other, higher and higher, just like the lamp the previous morning.

It was another earthquake! Grabbing Gabriel, I wrapped him in the thick white hotel towel and ran into the corridor, confused and stupid with panic. I knew what was happening this time and turned lunatic, running this way, running that, toward the stairs, toward the doorway, not knowing what to do, where to go, where was safe, *where in God's name was my husband?*

I learned later he was on a plane just about to land at the Mexico City airport. The pilot came on and drawled, "Ladies and gentlemen, slight technical problem with the runways uh. We're going to have to return to Houston." Paul had a radio and used the earphones to learn there was a second big quake in progress, although he couldn't say anything, since the plane was full of scarcely controlled people flying in to look for their families, and he didn't want to start a panic. He thought we were probably safe in the hotel, although he didn't like to dwell on the idea of the gaping crack in the lobby that had been plastered over so quickly. He was just as glad the airplane took off for Mexico again not long after they'd landed at Houston, even though it had already been a long day, he was exhausted, and he knew that everyone in Mexico faced more of the same.

When the quake finally stopped, I walked back to my room, clutching my child and feeling foolish. Once again, we were fine, although this time I could guess that many more people were dying all over the city. What was I doing here? What could I do? What had I done by coming here?

Over the years, I'd heard my Nannie shout those questions and read them in my Granny's letters. They were crucial in forming my outlook, my way of looking at the world. I became interested in peeling back layer after layer of experience in search of the elusive truth, an analyst, an observer, a resident foreigner, the same but different, not really needed but nevertheless handy to have around, at least sometimes, sort of.

But in Mexico, I felt I reached a deeper understanding of our common point of view. Or at least, I found the word that defines it. It occurred to me a couple of weeks after the earthquakes, when we'd finally moved into our house and I was able to meet with the administrator of a play school nearby. She was a bit exasperated with me for trying to enter my child in her school a month after registration had closed. I was obviously another arrogant *gringa* who believed she could get anything she wanted when she wanted it. Yet she was hardly going to turn away a child whose parents were reliably bankrolled from abroad at a time when more than a few people had been financially ruined.

"As a matter of fact," she told me, "we can take your boy. A couple of places have opened up. Two of our children were killed in the earthquakes."

My mouth dry, I took the position, I enrolled my son. And, as I say, there was a word I thought of, one that sits at the base of all my dealings with Mexico and the way I came to look at my grandmothers, who were buried—embedded—in Canada. I wasn't inside, I wasn't outside, I was simply there. A layer in the landscape, a geological fact, maybe a fault. But mainly, and from that point on, I was and remain complicit.

M O B I L I T Y

FOR THE FIRST COUPLE OF YEARS WE LIVED IN MEXICO, I
kept expecting life to fall into a pattern, and it didn't. Instead, we
did an enormous amount of traveling, Paul learning to take off at
a moment's notice to cover breaking new stories. He was on the
road almost all the time, covering a huge beat that sometimes
took him on long trips to South America and otherwise kept him
busy shuttling around Mexico, the Caribbean and the civil wars of
Central America—off to El Salvador or Guatemala or Nicaragua,
where the iguana was poor company, whacking its tail irritably on
the leaky tin roof.

I had more of a routine in Mexico, embedded early on in both
motherhood and writing. Yet we quickly learned that if Gabriel and
I were going to see much of Paul, we had to go with him. Not all
the time; it was too disruptive and sometimes too dangerous. But
we soon started racking up a large number of trips to small countries, visiting the hot spots, both literal and figurative. We stayed in
places that we never would have seen otherwise, including the
time that events took Paul to the Caribbean off-season, and our
travel agent managed to book us a package at an exclusive resort in
Grenada that would have been far too expensive in winter.

By then, I was starting to look on our travels as potential
material for the short stories I was writing. Originally, I'd tried
to write out of my background, thinking that someone should set
stories in Canadian suburbia—and they should. But my writing
seemed to work best when it was set somewhere else. I hadn't
started asking why, I was just growing conscious of a pattern. Yet
that was another reason to keep traveling, and as we landed in
sleepy summertime Grenada, I looked forward to staying at such
a rich and promising place, craning my neck as we rounded the
final corner. A line of villas wavered up ahead, a low-slung

mirage rising from the white sand beach to shimmer like ice in the tropical heat.

After we checked in, a courteous bellhop showed us to our walled villa, opening a gate onto a patio half-filled by a small swimming pool overhung with flowers. Behind the pool were huge shadowy louvered rooms where the bellhop showed us how to use the air conditioning, or to angle the evening breeze through the louvers. Everything was made of thick dark-stained wood that smelled so good I wanted to eat it like chocolate. As soon as the bellhop left, I pressed my face into a pillar and breathed in bark and cloves, humid breezes butting my legs like dogs with warm wet noses.

Exploring the villa, we found indoor hammocks and closets the size of rooms, towels thick as bathrobes and smooth wide floorboards. I kicked off my sandals, unused to such physical comfort, even in Mexico, where it required constant work to keep our well-proportioned house clean and functioning in the sooty air. Ease was usually beyond our budget. I soon noticed that most of the villa's fixtures were, as well, and worried that Gabriel would break one of the expensive-looking lamps as he played

Such a typically Canadian reaction: You suspect you don't deserve it, that you don't really belong. Or maybe it's just middle class. I loved the deluxe feel of the place, tracing my fingers down the billowing mosquito nets, touching the netted wind. But when we went to the open thatched patio for dinner, with starched tablecloths thickly set with silver and flowers, I didn't like to see that the clientele was uniformly white and the wait staff all black, including the older man who appeared at my elbow, suave and well-groomed, too formally dressed for the climate and reserved in his manner, although very polite. As he took my order, choosing not to meet my eyes, he gave a faintly indulgent smile at my choice, which simultaneously worried me—had I mispronounced something?—and made me think that he must be like an old family retainer, even though I'd never met a family retainer in my life. I had an idea that the inn's management was trying to recreate the air of a plantation, and wondered if that was why black tourists might not feel comfortable there. Also whether I should.

Yet the food was superb, small portions of fish and fruit freshly prepared. They cooked children's dishes for my son, even provided a distraction: a flock of blackbirds with intelligent cocked heads and bright yellow eyes that flew onto the half wall of the dining patio where it was open to the pounding sea, bold things that Gabriel immediately dubbed the cheeky birds for the way that they dropped on the floor close to the table, craning their heads up comically—for the way they flew *onto* the table, trying to snatch our bread.

"Cheeky birds!" he squealed happily. The younger waiters shooed them away, smiling and less formal, especially at breakfast, when they laughed and joked in a muted way with the sleepy, slow-moving guests. Some of the other guests struck me as being a little uncomfortable there as well, including an older American man who often sat near us, bowing his head as his wife hissed instructions across the table. I think it was probably his wife who dressed the poor man in khaki and white, but you could see a Hawaiian shirt in flamboyant halo around him, like the uniforms that cops always seem to be wearing even when they're not. His face was flushed with blood pressure and his wife ordered his food, which he didn't seem to enjoy. It was a pity, they were paying enough, and all he seemed to like was feeding the cheeky birds, tossing them balled-up pellets of bread.

"You'll encourage them," his wife hissed, turning to nod graciously at the waiter as he placed her plate in front of her, blinking at her flatware with quick, birdlike calculation before choosing a plausible fork, taking a bite, then giving the waiter a supercilious smile, as if she was used to better.

That's when I started to think about tourism as traveling in class. You spend a week or two vacationing at a social level above your own, living in a way that you can't ordinarily afford, with servants, daily restaurant meals, leisure. You only get a little uncomfortable, like the Americans and like me, if you jump too many steps up the class ladder all at once, maybe worse than uncomfortable if you pause to consider the way that your temporary rise presses other people down, making them take a supporting role to your star turn in the service economy that tourism creates.

I winced at the blinding flash of the woman's fork. The grandfatherly waiter avoided my eyes.

"Finished eating," my son cried, and I helped him down from his chair to take a ramble outside.

When I thought about that trip afterward, I had the feeling of something coming into focus, something that I needed to think about. Class mobility? It informed so much fiction, not to mention my life. But our lives were hectic enough that I forgot about it for another year, only picking it up again when we were driving through Panama on the way to visit the great prima ballerina Dame Margot Fonteyn, who had retired to a *finca* with her Panamanian husband, Tito Arias, a quadriplegic immobilized in a wheelchair for almost twenty-five years.

19

PANAMA WAS TORRID WITH REVOLUTION WHEN I ARRIVED— a very strange, upper-middle-class, pro-American revolution that was aimed at getting rid of the military president, General Manuel Antonio Noriega. Paul and most of the regional correspondents had been there for at least a month, covering the pot-banging, whistle-blowing demonstrations that had escalated into a general strike. The US was backing the revolutionaries, but General Noriega enjoyed strong support from the country's many poor people, not to mention the army, so the place was a bit of an anti-*gringo* tinderbox. Yet, day to day, the streets were calm enough and the tropical climate so inviting that correspondents' partners began to fly in for visits.

I say partners, but mostly it was wives. A growing number of women were working as correspondents, but the majority of journalists in the field were men, and the professional ethos was pretty *macho*. A few years later, when a correspondent friend was introducing me to her baby, cooing and talking baby talk, she looked up and said, "Listen to me!" Then, "You're not going to tell anybody about this, are you?" Not surprisingly, this virile attitude percolated into the spouse culture, as well. There I was, flying into a general strike with my four-year-old son, a little nervous, but also hoping to get a sniff of the type of conflict Paul covered all the time, avid to rubberneck a seedy *macho* equatorial world so very different from the female home I'd made in Mexico, as the Panamanian business class (male) lined up against the army (male) in another one of those endless damn struggles for power.

The first thing that happened when Gabriel and I got off the plane was that I was somewhat roughly searched by a tall customs officer with a ballistically pointed bust and a bouffant hairdo of a type I hadn't seen since elementary school. She called me "*amor*" and breezily confiscated the file of newspaper clippings that I was bringing in for Paul.

"These too, love," she said, taking my newspapers. "Subversive documents." Meaning that morning's *New York Times* and a copy of *The New York Review of Books*. Tickled by her allegation, I started arguing with the breezy customs officer, then with the airport's chief of security.

"It's not subversive," I told them. "It's *The New York Times*."

Sliding glass doors hushed open and shut as the other passengers cleared customs. Outside, I could see Paul pacing, appearing and disappearing in his correspondent's regulation jeans and white shirt. Eventually he glimpsed what was happening and barged through the doors. Leaning across a metal table from the security chief, he began arguing more loudly than I had, although he didn't get any further. Red-faced, he stalked over to a pay phone and called the army's chief of public relations, a major, who agreed to speak with the airport security chief, a sergeant. Soon the security chief took the major's call, and with a look on his sweaty face that was both belligerent and horrified, he asked, "How do I know you are who you say you are?" as I imagined his sergeant's stripes melting and flowing down his sleeve.

"*Tengo hambre*," Gabriel said suddenly. I'm hungry. The breezy customs officer bent down, looking concerned.

"*Eh, mi amor?*"

I was happy for an excuse to get away and steered Paul out the door, saying that we could get the clippings back later. But the empty airport was even stranger than the customs room. We spent far too much time flying into empty airports. The concourse echoed like a deserted mall, giving me that familiar dream-feeling of a massive palace that's been abandoned—but not really, not quite, there's something nasty encroaching on the fringes. Outside, we tossed our bags in the carpeted trunk of a rental car and drove into Panama City, its streets just as empty from the general strike. Unspooling down those empty streets reminded me of another dream I have sometimes, a slow-motion glimpse of a tall, pale, ghostly city in which there is a glacial reservoir dammed between brown hills, a turquoise reservoir in which I see a small blond girl standing halfway up a ladder that leans against nothing.

Turning a corner in Panama City, we came across troops in full battle dress guarding a government building, young men in camouflage who jeered as we drove past. Reaching city center, we drove down a canyon between high-rise buildings where a few restaurants opened their doors. We finally saw a crowd at the central market—an unusually serious, quiet, murmuring crowd which seemed even weirder when I realized that no one had brought children. Nearby, in a vacant lot, a circus roustabout threw not enough straw to four dusty attenuated elephants.

The whole place left me feeling unmoored, and I was relieved when Paul suggested that we leave Panama City the next day, taking a look at the Canal before heading into the countryside. The revolution seemed stalled and he could take a week's holiday, first at the beach, and later in the western mountains. Best of all, he said, we could visit the *finca*, the ranch, where Dame Margot Fonteyn had said that she would live out her days.

Here was a promise to hold onto, an expat being much easier to visit than the dream of revolution. Dame Margot had been retired for a decade by then, living very simply for someone whose career had been so eminent and rare. I wondered what she could possibly be like, a woman who'd had the discipline to dance until she was almost sixty, and who'd been celebrated, for much of that time, as the greatest ballerina not just in England, but the world. I had been disappointed the previous week when Paul told me on the telephone that he and a couple of other correspondents had already driven out to interview her. She was famous for turning away reporters, but they'd brought flowers, and two particularly charming wives had gone along, and to their surprise, she'd ended up chatting for hours. I wished I'd flown down a week earlier, I found her so fascinating—although I also felt more than a little uneasy about the tourism aspect. You went to Panama to look at the Canal and afterward you "did" Margot Fonteyn?

Yet Paul went on to tell me that Dame Margot had asked for copies of any pictures that turned out well. A week later, after a stop at the beach, I took my seat in the car holding an envelope containing some photographs and a thank-you note. Outside the town of El Higo, Paul recognized the unmarked dirt road and turned toward the *finca*, driving through a dappled forest of swaying young trees.

As we rattled down the rutted road, I was feeling a bit self-conscious, having read Dame Margot's autobiography at the beach. In it, she endorsed the theory that interesting people had interesting nostrils. I'd never really noticed my nostrils before, but a quick check in the mirror proved they were totally ordinary. On top of this, I didn't know very much about ballet. At least, I knew enough to realize that I really knew nothing, and that it would be wrong to trouble Dame Margot with my ignorance. I wondered what I could possibly say to her. I wasn't even a one-time dancer who just wanted to sit at her feet—although I admit to being curious about the state of her feet, a homely concern that she could probably have discerned by taking a look at my nose.

It really *was* tourism. The writer as tourist, sticking her nose into someone else's life, exploring another person's experience of mobility. As far as Panamanians were concerned, Dame Margot had married up. Despite all her honors and glory, she'd been born Peggy Hookham, a middle-class English girl, while her husband, Tito, was the one-time heir to the country's greatest political dynasty, a former deputy in the National Assembly and Panamanian ambassador to the Court of St. James, his father and uncle having been elected president of Panama six times between them.

As we drove along, I could almost hear a noxious little underlying hum: Maybe I can use this some day. Yet I couldn't help hoping, as we finally pulled up, that curiosity so intense was really the same thing as homage.

2 0

SHE WAS STANDING NEAR THE CARPORT AS WE GOT OUT, hanging back in the green shadows, her face obscured, her posture wary. Then she seemed to recognize Paul and walked out to greet us, accepting the envelope graciously, with an absent half-smile, before getting to the point.

"What's happening in the capital?" Dame Margot asked. "Have you been there recently? Tito will want to know, if you don't mind. Do you have a minute to stop?"

Her dark eyes were large and appraising, lively, ready to be amused. I'd read in her autobiography that her mother was half Brazilian, and later I would know Brazilian women, also beautiful, with the same light, upright figure and estimating eyes. Yet there was nothing Brazilian in the way she spoke, in a pleasing, tripping contralto that was at once unaffected, self-effacing and implacable.

"If you don't mind waiting a moment," Dame Margot said, already heading off, calling over her shoulder, "I'll just make some arrangements." When she returned, she led us away from the small whitewashed house and down a path through the forest. It was a very hot day, but she walked quickly, light on her feet, bone thin, wearing jeans, and looking at least a decade younger than her age, which was almost seventy. I can still remember the tapping cadence of her sandals on the soft brown earth ahead of me. People said dancers' feet could look deformed, but I thought hers looked like a working man's hands, all knobs and character, not deformed but used.

Tito sat in his wheelchair beside a table in a forest clearing, naked except for a big white towel laid across his lap. The arrangements, I thought, taking the seat Dame Margot indicated. She put Paul closer to Tito and Gabriel furthest away, although she watched, birdlike, with a gracefully inclined neck, as I brought out the colored pencils and paper we always traveled with, and Gabriel began to draw.

Her own seat was directly at Tito's elbow. From her autobiography, I'd learned that Tito had been shot in the neck in 1964, the bullets injuring his spinal cord and leaving him a quadriplegic. In hospital, a month later, he'd suffered a high fever that had cost him his voice. Dame Margot was one of the few still able to understand what he was saying; she was his interpreter. After a quick introduction, he whispered something that she repeated as, "So?"

So Paul told him the latest news about the general strike as Tito, through Dame Margot, asked a series of shrewd, sharp, witty questions. It was immediately clear that he—Roberto Arias, Robertito, Tito—was a feral politician, delighting in the most arcane details of party infighting, even though he'd been shot during an assassination attempt after winning his seat in the National Assembly.

At least, that was the official story. Paul had been told in the capital that the political rival who shot Tito was also the husband of his mistress, and that the motives of everyone involved were sophisticated and muddy. This was probably true, although the Arias family was so powerful that gossip hung around them like swamp gas. Tito's father had served two terms as president, while his uncle, Arnulfo Arias, had been elected four times. People said that if Tito hadn't been shot, he would have ended up as president as well, and years of political misery would have been avoided.

On the other hand, his uncle Arnulfo had been overthrown three of the four times that he'd been elected, so it's possible that Tito would have ended up as ex-president, as well. Then as president and ex-president again, maybe fleeing to Brazil, where he'd gone after his abortive coup attempt in 1959, when his family had been out of power. Tito's revolution, Dame Margot called it in her autobiography. At the time, they'd been married for about four years and she'd insisted on joining Tito off the coast of Panama, even though she didn't speak much Spanish or know anything about politics.

It was all an insouciant farce. One of Tito's boats was packed so heavily with arms that it sank, while the steering mechanism of a second somehow got damaged and it started turning in circles like a mad dog. Not surprisingly, they were spotted by the National Guard. Tito sped off in a shrimp boat, leaving Dame Margot to slip back to Panama City, where an embarrassed government jailed her. Soon the world was treated to the incongruous sight of ballet's prima ballerina assoluta being accused of gunrunning and deported to Miami.

Thirty years later, interpreting Tito's whispers, Dame Margot glanced over at her husband affectionately, burbling with laughter at his frequent jokes. Although she was the one to speak, I soon found that I was watching not her, but Tito. His cheeks were so chubby and his expression so ardent that he looked like one of the Lost Boys, his smile playing on an overbite, his eyebrows always working. I couldn't help looking at his hands, which lay on the arms of his wheelchair, clenched and spastic, the skin slowly growing darker as if his fingers had been dipped in stain. Tito's eyes were even more absorbing, the pupils caverns. He looked out hungrily, watching us follow what he'd said, his words unscrolling in his wife's repetition until she reached the inevitable punch line.

"He says," Dame Margot told us, giggling, "he says that General Noriega is so adept at sending out confusing signals, that in the end he confuses even himself."

When we laughed, an odd word came to mind. Tito beguiled us. His conversation struck me as the last echo of the courtiers' wit in the time of Shakespeare. Lordly, jaunty, heroic: I thought in terms of an antique vocabulary. Also of breeding. Tito had that well-bred air of mastery and entitlement. As he talked, an afternoon breeze arose, threatening his towel. Dame Margot often had to reach across and, smiling, flip it back into place. Of course she had to, but Tito still managed to give the impression that he could have taken care of it if he'd wanted.

He also let me know, through saucy looks, that he wouldn't have minded if the towel blew off. I had to glance away sometimes, watching Gabriel as he drew with unprecedented concentration, quietly filling page after page with birds and cartoon characters. Soon I began to wonder how much longer this would last. Lunch had been hours ago, and I was getting hungry myself.

"You want something," Dame Margot said. "It's warm, isn't it? A drink, perhaps?"

With a concerned look at Tito's towel, she flew back down the path, leaving an awkward silence behind her. Tito appeared self-conscious for the first time, and I think we were all relieved when Gabriel squirmed a bit and started complaining.

"It's not warm, it's hot," he said. "And I'm bored."

Tito laughed silently as I took up the notebook, asking about the drawings until Dame Margot reappeared carrying a tray. A glass of juice settled Gabriel, and the dish of cashews she put on the table.

"From our own tree," Dame Margot said, as she uncorked a bottle of white wine. "This isn't quite cold enough, I'm afraid, but I put another on ice for after."

As I raised my glass, the world shifted through its prism, and across from me I saw a lonely aging couple with all the glitter of their lives behind them. The Arias fortune seemed to have gone elsewhere. We sat in the forest because they had no air conditioning, and Dame Margot had been forced to leave Tito's towel to the breeze because there was no one to help with the wine. She'd written that Tito had three children from his first marriage, and they'd mentioned grandchildren, but who knew how often they visited? For the first time, I felt abashed at my intrusion. I'd come to be entertained, but I should have been helping to entertain them, and I didn't see how. Paul and Tito had already covered most of the political news. I realized that I'd better unearth a new topic, especially given the occasional flicker of Dame Margot's lips, which suggested that she found politics less enthralling than her husband.

Tito seemed ready to speak again when Dame Margot helped him to some wine.

"I loathe doing interviews, you know," she told Paul. "When you came the other day, I didn't really want to do it. But we're rather isolated here." Shrugging slightly, she turned to me. "You're not a journalist?"

I told her that I wrote journalism as well as fiction, mostly fiction lately. To my surprise, she questioned me about the fiction, what I wrote, where it was published—hardly anywhere—and I brought out the stammered fact that my first book had just been accepted for publication the following year.

"Let me give you a piece of advice," she said. "Never read the reviews."

"Did you really manage that?"

"Never care what anyone thinks of you," she insisted.

Tito laughed silently and, glancing at him, Dame Margot smiled back. But she was also watching me, waiting for an answer, and I told her that I seemed to be unusually dense about perceiving other people's opinions of me. I spent so much time watching the world that I never suspected anyone might be watching me back and was always disconcerted if it turned out that somebody was.

"You were going to say something else," Dame Margot said.

I told her that my mother had signed me up for ballet lessons when I was a child. I'd been thrilled until I heard my mother tell her friend that she was doing it because I was clumsy, and she hoped that this would help. I'd never really thought about being clumsy before. But we took our lessons in a room with a mirrored wall and I was forced to see that I was much taller and bigger-boned than the pretty little girls. I thumped rather than flitted, I was always half a turn behind, and I trailed behind the quicker ones like a disconnected caboose. My mother says that after two or three classes, I told her, "You can save your money. I'm never going to be a ballerina."

Half-smiling at the memory, I said, "I think you're right. I'd better not read the reviews."

"I've never understood why parents use the arts as punishment," Dame Margot said, glancing at Gabriel.

"I'm bored," he said. "When are we leaving?"

Dame Margot craned over sympathetically. "Boredom is something adults learn to deal with. It isn't really for children. Would you like some more cashews?"

Handing him the bowl, I said, "I feel guilty sometimes, trucking him around like this. He's going to all these fascinating places, but he won't remember them when he's older. Sometimes it even gets a little dangerous. When we were driving out of Panama City, we got 'Yankee Go Home,' things like that. But even when it's not like that, he'd just as soon be playing on his swing set."

Dame Margot leaned toward Tito. "He says it's quite all right," she said, then hesitated. "He says, you do him a favor by treating him this way. He says, you're teaching him that there's such a thing as injustice in the world."

After a pause, Dame Margot asked, "More wine?" as Tito's laughing eyes bored through us.

2 1

MY FATHER WAS IN A WHEELCHAIR BY THEN. I WAS THINKING of him the whole time I sat with Dame Margot and Tito. All three of them were about the same age, and since my father shipped over to England at the start of the Second World War, it's even possible that he saw the young Margot Fonteyn dance, her ballet company having been pressed into service to entertain the troops for the duration of the war.

I'm only speculating. My father hardly ever talked about the war, although I have an idea he would have tried to get out of going to the ballet. Really, he had nothing in common with the others apart from the wheelchair. We never even knew what was wrong with him, although that was partly because he refused to see a doctor for more than thirty years, having developed the same low opinion of the medical profession during the war as he had of the clergy. We only knew that gradually, throughout my childhood, his limp kept getting worse. Eventually he was shambling. People turned away from him. I suppose they thought that he was drunk, although this didn't occur to me at the time. I never saw him drink more than a single rye-and-ginger, or maybe a bottle or two of beer when it got very hot. Yet it was impossible to visit El Higo without making the comparison.

The story I grew up with was that my father had driven his motorcycle over a land mine during the Allied invasion of Italy. He was evacuated to a hospital in North Africa, where he was treated, and eventually—there? back in Canada?—diagnosed with osteoarthritis of the lower back. Later, the doctors didn't think that was all, and one neurologist even wondered if he'd suffered heavy-metal poisoning during his years as a machinist. He could also have been suffering from liver problems, having been treated for both hepatitis and malaria while he was hospitalized in North Africa. Six-foot-three, and his weight had dropped to ninety-seven pounds. Shaking his head, he told us once that he'd seen lightly wounded men force their arms through the mosquito netting in the hospital so they'd get malaria too and not have to go back to the front. After that, he clammed up.

It's strange to grow up in a house where no one talks about the most important things, although I suppose it's the same for almost everybody. My father never played with us when we were kids, not even with my brother. Mostly he worked, either at his full-time job, or stopping off after his shift to make a few freelance repairs at the job shops—medium-sized print shops with a couple of Linotypes—or going in at night to clean The House of Beauty. When he was free, we sometimes played cards, rummy or Romoli, but there was never any hockey, no games of catch, no sinking a few baskets in a hoop on the garage. I have no idea if he was in pain. He never said a word about being in pain, not a single word, ever. But he spoke less and less as the years wore on, and he'd never said much anyway.

Once I saw him hunched over the sports pages. Or was it the obituaries? "Look at this! I fought that guy during the war, over in England. He was the heavyweight champion of the Canadian army." Slow chuckle. "Got busted down from sergeant for that one. Fought him in a pub. They sent me to the brig. Beat him up pretty good, though."

Another time he was watching a TV special about the war. "Now look here, that's the invasion of Sicily." Long silence. "That's where I was. Right there."

I always thought of these things as clues, without exactly understanding that there was a mystery.

"Your father used to dress so beautifully," my mother said. "Like Gregory Peck. Oh, he was a *handsome* man. He'd walk down the street and all the girls would stare."

When I was growing up, he spent his days in work clothes, matching pants and long-sleeved shirts the color of green traffic lights. He ducked his head when we saw him in those, usually when we went in on Thursday to pick up his check from the back shop of the old Sun Tower on Beattie Street, and later the composing room of the new Pacific Press building on Granville. Both places were dense with noise from the big chunking Linotypes and the green-clothed men yelling around them. Both smelled of important metals that my father would get the printers to pour, molten lead flowing into molds that clanked out little hits of type, our names spelled backward and warm in our palms.

He never wore his work clothes at home, preferring dark pants and lighter shirts with the undershirt showing respectably through. Dressed like that, he would sometimes talk over the fence with our neighbors, a dentist on one side and the police chief on the other, although it grated on me that the dentist always called him "Ron," and for many years my father would say, "Dr. Jefferies." But when he was home he usually stayed inside, watching television from his gold-colored recliner.

"You see that? We used those guns during the Battle of Britain."

What I saw were his moods, his greenish-brown eyes darkening as if he'd got lost in a forest.

"I had grade eight, that's what I had."

"I had grade five. You listening to me? You listening? You're going to get an education."

"Your father was an intelligent man. His father pulled him out of school to work in the garage. It was the Depression. But he did his grade-twelve equivalency in the army. He had his high-school graduation."

"The Battle of Ortona. . . ." Another long silence, this time unbroken.

Years later, my mother showed me his wartime driver's license. "You see where he's written down this number? I always like to think it's a girl's phone number. I like to think he had some fun."

"We had *fun*. He used to play the Hawaiian guitar, the ukulele, singing all the time." My mother started swaying and singing, "*Ukulele lady with you*."

I couldn't picture him playing the ukulele. He had bulky hands, a working man's hands, the nails growing so thick and yellow he had to pare them with a kitchen knife. I remember the knobs, the humps of his knuckles, the wiry black hairs, the roughness, the pinkish healing burns and black lines of ingrained grease.

I remember him clenching those hands around my upper arms and shaking me when I ran away from the neighborhood kids. "You're going to show them. Do you hear me? You're smarter than they are. You're going to be a professor at the university. Are you listening to me? You get out of here and show them. You show them. You go show them."

I remember him shaking his head at a racist remark. "I've known a hell of a lot of Indians who aren't drunks, and a *hell* of a lot of drunks who aren't Indians."

"Your father used to be a shop steward in the union," my mother said. "I don't know why he stopped. He always enjoyed going to those meetings."

"Where do you think you're going? In whose car? Not to any parties, you're not. You're not going to end up like me. Driving the motorcycle into the wall. You hear that? Drove it into a god-damn wall. That's what happened. You drink, that's what happens."

That wasn't true, either. But I was sixteen and newly equipped with my driver's license.

"You make sure what happened to me doesn't happen to you. You show them. You show them, you hear me? University professors get four months' holidays a year."

Going to university was my first real experience of mobility, class mobility, rising from working up to middle. Or as a then-Marxist friend insisted, given my suburban upbringing, taking a half-step out of the petite bourgeoisie. Thomas à Kempis wrote—I used this as an epigraph for my first book—"They who travel seldom come home holy." It wasn't just tourism in this case, but real travel, a wrenching journey. Our family kept doing this. My grandparents, emigrating. My father, heading off to war.

I found the actual documents when I was eleven or twelve. I didn't even know whose trunk it was, stored in the basement, underneath the stairs. But I'd developed a mania for stamp-collecting, and I was certain there must be old letters inside, probably kept in stamped envelopes. That was how my mother kept her old letters, which I'd already ransacked from her dresser drawers.

It was a small dark trunk, probably dark blue, I think now a footlocker, trimmed with brass at the edges. My little brother and I knelt in the triangular alcove across from my father's workshop, breathing in the purposeful smell of dust and solder and greasy rags. The trunk was unlocked, and I flipped back the lid to find it filled with a jumble of cloth and paper. My brother started grabbing out the army medals, some of them like shields hanging from ribbons. He grabbed our father's red boat-shaped dress cap, like the hats he made us out of newspaper when we went in to pick up his check. Fumbling around, I found a curious silver keepsake maybe an inch square, a little accordion album of black-and-white photographs from Tunisia, one of them showing a lady with bare breasts. We examined them minutely.

Afterward, I found the letters, letters in envelopes, even a first-day cover. The First Trans-Polar Flight. King George VI. King George again. Green stamps with double portraits, a lady and a man. I felt drunk on stamps, an oily nasty basement feeling all mixed up with the lady's breasts. Pawing heedlessly through the papers, I snatched letters out of envelopes and threw them back, making a mess out of what had been a muddle. I tossed photos aside, and official-looking documents. Behind me, my brother frog-marched back and forth, the red boat hat falling in his eyes, the medals dragging down the thin cotton of his shirt.

"Look at me!" he cried and ran upstairs. "Look at me!"

"What have you got?" our mother asked.

He held up the medals while I—dragging behind him, not knowing why I felt so secretive—showed her my store of envelopes.

"Where did you get those?"

"In the basement."

She must have been preoccupied. "Don't get dirty," she said.

I grubbed back into the trunk. For several days, as I remember. Where was my father? It was a pity that he was seldom home to enjoy the expensive view from our living-room window. He loved the glimmer of Burrard Inlet, the arch of Lion's Gate Bridge. One of his favorite pastimes was counting the freighters at anchor in the inlet during a longshoremen's strike. But he was probably working again, paying off the mortgage, as my brother and I tore through his trunk, grabbing every envelope and finally, squatting and rapacious, turning our attention to what they'd contained.

What was this? Old black-and-white photos, one showing a young woman who had to be my Swedish grandmother, but beautiful. She was like a promise to me, her lips so ripe. But I also felt confused, trying to link her with the bent old Granny I knew. And who were these? A woman with my father who wasn't my mother and a little blond girl who wasn't quite me. What was this? A certificate of divorce? My father—and a woman named Queenie? Married before the war, divorced after. That was a sister in the pre-war pictures I didn't even know I had.

Trembling with upset, not looking at my brother, I understood that divorce must be shameful if no one ever mentioned it. And what about this? A military discharge? "Honorable discharge" with the "honorable" scored out in ballpoint pen? Who would have done that? I felt damp and driven as I peeled open a bundle of yellowing records going back to the start of the war.

Messenger reports back pain from riding motorcycle over cobbles. Evidence of early osteoarthritis. Recommending transfer.

Messenger reports continued back pain. Transfer recommended and denied. Malingering suspected.

Refusal to report for parade.

Malingering? Parade?

Transfer: gunner.

A photo of my father behind a big gun, ducking his head, his smile uncertain.

What is psychological?

I crouched like a beetle on the concrete floor, trying to take it all in. Rest leave? Promotion? Disciplinary action? Here it was again, refusal to report for parade. Followed by, Promotion, sergeant-major. Re-enlistment. Dogged man; excellent service. Intelligent, capable, officer material.

But what is battle fatigue?

Now he was excused from parade. There were complaints of worsening back pain. And in different handwriting, malingering again. Angry letters: "Five-year record refusing to report."

Jaundice diagnosed; case severe. Evacuated, North Africa.

"I saw guys stick their arms out the mosquito nets to get malaria so they wouldn't have to. . . ."

Returning the documents to their envelopes, tidying the pile, ignoring my quiet little brother, I felt so unmoored that I never told my father what we'd found. I think he knew. A few months later, when I went back to reread the records, the trunk was gone. I never saw it again, nor the certificate of divorce, nor the discharge, nor the picture of my grandmother.

I've been collecting other old photographs lately, all the family snapshots I can find. As I study them, I wonder what people really went through, where they went that we could never follow, these travelers. My grandmother doesn't look as beautiful as I'd thought in the pictures that survive, but my father—forthright, jaunty, posing with his pipe—is as manly and as handsome as the hero of any old black-and-white movie, and so much more human, and I finally know enough not to feel ashamed of that.

2 2

I HAD A TICKET TO SEE DAME MARGOT DANCE ONCE IN London. This was in the seventies, near the end of her career, when I'd rented a furnished flat in Notting Hill after my back-packing trip around Asia. I bought cheap student seats for all the West End plays, practically hanging from the rafters to see little dot figures play Chekhov. Another time, I made my way to the head of a damp queue to get tickets to see Dame Margot dance with Rudolf Nureyev, her most famous partner.

I once saw Nureyev dance *Coppélia*, maybe with the National Ballet of Canada. His black hair snapped around his face—even his damn hair was dancing. I think that might have been the first ballet I'd seen, except maybe a *Nutcracker* somewhere, but at the perfor-mances that I started going to in London, I discovered that I could be riveted by dance in a way I don't quite feel with music alone. The synchronization of notes and steps fills my mind, colors flow-ing together into something I can only describe as a trajectory. This feel of interior motion erases all my busy-busy thoughts, so that during a performance, I'm lifted above the words that sometimes plague me. What this means, of course, is that I've never paid intellectual attention to the dance. If pressed, I could name a cou-ple of steps, but I usually don't bother with that, and often don't remember where I've seen a performance, including Nureyev in *Coppélia*, so that it might even have been in London, a week or so before the performance with Fonteyn, when I remember being in my local tube station on the way home from seeing him dance.

There's a second reason I'm not sure what performance I saw that night. Just as I was going through the turnstile, I was startled by the sight of an absent-minded figure heading the other way—skinny, hunching Paul, whom I hadn't seen since he'd headed off in one of his tiny cars, leaving Vancouver. I didn't have a clue that he was in London and touched his shoulder before he disappeared. After blocking the other passengers for a couple of minutes, shuffling, pleased, both of us lonely, we got ourselves on the same side of the turnstile and headed off to the pub, where he told me that he'd just arrived in London after backpacking through Europe. He was so exhausted that he'd fallen asleep that evening during what was supposed to be a very good film at my local cinema. *Cadaveri eccellenti?* What a coincidence, I'd been meaning to see it too.

So much for the journal in which I'd been writing down the name of every performance I attended. So much for the next twenty-odd years. But there was a cost. A week later, in Paul's new flat, I screamed.

"I had a ticket to see Fonteyn and Nureyev dance tonight and I completely forgot."

When I told Dame Margot the story, she laughed delightedly, with Tito looking indulgent beside her.

"But you saw Rudolf," she said.

"Several times. In *Coppélia*, *Romeo and Juliet*, *Swan Lake*. . . ."

I had a sudden memory of the closest brush I'd had with Nureyev, one dirty night in the early eighties in Toronto when I was driving home late. I started to turn right when a caped figure ran directly in front of my car. Throwing on the brakes, I screeched to a stop, and the figure fell across my hood. To my horror, I looked straight into the startled face of Rudolf Nureyev. He quickly dusted himself off and continued across the street, but I was badly shaken and idled at the corner until a driver honked behind me.

If you had to be responsible for putting someone in a wheelchair, who would it be? The world's greatest *danseur*, a traumatized war veteran or the future president of Panama?

"*Swan Lake*," I repeated stupidly, as if I really didn't know the faintest thing about ballet, and either lost the chance to hear Dame Margot talk about Nureyev or—I think more likely—gave her an excuse not to. Instead, she began to speak about Mikhail Baryshnikov, whom she didn't seem to know all that well.

"Of course, all the girls are mad for Misha these days," she said, telling rather forgettable stories, but kindly assuming that I would care. Instead, what I thought was, *men*. We've spent almost the whole afternoon talking about men. George Balanchine said, "Ballet is woman." But is it? When almost all the choreographers and impresarios aren't?

"I finished all my paper," Gabriel said, and put his pencil down firmly. I saw at a glance that he'd reached his limit, and we said good-bye to Tito before stopping back at the house. In the tiled front room, I paused by a low table covered with carved wooden animals, folk sculptures of lions and horses emerging from the cool unpainted wood.

"My collection," Dame Margot said, gesturing toward them with perfect grace and humor.

"I collect them too," I told her. "Mainly from people who sell them by the side of the road in Mexico. Does that happen here?"

She gave me directions to the junction on the highway where the carvers sometimes set up shop. But it sounded as if I'd miss their day, and I told her that in any case, the Mexican craftsmen made such crazy painted creatures that an unpainted one from Panama would probably look sad among them.

"Here, then," she said, pulling an orange-painted bird off a post on the veranda. "Somebody brought me this the other day, but I don't do colors, you know. You might as well take it."

Without listening to my thanks, she took us to our car, then slipped back down the forest path toward Tito.

A year later, after we'd moved to Brazil, I found carvers in the state of Minas Gerais who worked in unpainted wood and bought a bird-filled tree that I hoped Dame Margot might like. I tried to find someone to take it to Panama, but there wasn't much traffic in that direction, and then it was too late.

She died of cancer in February 1991. The obituaries said that she'd been ill for several years, which probably meant she'd been ill when we met her, and they all mentioned the gala that had been held to pay her medical bills, when, far from Panama, she'd sat perfectly erect in the Royal Box between Princess Diana and Princess Margaret. Three years after Dame Margot's death, when her will was probated, a letter appeared in the London papers claiming that the gala had been unnecessary, since she'd left behind a share in substantial family property. The trust fund managers wrote back saying that she'd been unable to liquidate the property during her lifetime. They said that she'd been destitute but had hardly touched the money from the gala, which she'd requested be used to help young dancers.

Dame Margot had survived Tito by two years. He died of cancer in 1989. The obituary I read said that his mistress committed suicide the day after he died. This was quite a young woman, a socialite, who apparently moved into the house to take care of Tito whenever Dame Margot left Panama. She moved back out when Dame Margot returned, but in the end, she said she couldn't live if he didn't and took her own life.

Thinking about that poor mistress, I wondered if men tourist women—or at least, if some of them might. I didn't think that men could marry up the way that women could. I'd never met anyone like my hairdressing Uncle Walter who was taken seriously, his social position rising to equal that of his wife. But men could slum, couldn't they? Sample downward, sample women, troll through the working classes, indulge in *nostalgie de la boue*. That's certainly what John on the freak bus did. It finally occurred to me that despite his scorn, he was really a tourist himself. He'd just decided to climb down the ladder for a while instead of up.

There's an obsession here, I admit, mobility in all its facets. Reading Tito's obituary finally made me see that. I also began to realize that this was the reason why my more successful stories were set on the road: You have to write out of your obsessions. Amazing how long it takes to figure out why you've kept doing something. But eventually I realized that writing turns on defining what absolutely rivets you and insisting on making it your subject—which isn't as easy as it sounds. How easy is it for anybody to figure out who or what they love? There's so much noise out there, so much salesmanship and insistence on buying someone else's line. Dame Margot told me, "Never care what anyone thinks of you." I finally saw the corollary, what she was telling me to do. Ask yourself, What do *I* think? I'm not sure there's anything harder than figuring that out.

SMOKE

AND

MIRRORS

THE FIRST TIME I ACTUALLY SAW BRAZIL WAS WHEN WE FLEW down to look for an apartment. All the time we'd been in Panama, we'd been waiting to hear where we'd be going after Mexico, whether back to Toronto or somewhere else. The call came through when we got home. Rio de Janeiro.

I still remember the overnight flight into Galeão airport, landing sleepless, our bodies heavy, bags even heavier, eyes dry and itchy. Outside, in the cab, I quickly got a headache from the queer moonstone shine of the rising winter sun, the razor line of the horizon that nicked my eyes as we drove along the shoreline. As we curled toward town, everything seemed disconnected and surreal: hills nested with shantytowns, water-stained tunnels, a forest of high-rise apartments, all of them built so close to the expressway that as we clicked by, people seemed frozen in the moment like window displays, shards of life—slouched over a table, pulling up a bra strap—mannequins who finally fell away as we reached our hotel in Ipanema, where a sullen gray surf crashed in from Africa, looking cold, in that season, as stones.

In the three years that I lived there, racked by frequent headaches, overcome just as often by delight, I felt that Rio was a place of flashing clarity, but clarity without any promise of clarification, a brilliant puzzle. I wasn't the only one who thought so. A few years later, back in Mexico, I was craning to look up at the bloody frescoes on a church ceiling while part of a literary delegation headed by the poet P.K. Page, who had lived in both Rio and Mexico more than thirty years before. Turning in circles beneath the black-and-red dome, P.K. said that Mexico was night to her, baroque depth, clotted, sanguinary textures, while Brazil was day, light, mirrors, shine, reflection.

I thought that this was especially true since mirrors often craze in Rio's humidity. The apartment we found was part of a huge condominium complex, three towers backing onto a recreation area, and among the few foreigners living there was a German woman named Anna, a cracked surface if ever there was one, damaged, I think, by moving abroad, and Green Party guilt over her husband's job at the nuclear reactor south of Rio. Anna was scornful of her own middle-class life and obsessed with women who worked as maids. She was different from any expat I'd ever met, and I kept trying to understand what she was up to. Also figure out why she bothered me so much.

The Mexican writer Carlos Fuentes once wrote about a woman who winced away from mirrors after she reached a certain age. Maybe I winced away from Anna for the same reason: She reflected something that I had become and didn't want to be. It's certainly true that I got lost so far from home, more displaced than I'd ever been, maybe a little wandery. I didn't just have the occasional intimation of my Nannie's presence. I sometimes felt she'd moved into the apartment.

Mirrors, P.K. would say. Day, light, shimmer, shine—shatter.

2 4

I'D HEARD ABOUT ANNA BEFORE I MET HER, GOSSIP FROM A friend in the building about a German woman who'd been drinking with her maid and the maid's mother by the pool as her children went swimming, all the women getting so drunk that the maid finally started yelling at the German, calling her a drunken cow, a drunken bitch, while the woman laughed and laughed and laughed.

We'd been living in Rio for almost a year by then, and life looked pretty. The condominium was built into an old landscaped quarry halfway up a mountain, lifted above the heat and bustle of the suburban flatlands below. Our tenth-floor apartment faced onto the recreation area at the rear, where there were a couple of tennis courts, a children's playground, and a pool and bar area called the *clube*, where the women got drunk. The whole area was so tended that it seemed otherworldly, the cobbled pathways shaded by tall clipped palms and flowering trees. In season, the trees bloomed pink and mauve and candlelight white—frangipani blossoms on bare branches sending up such a thick rich scent that the first night I smelled it, I thought that someone was burning incense in the apartment below.

I loved looking down on the recreation area from our balcony, especially during Rio's crazy storms, when loud winds funneled into the quarry, pitching leaves and flowers onto the rain-slick paths as if a painted backdrop was shredding. On sunny days, bright birds and butterflies flocked around the flowers, many butterflies the size of birds, huge blue morphos blundering down the mountains like pinches of animated sky. It was so unreal, so Disnified. In fact, it was a high-rise version of a gated community, where people tried to cotton-wool their children. God knows, there was lots to protect them from, even down the hill in the wealthy suburbs of Leblon, Ipanema and Copacabana, which formed a grid of plush apartments and shopping streets where people kept to the main thoroughfares at night, and even in the daytime, you couldn't predict what might happen.

That was part of the reason for my headaches, the constant threat of violence, an underlay of stress that gave life in Rio a sick thrilling buzz. One day, I was walking along the main shopping street of Leblon on my way to pick up Gabriel from kindergarten. For some reason I noticed a guy on a motorcycle pull up at a traffic light between me and a white car, just outside a neighborhood bakery where I stopped for bread almost every day. As I watched, the motorcycle guy pulled a flash of metal out of his black leather jacket and aimed it at the driver. I don't remember any sound, just the red. Head red, I thought hysterically, gaping as the driver slumped and the motorcyclist gunned away. Everyone else went about their business, but I was paralyzed with shock and fear until an elderly well-dressed woman came up beside me, linking her arm through mine and saying, "We're going to keep walking now and chatting about the lovely day, the weather being beautiful, isn't it, dear?" until we reached the corner and she released me to stumble the final few blocks to the school.

It might have been a drug deal gone wrong, or a business deal. Paul's assistant came in one Monday morning, red-eyed and saying that the brother-in-law of her best friend had been shot to death on the weekend. Gradually, the family learned that his murder had something to do with an apartment he'd been buying. Another time, the minibus on our hill was hijacked by an armed man, who robbed everyone on board, almost by-the-way, before making the terrified driver tell him everything he knew about the schedule of a friend of mine, a coffee trader's wife with three young children who often hopped the bus. The driver was brave, alerted my friend and disappeared. My friend and her family moved to a smaller city. A while later, another child was kidnapped at the bottom of the hill as she waited for the school bus. She was the daughter of two professionals, not rich, but middle-class people, and she was held under dreadful conditions for five days before her extended family sold enough cars and jewelry to scrabble together a ransom.

It all left me nervous, hair-trigger, driving Gabriel to school during bad periods at a slightly different time by a slightly differ-ent route; the American embassy issued periodic warnings. Even so, the middle class and the tiny elite were spared the worst of the violence. The very poor people who lived in Rio's endless shanty-towns faced dreadful calamities. They were caught in frequent gunfights as gambling lords battled over turf, or watched their sons die as soldiers in the drug wars, or saw their neighbors taken out by death squads, execution-style. The most famously dire shantytown, Roçinha, was just over the mountain from our condo, and we sometimes heard the gunfire crack against the granite on an otherwise pleasant Saturday night.

So there was that, too. There was the woman I'd originally met at the condo who worked as a nanny for friends of ours living across town. The woman's family still lived in a *favela*, and one day a bunch of off-duty cops broke into their house and shot her sleeping brother dead, believing him to be a drug dealer. He wasn't, although there might have been a dealer who looked like him. My friend phoned to tell me what happened, and when I stopped by to give the poor nanny my sympathies, she started weeping hysterically, asking me over and over if I knew of any job openings back in the condo, even though she got on very well with my friends, and her brother had been murdered miles away from any place she'd ever work.

"I'd feel so much safer there," she kept saying. "It's just so much safer there. It's just so safe."

And so we huddled together, employers and nannies, strained and fearful, buzzing like bees in a hive. The overcrowding made it worse—at least for the maids. I knew of households in Copacabana where fourteen-year maids slept on the kitchen floor at night, or doubled up in the tiny five-by-eight-foot service quarters. That was the way things worked in Rio. There was hardly any daycare, and in such a densely populated city, there wasn't much space, either. Stress, overcrowding; overcrowding, stress. A Brazilian maid showed me the pinkish-brown scars on her inner arm from the boiling water a former employer had thrown at her, almost identical to the scars Maria had shown me in Mexico. Just like in old Sweden, other maids were raped.

Even before we met, I had an idea that when my neighbor, Anna, got so drunk with her maid at the pool, she was making a statement about the way maids were usually treated, and of course she was right. The whole system was worse than lousy. It was a tragic waste, this scaffolding of servants holding up society, the women often overworked, shamefully housed and badly paid. Even at its kindest, it could break your heart. A pediatrician in our condo had a job in public health, and the woman who worked for her told me once, "I always wanted to be a nurse, and it wasn't on, but here I am working for a doctor anyway. Sometimes we have emergencies, and she wouldn't be out there if she couldn't count on me absolutely with the kids."

She looked proud saying this, chin up, and as I glanced around the playground at the other nannies, you could see them listening, their envy, she had status there, and it made me want to cry.

2 5

I MET ANNA IN OUR KITCHEN DURING GABRIEL'S SIXTH birthday party, not long after the pool episode. The party was one of my social goofs. It was the first birthday party we'd held in Brazil and I tried to go Canadian, inviting a few of Gabriel's buddies over to the apartment late one Sunday afternoon. I didn't know that the kids' whole families would come, or that other people would drop by when they heard that there was a party, wanting to be friendly and to add to the fun. Before long, I had to run around borrowing cases of soft drinks and beer and potato chips from neighbors, meaning that several of them came, too.

I think that's how Anna and her kids arrived, with a case of beer. Eventually we had about fifty people crammed into the apartment, laughing and rattling ice in their glasses. Paul took some of the noisier kids outside to play soccer, others crowded around a video, and I found a few holed up in odd corners blissfully eating one potato chip after another out of crinkly family-sized bags.

Meanwhile, the nannies held a party in the kitchen and the mothers alternately gossiped in the living room and snooped around the apartment. Occasionally one or the other would laugh and give me a hug, saying happily, "*Que bagunça!*" What a mess.

I didn't have time to talk with anyone, running around, filling drinks. But eventually I realized that a German woman was sitting in the kitchen, a wide woman of middle height with carelessly cut dark hair and small unreadable eyes. She was drinking beer with the nannies, legs planted far apart, elbows on her knees, listening intently to their jokes and laughing raucously when she finally got the point, three or four beats late. I realized that she must have been the woman from the pool, and when I introduced myself in passing, she answered overpolitely, calling me "*Senhora*."

"Actually, it's Laayzlee," I repeated slowly in a mock Brazilian accent, so it sounded almost as strange as her *senhora*. "I'm sorry, I didn't catch your name."

She belched. Some of the nannies looked embarrassed, some titillated.

"Excuse me," the woman said, although I couldn't tell if she meant it or not.

"No problem," I told her, and left.

Gradually, people drifted out, saying what a good time they'd had, what a spectacle, what a mess. The German woman was the last one left, very drunk and still sitting in the kitchen with the woman who worked for us, Adélia. Paul and I were sweeping up when a short red-faced man opened the door without knocking.

"Is my wife here?"

"I think so," I answered. Without saying another word, he collected her and left.

That might have been the end of it, except that the next day, Adélia popped her head in the door of Gabriel's room, where I was trying to figure out where to put all the birthday presents.

She said that the woman, whom she called Anna, wanted to cook a birthday dinner for her on Thursday evening. I thought she said Thursday. She wanted to make sure I didn't need help that night, that I wasn't planning anything, which I wasn't.

"I didn't know it was your birthday this week," I said. "*Parabens.*" Happy birthday.

"*Obrigada*," she answered, and went out.

Adélia hadn't been working for us long, just since Carnival, not quite four months earlier. Another woman had been with us for about six months beforehand, a dreamy woman named Fátima, but she'd arrived in the middle of a love affair and had done *macumba* work all over the apartment to bring on a proposal—smoky candles left to burn down, the man's name written on scraps of paper in the shape of a cross and put under the phone so he'd call:

$$
\begin{array}{ccccccc}
 & & & A & & & \\
 & & & N & & & \\
 & & & T & & & \\
A & N & T & \hat{O} & N & I & O \\
 & & & N & & & \\
 & & & I & & & \\
 & & & O & & &
\end{array}
$$

During Carnival, Antônio had asked her to move in with him. She came back for two hours, packed up and left. We interviewed Adélia a few days later on the recommendation of the doorman and were impressed with her candid manner. Sitting across the dining-room table, a strong-looking, casual, almost pretty woman, she told us that she'd been working in a building down the hill, but the people were moving to São Paulo. She didn't pretend to regret this, telling us that the position had been okay, the kids cute, but they kept the refrigerator locked and she'd never got enough to eat. I said something indignant. It happens, Adélia told me, and shrugged.

The doorman had described her as a *mulata* in her mid-twenties. At the time, I thought *mulata* simply meant mixed race, which seemed to fit, given Adélia's lovely umber skin, her thick black hair and amused, changeable features. I hadn't yet realized that since nearly everyone in Brazil is racially mixed, *mulata* has taken on a special meaning. The doorman had really been saying that Adélia was sexy, sure of herself, everything a woman was supposed to be, maybe even more. He thought she was hot—not least because he probably knew she was involved with another of the doormen, a married man. It took me a while to learn all this, but by then I wasn't surprised, having come to believe that Adélia was really very far from candid.

That sounds too harsh. Adélia was very good at her job, understanding, for instance, that we wouldn't know you could get weekly deliveries from the butcher and arranging it herself. I'm sure she would have run a successful business if she'd been born in Canada. As it was, she was a woman with a primary-school education from the poorest part of Brazil, the bleak ranch lands of the *sertão*, the northeast, where the superb desolation was endlessly lamented in cowboy songs. Making it to Rio had been a big victory for Adélia, and I ended up thinking of her as a survivor, hard-working, a bit of a loner, an observant and sometimes satirical person who found much to amuse her in life. I also thought she was probably far more intelligent than most of the people she'd grown up with, which is the sort of thing that can get anybody into trouble.

On the Wednesday evening after his birthday party, I took Gabriel into the kitchen to make him a snack before bed. Adélia appeared, all dressed up.

"It's time for Anna's," she said. "Would you like to come and cut the cake now?"

I was completely unprepared, having mistaken the date and assumed that I wasn't invited anyway. Adélia's present was unwrapped and Gabriel already in pajamas. But I said that, of course, we'd love to stop by. After Gabriel and I got dressed, the three of us went downstairs and knocked ceremonially on the front door. No answer. We went around back, to the kitchen door, which Anna opened on the ominous smell of meat cooking.

Adélia said hello to Anna, who greeted me gruffly. Nevertheless, I took her aside and said, "Look, I'm not prepared for this. I got the day wrong, I've already eaten, I have to get my kid to bed. Why don't we just have a glass of wine to toast Adélia, then I'll head off."

She had such unreadable eyes and was already drinking, and I wasn't sure she understood me. "I heard her say to her friends in the kitchen on Sunday that it was her birthday this week, and she was sorry, she couldn't afford to take them out to dinner," Anna told me in labored Portuguese. "So I said I'd do a dinner for them, why not? Adélia would never have told you, being ashamed of her situation, the way maids are, and her salary being so low. . . ."

"If having a party was a priority for Adélia, she could have had one. I would have helped her if she needed help, although I don't think she did." I spoke quickly, stung by the dig about the salary, which wasn't true, and didn't add that I thought Adélia might have been trying to get out of holding a party with one of those throw-away excuses that people use, and that Anna had misunderstood. After all, I told myself, Anna meant to be kind, and I'd made a mistake about the date of the dinner, even though my Portuguese was better than hers.

There was another knock on the door, and Adélia's friend Delma came in. As we greeted her, Anna poured glasses of champagne, and I took mine with relief, toasting Adélia. But what was this? Anna brought out cake as well, *two* cakes, identical tortes of chocolate and whipped cream piled up to Alpine heights, while the beef still roasted in the oven.

"We'll cut this now so the *senhora* can leave for her important business," Anna said scornfully.

"But that's ridiculous," I replied. "I'm not going to ruin Adélia's dinner."

I started to gather myself to leave when Gabriel saw the cakes, eyes widening.

"Don't you want some cake?" Anna asked. "Doesn't it look good? Don't you want just a little piece? Or maybe a great big one? Sure, you want a great big piece of cake, don't you, blondie?"

So much for leaving. We sat down around the dining-room table, Adélia looking watchful and amused, almost titillated, her nostrils flaring. Just as we'd settled, Anna hopped up and went back into the kitchen, reemerging with a woman who must have been sitting behind the kitchen in the service area. The woman's sardonic voice preceded her. "I don't want any part of your friendship, just give me my paycheck." Anna laughed happily and introduced the woman who must have been her live-in maid, the other woman from the pool.

Now our party was almost complete. One empty chair remained, filled in a moment when Anna's husband wandered absently out of his study. He looked over the company, frowned at the table, sat down wordlessly and began to eat a large piece of cake. Since I was sitting next to him, I asked, "Are your children in a crèche or school yet?"

"Clearly they are not in school," he said in English. "The oldest one is in a crèche." He resumed eating, and when he finished his cake, he left.

The conversation stuttered along, mainly between me and Delma, whom I knew a little from the playground. I often went down there in the afternoon with Gabriel, when the other mothers weren't home from work or whatever and Gabriel's friends were tended by nannies. It was the nannies' social time and I was a bit of an intruder, a bit nosy, eavesdropping—they suspected and I admit—but a foreigner, clearly unsocialized and probably rather harmless. Delma was older than many of the others, my age, early thirties, and a mother herself. Anna's dinner party seemed to embarrass her, everything upside down. Cake before meat and the wrong people calling each other *senhora*.

"Lovely cake," I told Anna, since it was.

"She doesn't understand a word you're saying," her maid answered. "Her Portuguese is terrible, and she doesn't get accents."

Anna laughed.

"Well, it is. You make a fool of yourself all the time, you stupid cow."

"Cleusa is a joker," Anna said, laughing even harder.

"My name is Creusa. You can't even get my name right. If I started charging you extra for every mistake you make in Portuguese, I'd be a millionaire in no time, and you'd be out on the street like the prostitute you are."

"Listen to her!" Anna cried, laughing so hard she had to wipe tears from her eyes. But Creusa saw that I understood every word and cut back on the witticisms. In fact, we grew rather silent, until fortunately Gabriel finished his huge piece of cake and climbed into my lap.

"I want to go home," he said loudly, and we excused ourselves, fleeing the second disastrous birthday party of the week. As the door closed, I heard the cliché burst of laughter, Anna the loudest, but with Adélia and Delma audible beneath. I felt a little exasperated with Adélia. She and Delma would probably relish their dinner, then laugh at Anna behind her back, too. Not that I could blame them.

2 6

WE KNEW ADÉLIA WAS PREGNANT BY THEN. WHEN SHE'D
been working for us for about two months, I'd noticed that she was
putting on weight but assumed it was because we didn't lock the
refrigerator. Nor did I enquire into the *macumba* she was doing, clay
bowls filled with rice and chicken parts hidden in the back of the
oven. She sometimes put a couple of unlit red candles on either
side, but I thought that was her business too, even though I didn't
like it, red candles meaning black magic, wishing someone ill. The
woman who'd worked for us previously, Fátima, had lit only wistful
white candles while spraying perfume around the laundry room.

Not that it had done her much good. A few weeks after Fátima
took off, she returned with a black eye and bruises, saying that this
Antônio guy was no good and asking for her job back. I explained
that we'd already hired Adélia.

"You'd be better off with me," Fátima replied, but I didn't
think so then and helped her find a job somewhere else.

We went on home leave to Canada not long afterward, and
when we got back, Adélia's pregnancy was unmistakable, her belly
high and round under a billowing T-shirt. Judging from her size,
she must have been pregnant when we hired her, probably fired
from her previous job because of it; some *senhoras* checked sani-
tary napkins. Her lack of candor disappointed me, although I
couldn't really blame her. In Mexico, we'd hired Maria when she
was pregnant, but Adélia didn't know that, did she?

I went into the kitchen and asked her if we could sit down,
knowing that my height made me intimidating, along with my bad
habit of frowning when I was trying to concentrate. We had to talk
about maternity leave, and I hoped we could keep it businesslike.
But when I asked Adélia if she was pregnant, a confusing story
poured out, all about how she'd tried to get an abortion several

months earlier and her doctor had refused. Not because abortion was illegal in Brazil, although it was, but for complicated reasons involving a kidney condition and a previous pregnancy that had ended in a miscarriage at six months. Now the doctor was growing alarmed at her condition and wanted to perform a "micro-cesarean" to end the pregnancy. Otherwise, she'd have to spend the next three months in bed and might not survive her labor.

"I need 650 cruzados," she said, a couple of hundred dollars.

It didn't matter whether I believed her, although I didn't. Her shoulders were hunched, her eyes darting. But I could also see that she was desperate, defensive, flailing around for help—and, doing the arithmetic, somewhere around five months pregnant. How had things reached this point? Probably the baby's father had abandoned her, maybe quite recently. Now she was trying to make up a story that would allow me to help her the way *senhoras* could. Sighing, I asked her if she wanted me to arrange an appointment with an obstetrician, and she seemed relieved.

Over the next few days, Adélia's story began to change, maybe as she grew convinced that I wouldn't kick her out. After her first appointment at the clinic, she told me that the obstetrician wouldn't do an operation. When I asked why, her eyes darted back and forth, then she shrugged and told me that there had actually been two doctors before this one: her own physician, who had refused to do the abortion, and the micro-cesarean guy, whom she'd found while we were in Canada, and who began to sound pretty much like a backstreet abortionist. I felt I was finally getting the picture when his fee dropped to 350 cruzados. Then an upstairs neighbor invited me over for coffee.

This was the well-coifed woman who employed Delma. It turned out that Delma had been talking with Adélia while we were in Canada and had eventually got her to admit that her own doctor wouldn't do the abortion because he felt she'd already had too many, another would be risky. Now she was at least six months pregnant, not five. I would have helped Adélia with money if she'd really needed medical treatment, but under the circumstances, I phoned around about adoption agencies and gave her the names.

"I want to have a girl," she said dreamily. Then, turning angry, "No one else is going to bring up my kid."

I thought she had a point, especially considering who was helping to bring up mine. I no longer believed very much of what Adélia said, although I understood her desperation better the more we talked. She was completely on her own, no fallbacks, saying with convincing bitterness that she knew better than to expect anything from the baby's father. Her family wouldn't lift a finger either, not even to help with maternity leave. Her father was a loser, a drunk, a clown. He'd just take her money for booze. And her mother was pathetic, hunched over her stupid vegetables in that filthy little market. Why hadn't she left? People could leave. Adélia had left, and she wasn't going back, *de jeito nenhum*, not for a second. She'd got herself into the condo and no one was going to make her slink back out. Why should she? As if half the *senhoras* didn't get knocked up before they got married. She had nothing to be ashamed of. She didn't need to disappear on maternity leave, no way. She'd have a week in hospital, then she'd come back to work. She was a hard worker; I knew that. And this was a perfect place to raise a baby, the people aside. Delma making up stories about her; she'd never forgive *that*.

Sitting there, palms open in my lap, I could feel my invisible Nannie watching us, a shivery intimation, clear yet somehow changeable, fluid as the heat of a Rio winter day. One minute I sensed her as a harsh old lady, her pale blue eyes as cold as icebergs, something ignorance crashed against. You miserable geddle! Miserable! Ged-dle! It was clear she had no use for Adélia. The sly little baggage! A liar for your nanny? Get rid of her now!

The next minute she softened and grew vaporous, unformed, her belly full of her first son, the one whose grave she'd cry on. I could almost see her lips form a forgiving smile. Let her stay. I should have stayed. I wish I'd stayed.

No, that was my Swedish grandmother, her full red lips and pregnant words. I was making a mistake. But then, Nannie had made her own mistake, hadn't she? At least in the terminology of the time. My aunt had let me in on the family secret not long before, and memories of both my grandmothers flowed confusingly together, mixed up with Adélia and the buzzing condo. Sitting in the kitchen, I could almost hear the old Scottish biddies cackling outside the back door. Havna ya heerd? Margaret Mary made a mistake. Ach, tha puir parents! What's ta be done with tha geddle? Wu'll see a wedding, I heer. Tha bairn wull be a wee bit airly, but ach, so munny bairns coom airly these days.

At first I couldn't reconcile the funk of passion with the lily-of-the-valley scent my Nannie usually wore. My eldest uncle was "premature"? Over the years, I'd assimilated all sorts of contradictory stories about my grandmother—such a large personality!—but this one was different. My aunt told me that she'd been twenty years old, a tall girl for the time, clever and decisive in her movements, when she'd fallen in love with a fair-haired boy from the nearby town, who was her younger by two years. He was the son of a respectable jeweler, and when Margaret Mary got pregnant at twenty-one, no one tried to pretend he wasn't the baby's father. So the yearning was public, if the pledges stayed private, the passion secret, stolen—these were my grandparents?

Nor could I understand the delay, the whiff of ambivalence or of reservations stubbornly outlasted. They married the day after my grandfather turned twenty when my grandmother was six months pregnant. Afterward, the family shipped the young man off to an accountant's job in the city, and later to Canada, where he gave up his dream of becoming an architect and drew model ships at night. Margaret Mary joined him a year later on the last street of Winnipeg, spending hours gazing out at the prairie before raising her .22 and shooting gophers through the eye.

For years, I'd thought that the contradictory stories about my grandmother were simply pieces of human inconsistency, par for the course. But in Rio, I began to sense a trajectory to her life. Margaret Mary must always have been stubborn, and for a while, her self-assurance made her unconventional too, attracted to someone younger at an age when two years makes a difference. I could imagine how much she'd liked being the dominant figure, the one in charge. Yet I couldn't help saying, Good for her. Girls were supposed to repress themselves and she didn't. Good.

She must have been passionate. Surely, maybe, I can't know. Headstrong and ingenious, certainly. Good Lord, her son was conceived in the middle of a Scottish winter. Where on earth did they meet? Maybe under the ignorant nose of the one who decided to punish them, making them wait to marry until the pregnancy billowed shamefully forth. Her young husband must have felt relieved to take off for the promising city of Winnipeg—the future Chicago, as they said then, a key depot on the intercontinental railway—and it couldn't have been easy for my grandmother to watch him go. Left behind in the Old Country, she doted on her son, the physical proof of her husband's passion. But the bairn was a symbol of a different sort to the rural community clucking around her, such a loud crying out of her mistake that she must have felt a little isolated, and maybe steeled herself into defiance. I could almost feel her sense of emancipation as she made her first Atlantic crossing.

Yet Margaret Mary arrived in Winnipeg just as the Panama Canal opened. That first warm mix of Pacific and Caribbean waters swamped whole families, entire futures, and turned promising cities into backwaters. In 1914, with transcontinental freight diverted through the Canal, the railways began to lose their importance, and that was the end of the "northern Chicago." Aldine Street, where my grandparents lived, is still one of the last streets in Winnipeg. The city never grew much further east. Things slowed down for the family as well, with the next children, my mother and her twin sister, arriving five years later. When my grandfather finally got his own bank, it was in a very small town.

I wondered if Margaret Mary was disappointed, or if the town seemed like just another way station at first. She certainly made the best of it for a long time. This is when the stories describe her as a strong woman, an upright figure whose eyes were the windblown blue of northern lakes in summer. She was popular and respectable, if prone to sad bouts of longing for the Old Country. Oh me! she began to cry. Oh me, I should never have left home! In these moods, she could be hard on her children, teaching my mother to tell time by pressing her fingers into the raised numbers of a clock until they bled. "You silly dunkey!" she scolded, pushing my mother away. Yet as late as the Depression, she was a model of charity, the soup warming on the burner, the hobos' mark etched into her gate, an experienced woman who understood how intercontinental tidal waves could swamp young hopes, even as she scolded her husband, the drinker, who really should have known better.

Living in our Rio condo was a bit like living in a small town. A woman on the playground once mentioned Paul's next trip before I knew about it myself. After that, I always greeted her by asking about my husband's plans; it became our standing joke. The problem was, she often knew. I laughed but also began holding myself aloof from condo life just at the point I might have been welcomed into it, going off to run along the seawall instead of joining the aerobics classes in the *clube*. For the first time, I began to enjoy my foreignness, glad that condo society couldn't quite place me. It allowed an inch of privacy, at least.

My father? Oh, he was retired and unfortunately in poor health, a painful thing to talk about. Weren't you lucky that your father was so active! Playing such a great game of tennis! There was Gabriel—what was he saying? Excuse me.

But I also remembered the old story about the Scottish cousins visiting from the States and finally understood why my grandmother couldn't wait to get rid of them, terrified that they would drop some hard word of truth and shatter her carapace of polished evasions. The strain must have been awful, the constant fear that they—that *you*—would make a mistake. But it must also have been tempting to let it all pour out, laughing at the way you'd fooled them, letting them know you thought they were fools.

My father? Oh, he was a machinist in the back shop of a newspaper, much like the workers in your factory whom you once so charmingly referred to as troglodytes. He and my mother also worked as cleaners, exactly like the woman you slapped across the face the other day for breaking a wine glass, you stupid bitch—growing shorter as I spoke, and broader, my hair darkening and my eyes drawing closer together, smaller, impenetrable now, as I sat at the *clube*, drink in hand, and laughed and laughed and laughed and laughed, doing no one any good at all.

I sighed, and noted the flicker of irony in Adélia's eyes: So the pampered blond *senhora* feels put out by the complex problems of the poor. In truth, I didn't know what to do. How did you define proper cause for firing someone? On paper Adélia did her job very well, an efficient and usually good-humored woman. I wasn't so sure about good-hearted, yet the moralistic intimation of my grandmother scared me. I didn't want to turn out like her, growing so convinced of my own PR that I felt justified in coming down hard on everyone else.

In the end, I fell back on the best interests of the children, both the baby and Gabriel, insisting that Adélia take her full maternity leave. When she saw that I meant it, she found a woman in the northern suburbs who would be happy to board her, a recently widowed single mother who needed the money. The woman even said that she'd take care of the baby after Adélia's leave ended. Adélia would stay there on weekends; it was a three-hour bus ride away. I wasn't sure that she'd be able to leave her baby after four months, I couldn't have, but I also thought that we could figure out what to do when the time came. We had until the spring, and in the meantime, things returned more or less to normal, except that I felt increasingly isolated, too stressed, too foreign, and when Adélia started doing *macumba* again, she used not just red candles, but black ones.

27

MACUMBA HAD FASCINATED ME EVEN BEFORE WE MOVED TO Rio. I knew that it was a religion based on Yoruba beliefs brought over by African slaves which had got mixed up with Catholicism and indigenous spirituality, so that modern followers made offerings to a twined pantheon of gods. Iemanjá was at once the goddess of the sea and the Virgin Mary, wore sky blue, favored pearls and loved her children so much that she sometimes took them to her bosom, drowning them. I was attracted by the ambiguity and the way that the African trickster gods didn't quite translate into Christian iconography. The god Exu was often represented as the devil, but he was really a supernatural messenger who sounded more like the Navajo Coyote or Northwest Coast Raven, mischievous, unreliable, humorous and carnal—not to mention married, sort of, to the goddess Pombagira, the patroness of prostitutes, childbirth and sex, whom I thought of as wild female energy unleashed. Call on Pombagira as you put a drop of menstrual blood in a strong cup of coffee, and after your husband drank it, he'd stop cheating.

Adélia's offerings were made to Pombagira. I'd assumed that I'd have to go somewhere to learn about *macumba*. But no, it was happening right in the kitchen. And despite the philosophical overpinnings, I could see that *macumba* was pretty practical-minded. You made offerings to try to get something, hoping to exercise some power in a pretty powerless life. Yet I suspected it was also more than that. Adélia was clearly more complicated than that, and the person who sent me deeper was my friend Estela.

Estela was a white witch. I first went to her for lessons in the tarot, wanting to learn the cards so I could flesh out a character in the novel I was writing. I felt more or less justified in calling it research, since I'd published my book of short stories by then, launching it during our home leave. Yet behind the justification was something else, the sick thrill of living in Rio, the realization that anything might happen, any moment. Everything else did—murders, kidnappings—why not this? Until then, I'd had no more use for the occult than my father, but I don't think Estela would have taken me on if she hadn't sensed a willingness to suspend judgment—or maybe the fact that I hung suspended. I was hanging by a thread, breakable as glass, a wind chime jangling in the breeze.

Tiny Estela was hospitable and good-hearted, the granddaughter of a great rubber baron and divorced mother of several grown children. She'd been an expat in New York for many years and was working on a novel, so we had a lot in common. Not everything. Estela felt that between her novel and the tarot, she was attracting so many influences she needed to keep an iron rod by her bed, a lightning rod to deflect evil, but despite my stress, I felt that keeping an iron rod was a little silly in our fortified condo and declined to do the same.

I went for weekly lessons, learning the archetypes on tarot cards, the hanged man, the devil, the empress. Estela let me in on the tricks of the trade, the universal fallback musings (I seem to see someone blocking you at work. Your house could eat up an absolute fortune if you'd let it. So you're worried about problems *down there*), but for her, this was just a way to start, warming up the motor. She was hoping for something deeper, going beyond the tricks and trial balloons and psychological counseling to something much harder to explain, like the time she said to me, out of the blue, in the strident voice that I'd learned to recognize, "Your father has fluid on his lungs, *be careful*," right after I'd learned about his pneumonia.

I saw the whole process too often to forget the many wrong guesses, the older male from my past who was going to arrive with a piece of good advice that I still wouldn't mind hearing. I could also see that virtually all the correct bits came out of Sherlock Holmes-style observation and deduction, not to mention from things people let drop during their readings, which they didn't seem to hear themselves say. But sometimes Estela frightened me by going beyond that, saying unexpected things in that weird voice, as if she was tapping into a field of information that we can't normally enter—a concept that I ended up accepting because when I saw her do it, and on very rare occasions did it myself, it involved a hyper-perception of something that was then true, never any reading of the unformed future.

Estela told me in her strident tone, not long after those awful birthday parties, "You need a good cleansing." Not a shower. She was using a *macumba* term, *uma limpeza*, meaning that I needed a spiritual dust-off.

"But I'm not an expert," she added more mildly. "You should go see *Pai* Geraldo."

She told me that Geraldo was a *macumba* priest, a *pai-de-santo*, father of the saints. He was a famous figure in Rio, with a

Copacabana apartment and a spiritual center out in the northern suburbs. I booked an appointment in Copacabana, not really sure about this cleansing business, but titillated, nerved-up and always ready to try something new. Soon I was let into a plush, velvet-curtained living room with high ceilings, a crystal chandelier and glistening silver everywhere, silver candlesticks and silver vases filled with white roses, all of them presents from devotees.

At least, that's what his assistant said, a little meaningly, adding that Geraldo would be ready for me soon. In a few moments, she led me into a plainer room, where the priest sat waiting behind a desk. "Priest" is the usual translation, yet as Geraldo looked up, he reminded me of a Southern Baptist minister, a solidly built, hard-bellied man with shrewd dark eyes whose practiced glance left me feeling all awkward elbows and knees. His powerful hands were clasped on top of bead necklaces sacred to different gods, the neck-laces forming a circle inside which were placed other, bigger beads and curiously shaped stones, polished tiger's-eyes among them.

As I sat down, Geraldo threw the *buzios* inside the bead circle: cowry shells from Africa. He studied them a moment, then spoke in a rush.

"You have brought a cargo of bad spirits down upon you, they are a heavy weight, blocking your path, they are bringing you bad luck, you are bringing bad luck down on other people—do you have any questions?"

"What's bringing it down on me?" I asked.

He threw again and hesitated. "You are diverting bad influences from other people onto yourself. Do you have any questions?"

"I'm doing this?"

He hesitated again. "You are inexperienced here. You're in over your head. You don't really mean to do this, there's no blame, but naturally there are consequences. Do you have any questions?"

Feeling a little humbled, I asked, "What can I do?"

Uma limpeza. The cleansing. Estela had told me *pais-de-santo* made most of their money from cleansing ceremonies at their temples or centers, primal, herb-fueled ceremonies where they drummed and danced and sometimes sacrificed small animals, blowing ritual smoke in your face. But she said that Geraldo was genuine and that I should believe him even—she laughed—if he contradicted her. I still wasn't sure whether I believed him, but I asked Geraldo for the map to his center. Drums? Animal sacrifice? Research; I should probably go.

Geraldo threw the *buzios* again and told me that my spiritual mother was Iansã, goddess of the wind. She was a distant blond, identified with Saint Barbara and Diana the Huntress, felt to be rather chilly. She liked to dance and wear men's clothing, moved like lightning from place to place, and was stubborn, solitary and just.

Another throw. "Your father is Omulú," he told me, looking surprised. The *macumba* books said that Omulú, lord of the underworld, had few children. He was a suspicious, pockmarked old man, his face hidden under a straw hood decorated with cowry shells, who was summoned in times of plague, able to cure the worst diseases, though not always willing to. Omulú was very powerful, summoned as well for black magic, graveyard work—Estela said dead folks were still dug up—but he was capricious and judgmental, and could easily turn against you.

Geraldo surprised me by shifting in his seat, looking worried.

"If Omulú is your father, you really have to come to my *terreiro*," he said. "We have to cleanse you, or you'll hurt people when you could be helping."

Seeing the honest concern on his face, I blushed to realize how fatuous I was, how condescending, what a stupid mixed-up foreigner. I'd been playing with *macumba* as if it were an exotic game, a sad attempt by powerless people to gain some control over their lives. But people *believed* it. With her hidden offerings and black candles, Adélia was doing her damnedest to hurt someone. She was filled with fury, a waxy hate, longing for revenge. Against whom? Closing my eyes, I shivered to finally understand how badly she wanted to light those candles in the back of the gas oven.

"Thank you," I told *Pai* Geraldo.

"You can pay here," he replied. "Fifteen cruzados."

28

ADÉLIA WENT INTO LABOR A DAY LATER. PAUL AND I WERE sitting in the living room with friends, discussing the final details of a driving holiday that we were about to take together. We thought Adélia was due in a month or so and that we'd be back in plenty of time.

She'd been hanging around all evening, looking tired, dark circles under her eyes, but that was hardly surprising for someone who was supposed to be eight months pregnant. At midnight, Delma appeared in the living-room doorway, and I knew instantly what that meant.

"How far apart are the pains?" I asked.

"Three minutes."

"Three minutes!"

"She's been in labor all evening, she just didn't tell anyone."

The strength of my exasperation surprised me, but under the circumstances, I buried it quickly. Our friends offered to baby-sit, and Paul and I got Adélia in the car, racing off for the maternity hospital she'd chosen, about a twenty-minute drive away. The problem was, Adélia couldn't remember what street the hospital was on, and Paul and I hadn't made a dry run, thinking we'd do that after our holiday. So with Adélia panting and scared, we drove in grids around the neighborhood, finally stumbling on a gas station where they were just closing up for the night.

At first, the men turned their backs on us. But when I leaned out the window and screamed that they had to help, *the baby was on its way*, the biggest, most stubborn-looking back turned around and showed a very kindly face. The man gave us concise directions, and after turning left a couple of times, we arrived at the hospital.

It was completely dark, lights out, surrounded by a high spiked fence and locked up tight behind a gate. Leaping out of the car, I rang the buzzer on the gatepost. And rang and rang and rang and rang. Adélia's pains were now ten seconds apart and the lights stayed implacably doused. Paul finally spotted the buzzer cord hanging disconnected from a tree. He decided to climb the ten-foot fence, which was made of wrought iron with closely placed spikes on top.

The first time Paul made it to the top, the rusty spike came off in his hand and he fell into the bushes on our side of the fence. Adélia panted and groaned, and I was convinced that I was about to deliver the baby on the sidewalk. But on his next try, Paul made it over the fence and ran to the front door. In a moment he reappeared, telling me that he'd awakened a sleeping woman in uniform. She didn't seem at all surprised at his appearance and said that he could let us in.

It felt better to be inside, even though Adélia's pains were coming in constant waves and there was no sign of a midwife or a doctor. She was astonishingly controlled, but I was about to start screaming again when a sleepy resident finally appeared, stubbing out his cigarette and doing a quick examination before saying what was rather obvious, that the baby was about to be born.

"It's premature. You might need an incubator," I said.

"Doesn't look like it," the resident replied, adding that we had to leave.

"Shouldn't I wait?" I asked. "Can't I stay with her?"

"What for?" he asked, pushing me out the door.

The next morning, I woke up feeling completely exasperated with both Adélia and the Brazilian medical system. She should have managed things better. The entire bloody country should have managed itself better. They called that a hospital?

I'd never felt so much like a foreigner before. My repressed anger finally broke through, shattering the romance of travel and expatriation with a great self-pitying crack. What am I doing here? I asked myself. Oh me, I should never have left home.

Stop it, I told myself. I refuse to let this place, that woman, turn me into *her*. Instead I called the maternity hospital, and after a long delay, they told me the baby was a girl, as Adélia had wanted. But they wouldn't give out any other information over the telephone, so Paul and I picked up Gabriel from school and we all went out to the hospital together.

Fortunately, the resident who delivered the baby was standing by the front door. He recognized me and fetched a nurse, who said, "Just wait a couple of minutes while I brush my teeth, then I'll take you upstairs."

I rolled my eyes at Paul. Everyone else was ignoring him, treating him like a social error. When the nurse returned from the bathroom, she said that "the men" had to wait outside, which tickled Gabriel. Then she took me upstairs in an ancient creaky cage elevator, clicking past several levels of green-painted walls to arrive outside the maternity ward, where she dropped me off and descended with a screech.

Adélia was standing near a closed double door, dressed in slippers and a nightgown.

"My God, Adélia, why aren't you in bed?"

"I don't have a bed yet," she told me. "The other woman hasn't left, and it hurts less to stand, anyway."

"That's completely ridiculous," I said, looking around for someone to berate. But there wasn't anyone in sight, and when I checked, the double door to the ward was locked. No one came when I knocked and rattled it. Finally I pounded on it with my clenched fist. When there was still no response, I began pacing back and forth, finally pulling myself together enough to stop in front of Adélia, congratulating her on the baby and asking how she was doing.

Adélia hadn't seen the baby. They'd taken her away and hadn't said how much she weighed or whether she was in an incubator, although they told Adélia she could take her home in a week.

"Completely bloody absurd. Who's in charge of this place?"

"I'm calling her Sara," Adélia told me plaintively. It was the name of the pediatrician in the condo.

Recollecting myself, I said, "*Parabéns*. It's a lovely name." But Adélia only shrugged.

We'd known they would keep her in the hospital for a while, and I told her that we'd still like to go on our week's holiday if she felt she'd be okay. I'd asked around that morning and found someone's sister, an unemployed nanny, who could pick Adélia up from the hospital and stay with her in the apartment until we got back a day or so later. Adélia agreed that this would be fine and that we could figure out everything else once we all got home.

"Do you want me to see downstairs whether I can find out more about the baby?" I asked.

"I suppose so," Adélia answered, sounding weary. Catching the helpless look in her eye, I wondered whether she'd ever understood that this would end in a baby. I wondered if any of us ever do.

Downstairs, no one would tell me anything either, and people kept asking us to leave. But I was far too angry to leave and finally managed to track down the chief resident. He listened closely, looked as if something clicked and actually went upstairs himself to get some information.

"She's a lovely little girl, just lovely," he said, coming back down. "Five and a half pounds, full term, very healthy, ready to turn your lives right upside down."

As he left, I said to Paul, "The only goddamn reason he can imagine we'd be interested is that we're adopting her."

"Are we?" Gabriel asked hopefully.

Of course it didn't end very well. How could it? When we got back from our short trip, we found Adélia waiting in the apartment with the baby.

"Do you want to see?" she asked Gabriel in a high, sugary, wheedling voice. "Do you want to hold her? Why don't you hold her? Sure you can, she's your baby friend."

Looking important, he cradled the tiny newborn, while I stood above him, arms crossed. Adélia had never asked me why we'd had only one child and I don't know what I would have said if she did, or if the question of adoption really *had* come up. That sometimes you play the hand you're dealt? But Adélia wouldn't understand, I thought, being someone who always upped the ante.

Now she smiled sweetly. "She's a very good baby. She barely cries, and I feel fine. I can start back to work in another week." Her smile fading, she added, "And you can get rid of that creep who's supposed to be helping me. She's no help at all."

I took the baby from Gabriel, feeling more unsentimental about a newborn than I ever imagined it was possible to feel.

"Why don't you go help Daddy unpack?" I asked Gabriel, who went away reluctantly, waving at the baby. Then I turned on Adélia.

"What do you think you're doing? Can you imagine what it would be like for two little children, spending two years together in a small apartment and then splitting up? We went through that when we left Mexico. I'm not letting you do that here."

Adélia started speaking, but I cut her off. "Have you been in touch with your friend? Is she ready to take you and the baby, or does she need a bit more warning?"

Adélia mumbled something, almost snatching the baby away.

"There are people who would kill for four months paid maternity leave," I said.

"I'll call her tomorrow," she replied, half-spitting with anger.

Instead, people began calling me and whispering behind my back. To my intense irritation, I soon learned that Delma had found Adélia crying in the apartment the day she got home from the hospital, and that Delma and her well-coifed employer had taken her to their place, where Adélia had said that the other woman we'd hired to help was actually her replacement, and that we were throwing her out into the street as soon as we got back. So the well-coifed woman had phoned around, gossiping, and I found myself harangued by the officious woman who had helped me find the obstetrician, someone I barely knew, an Englishwoman who told me that I was a miserable sod, and when I'd cleared a few things up, that I was dense.

"You didn't really believe she'd found a woman to stay with, did you?"

When she'd lied about everything else? I'd thought it was possible that she hadn't found anyone, but I'd given her the benefit of the doubt, especially since nothing sounded more likely, at least to me, than a single mother needing a little extra cash.

I seemed to be the only one to think so. Yet I soon found that opinion around the condo was divided on the presumed lie, with a surprising number of people inclined to blame Adélia for being a liar and to believe that I was merely a bumbling foreigner. A few mothers and nannies started whispering to me about the baby's marked resemblance to one of the doormen, a married man with two little kids and a popular wife. I didn't want to hear this, but also did: that Adélia had so many boyfriends no one was sure who the father was until now, including her, that she and Delma were disliked in the condo, they gave themselves airs, they were snobs, and that lately they spent all their free time with that German woman, who was crazy, a drunk and a terrible influence; her poor children. One time I ran into the pediatrician, Sara, who looked amused, shaking her head and telling me, as she got off the elevator, "You should have kicked her out as soon as you knew she was pregnant."

It turned out that there really was a woman in the suburbs. Adélia spent two more weeks in the apartment, assuring me that the woman would be ready for her soon, then left one day when I was out. I found most of her clothing gone, although not all of it, along with my suitcase. We'd already given her a big check, the first instalment of her maternity pay, promising more when she was settled into her leave.

This time I ran into Anna in the elevator. To my amazement, she didn't smirk and grunt and sneer, but instead looked at me steadily.

"Adélia has gone to the north zone," she said. "Her friend's husband came to pick her up."

Husband? "Thank you," I said.

"If she comes back, I have found a job for her. A German man's wife and children have gone home, they hated it here. But he is here until February, and is willing to take her into the apartment to do a little light cleaning and cooking. He will only pay one minimum wage, so she doesn't want to take it. But I think"—sneering slightly now—"that you will not take her back."

"The way things stand, I've decided to help her find another job by the end of her leave."

"This is merely a temporary job. You might have to help her find something in six months."

"I'll do that."

Leaving the elevator, she nodded and said, "*Senhora*," but this time merely ironically.

This is what happened: Adélia came back in a week, saying that she couldn't stand the confusion in the woman's house and demanding her job back. She didn't want to leave the condo, she had as much bloody right to live there as anyone else. But we pointed out that if she left to work for the German man, we would pay her a large lump sum in lieu of maternity pay, and as I suspected, it proved too tempting. She signed the legal letter, packed up and left.

As I watched Adélia going out the door, I thought to myself, I have no use for that woman. I hope I never see her again. I'm tired of this place and I want to leave.

Also, you wanted to know what it was like to be an expatriate. You wanted to know what your grandmothers went through. You wanted to know what it felt like to be *them*.

As the door slipped shut, I sighed and shook my head, offering a skeptical prayer.

Pombagira, guard your child.

29

AFTER ADÉLIA HAD FINALLY GONE, THE APARTMENT FELT AS if we'd done the *limpeza* that Geraldo had suggested. I calmed down, remembering the many wonderful things about life in Brazil. Then tragedy—or whatever you call the eruption that was Adélia—repeated itself as farce.

Noemi was working for us by that time, a lovely woman who'd worked in a São Paulo jeans factory for sixteen years, edging her way up from machine operator to supervisor before the most recent economic crash, when everyone in the factory had been laid off and offered their jobs back at less than half salary. Noemi decided to try Rio instead.

I found it such a comfort that she knew what a real workplace was like. She did her job, maintained a collegial relationship with other people in the workplace (me) and felt that her private life was both her own business and her own responsibility. Almost all of the other women in the condo had only ever worked as maids, and they usually came from families where generations of women had worked as maids, or as laborers in the sugar fields, and especially after meeting Noemi, I began to wonder whether slavery still echoed through the maid-employer relationship, in all the self-serving paternalism and cruelty and matted lies, since it had only been abolished in Brazil a little more than a century before.

It's also true that Noemi and I got along because we were quite a bit alike, both of us rather blunt yet slow to take offense ourselves. She also had a great sense of humor, which under the circumstances proved fortunate.

One evening, moments after she'd left for a date, Noemi slammed back into the apartment spattered with egg. Half-laughing, half-furious, she told me that the egg had been deliberately thrown from "that German woman's" balcony. She hadn't seen anyone throw it but knew that Adélia came back for visits, and that she'd talked about how much she hated Noemi for taking her job. When it happened again, Noemi's friend was almost certain that he saw Adélia on the balcony, and condo society grew fully convinced when both eggs and water started raining down on the wife of the doorman who was presumed to be the father of Adélia's child—and, as it turned out, of several other children in the neighborhood.

"As if the poor wife doesn't have enough to put up with," Noemi said, on a day when both the wife and she were hit. "Not just baby chicks, but eggs." Noemi gave a belly laugh, wiping off more yolk. "This is the closest I plan to come to hatching anything around here."

Adélia denied throwing the eggs, saying that she had no interest in either the doorman or her former job, and hinting that the man she now worked for wouldn't be returning to Germany alone, or going back to his wife. As it turned out, the man's friends hustled him back to Germany without her. Despite her scheming, or because of it, Adélia never had much luck.

Yet after a short try at another job, she moved back into the condo, going to work for Anna. The egg thing gradually tapered off, but people started seeing Adélia, Anna and Delma drinking in the strip of restaurants at the bottom of the hill, hanging out with some pretty miscellaneous men and staggering home at 3 A.M. Noemi seemed to think that Anna was going to have to take Adélia to Germany. Either that, or Adélia would tell the husband what was going on.

"Last night, I saw that German woman necking with the big fat guy from the gourmet shop, right there by the canal," Noemi told me. "And her married—and a *foreigner*." Her easygoing liberality finally deserted her, as if she'd caught Dorothy in the bushes with a Munchkin, transgression having reached new heights, or depths, down on the suburban flatlands.

I don't know whether Adélia went back to Germany with Anna—or with Anna's husband, as the betting soon was—since we left Brazil before they did. As a matter of fact, so did Noemi, who had the great good luck to land a job in Italy, where she went to care for the aging parents of an Italian-born executive living in São Paulo. Noemi had no intention of ever returning to Brazil, telling me before she left that she was going to marry some well-off Italian and have her children there. She promised to send me her address, no doubt followed by her wedding pictures, showing yards and yards of lace.

I never expected to hear from her again, and didn't, although I'd hazard a guess that expatriation proved far harsher than she anticipated. I also figure that Anna would tell this story differently, all parts, even Noemi's. Cracked mirrors show such different reflections, depending on the angle of view. In Anna's version, Noemi might have found what she was looking for. In a certain self-lacerating light, my Nannie might have, too.

But what do I know, really? I keep thinking of something else that P.K. Page once said, this time at a literary gathering in Toronto. She was as forceful and as gracious and funny as she'd been during our week in Mexico, a tall woman commanding the room. After we'd talked for a while, P.K. leaned toward me confidentially.

"If we keep meeting like this, we're going to start thinking we know each other," she said, and disappeared into the crowd.

FRONTIER

STORIES

AFTER WE'D BEEN IN BRAZIL FOR TWO YEARS, IT WAS TIME TO start thinking about what to do next. That was the dispiriting part of foreign postings. You no sooner cracked the surface of a place than it was time to leave. I could see how you'd get tired of that, bobbing from country to country, a cork that might one day start smelling a little too strongly of booze. The expat circuit had more than its share of drinkers, and what was worse, a surprising number of them were the children of expatriates, diplomats' brats who said they'd never belonged anywhere. We began to worry about Gabriel, wondering whether he was growing rootless, his identity confused. He was very happy in Brazil, but everyday things, like a visit to the dentist, made me wonder if this might one day cause him grief.

I was lying in the chair one day when my dentist told me that she'd applied to immigrate to Canada. She liked country music, she said, putting on a Blue Rodeo tape, twang twang as she drilled. Plus, it was almost impossible to build up a practice in Rio. You did your best work for people. You knew in your heart of hearts that you'd done a textbook root canal, straight as a bullet, absolute minimum of swelling. You'd saved a tooth, saved a smile. But Brazilians were all such surfers, riding *ondas*, waves, trends. They'd hear about some hot new dentist and they'd simply have to try him, leaving without a word of warning and taking their friends along with them. She'd heard that things were different in Canada. Clientele was loyal. She wanted to go north and build something, not just run to stay in place.

"Plus, there's my son."

He sat on a stool beside her, doing his homework on the white laminate counter, a serious little boy of about seven or eight, Gabriel's age, but smaller and slighter, a self-contained child with dark eyes and a long tanned face who bit his tongue as he worked. He was practicing his curlicued European-style penmanship, drawing methodical circles around dotted outlines for a full two pages before straightening up and starting to chant his times tables, his voice rising firmly when the drill got loud, "Three times three is nine, three times four is twelve, three times five is sixteen. . . ."

"Fifteen," his mother interrupted, leaning over my open mouth.

"Fifteen fifteen fifteen," Gabriel chanted, sambaing around the room, doing hopscotch jumps on the linoleum tile to the rhythm of Blue Rodeo, beating his fists on an invisible drum at the whine of the drill.

"My son deserves a better education than we can pay for here," the dentist told me loudly. "Schools are getting so expensive. We're always running to stay in place. That's middle-class life in Brazil."

"Three times eight is twenty-four, three times nine is twenty-seven. . . ."

"Botafogo, Botafogo," Gabriel sang, as the country tape crackled. The name of his favorite soccer team. He belted out their theme song, then echoed a TV announcer. "*Goooooooooooool!*"

"You're a Botafogo fan!" the dentist cried. "So am I!"

"*Four* times *one* is *four*, *four* times *two*. . . ."

"Oh lay, oh lay oh lay oh la. . . ."

"Your son is more Brazilian than mine is," the dentist told me ruefully. "But maybe mine will do better in Canada?"

Paul and I agreed that we should return to Toronto at the end of the posting. We made a few trips around South America, saying farewell to friends and visiting some places we'd always meant to see. On one trip, I took Gabriel deep into the Amazon. I'd never spent much time there and wanted to cram in some last-minute research for another novel I was hoping to write.

Paul's editor called not long afterward, asking if we'd like to stay in Rio for another year. The offer was tempting. We'd ended up fascinated by life in Brazil, all the nerved-up challenging chaos. Maybe we should stay and see if we could delve a little deeper. Or a lot. Something the editor said made Paul think that if we wanted, we might be able to string it out even longer.

"*Mamãe*, I need a costume of cowboy for São João Day, or maybe the spaceman," Gabriel said. "You can *costurar* me one, okay?"

My father told me once that he'd spoken Swedish as a boy, but had later forgotten how.

3 1

I'D WANTED TO GO TO THE AMAZON FOR MOST OF THE TIME we lived in Rio. The problem was, Gabriel had to go with me. I never left him at home with the maid while I traveled the way some other expats left their kids. Yet this complicated matters, not least because we couldn't tag along with Paul, whose trips to the Amazon usually involved days of bouncing a rental job over pot-holes in thirty-five-degree heat, making his way from one distant interview to the next. With our time in Brazil running out, I finally phoned a friend named Doug, an American who owned an ecolog-ical tour company, asking if he knew of a place suitable for kids. As it turned out, Doug was preparing to take off on a tour operators' junket to a new resort in the southern Amazon, and by billing me somewhat prematurely as a travel writer, he got us invited along.

It was a stretch in more ways than one. When I first got to Rio, I'd thought that the expats who left their kids with maids while they traveled were being neglectful, although I also wondered if I was being overprotective in taking mine along. Later on, I realized that I wasn't exactly protecting Gabe, nor were the others selfish. Trips to the Brazilian interior could get dangerous. There was the time we went to the Pantanal—a huge wetlands in south central

Brazil, a birders' paradise where I thought Gabriel would enjoy the wildlife. Our plane was delayed taking off from Rio, and delayed again at Belo Horizonte, apparently so they could fix a gauge, and delayed a third time in Brasília. After we'd finally taken off from Brasília, a little boy who had been allowed in the cockpit was suddenly pushed back out. The boy said quite happily, "There's smoke inside, and the pilots put on gas masks." We didn't seem to be gaining much altitude but were making a slow, low turn back toward the airport, everyone on board silent and tense.

We landed with a bump on the longest runway surrounded by the revolving red lights of fire trucks. In the terminal, the grandparents of the little boy from the cockpit rushed up, crying that smoke had been pouring out the front of the plane; they'd been watching from the observation deck. They grabbed the kid, saying that they were going to drive him the eleven hours home to Cuiabá, our next scheduled stop.

As the rest of us milled around, the plane took off again on a test flight with our luggage still on board. It circled the airport a few times before it landed and we were given our luggage, then sent to a hotel. The next morning, after taking off in what was clearly, thankfully, a different plane, the flight attendant cooed, "Welcome on board your Varig flight to Rio Branco," Rio Branco being an Amazon outpost thousands of miles northwest of the Pantanal. The attendant allowed as how we'd only land at our destination, Cuiabá, on the way back from Rio Branco, which was something like flying from Toronto to Thunder Bay by way of Vancouver. Gabriel grew overtired and nervous on the day-long flight, and as I tried to calm him, it occurred to me that this didn't qualify as one of the educational injustices that Tito had advised, and I wondered what the hell I was doing to my son.

Luckily, the first leg of the Amazon flight was fairly routine, aside from the oily smell of dried fish that gradually leaked out of an overhead compartment and adhered to our clothes and hair, even got under my fingernails, which I found terrifically interesting since I didn't think I'd scratched. Yet when Doug joined us in Belo Horizonte, he told us that he was wearing the only clothes he had left, his house having been cleaned out by burglars the day before. And when we landed in Cuiabá, the trip started backing up. We were scheduled to catch the inaugural run of a Canadian-built Dash 8 that was opening a new route between the burgeoning towns of the central Amazon. But it turned out the plane was still hopscotching down from Belém, delayed at every new destination by a toast from the mayor. Cuiabá was the southernmost stop before the plane turned north again, and the arrival times on the board kept changing. Gabriel was getting a little impatient—he hadn't exactly asked to come here, had he?—but at least we met the rest of the tour, and the manager of the resort we were trying to visit found us a lounge and some drinks.

All but one of the other travel types were Brazilian women. As we introduced ourselves, they squealed happily over Gabriel, the little blond foreigner with the perfect Carioca accent. A gorgeous young travel agent named Daniela, whom I immediately thought of as the girl from Ipanema, began to quiz him teasingly about his favorite comic books. Do you like Monica best or Cascão? Cascão? But I adore Monica. Gabriel grew animated, a self-confident seven-year-old who was used to finding friends wherever he went. I was glad of that. Yet I also disliked the type of attention he was paid throughout Latin America, even though it often got me invited places I'd never have gone on my own. It struck me as unhealthy, this widespread abasement before the blond male— unhealthy for Gabriel, unhealthy for other children. Standing to one side of our group was the dark-haired, dark-skinned daughter of a travel agent from São Paulo, a shy child Gabriel's age who watched the gorgeous Daniela slavishly, adoringly, and without raising a flicker of response.

I'd meant to enjoy this trip to the Amazon, but the long stop at Cuiabá put me in a sour mood. I also didn't take to the other foreigner on the tour, an American named Stu, a boyish-looking bald man who wore shirts and shorts with so many pockets that I soon concluded they were breeding. Like Doug, he was checking out the new resort, assigned to decide whether it met the standards of the international tour company he worked for. Stu quickly proved himself to be an *über*-guide, keeping an eye on everyone's beer level and handing out snacks as we waited—and waited, and waited—in the farty heat. I found him excessively obliging, giving the kids too many soft drinks before the plane finally landed, its propellers gently slowing, the pilots already noticeably relaxed as they wafted into the lounge. Stu refueled them, and when the boarding announcement came, he bounded up the stairs of the plane, seating our party as if he was in charge. No, you're not, I thought, shepherding Gabriel on board.

"*Tudo bem*, Gaby?" Daniela asked, popping up from the seat behind. "You're not afraid of airplanes, are you? What a brave boy. *Macho*."

In a restaurant not long before, Gabriel had hissed loudly for a waiter, a Brazilian custom I particularly disliked. I felt mortified when the waiter arrived, a bent old man who looked as if he'd been beaten down by life.

He was smiling broadly. "At your service, *macho*," he said.

"Are people frightened of airplanes?" Gabriel asked Daniela. "Why? I'm not. They're fun."

"*Bem brasileiro*," Daniela cried. He's so Brazilian. "*Olhe só!*" Look at him!

Shaking my head and smiling, I got Gabriel busy coloring and started work myself, pulling out my notebook and drawing quilt-like sketches of the land below. Forgetting my mood, I grew absorbed in the scenery as we flew over the Chapada dos Guimarães, a dry tableland that gleamed golden in the afternoon sun, its spare beauty only gradually giving way to cultivation. When it did, our flight path took us over ranches, *fazendas*, the symmetrical fields of emerald green specked with tiny crawling machines and flea-sized cattle, huge spreads bordered by iron-red ribbons of roads that led to other huge spreads all the way to the curving horizon. Periodically our cross-shaped shadow fell on rough-looking service towns, rectangular places only a couple of dirt streets deep but long and straggling, with lines of metal roofing lustrous in the sun.

I wondered whether many people outside Brazil understood its enormous size, or had any idea of what the famous burning and colonization of the rain forest really looked like. Pretty much like a red-and-green version of the Prairies, actually. *Fazendas* marched north on burnt-over land, the green pasturage only slowly giving way to untouched forest, a patchwork, for a while, of red-rimmed fields and stands of trees, with fewer roads and more landing strips laced into the green. Doug recognized the forest as transitional, a tropical moist forest with a dry season several months long. The trees below were shorter and more sparse than the ones in a true rain forest, where you can count on regular rainfall all year. But we finally crossed a climatic line and looked down on a modulation of high green trees that was the southernmost extension of the Amazon rain forest, canopy forest like green brocade thrown onto the ground below.

Soon after the landscape changed, we landed in Alta Floresta, a town of 150,000 people that hadn't been there fifteen years before, one of many new towns, cities, in metastasis throughout the Amazon. A small resort on the outskirts of Alta Floresta would be our base for trips into the bush. The resort manager, Edson, told us that his family had founded Alta Floresta as a model settlement, offering laborers from the *sertão* a chance to work on a plantation of ecologically sustainable crops. Unfortunately, gold was quickly discovered nearby. Prospectors and miners flooded the area, as they have throughout the Amazon, sluicing the beds of nearby rivers and polluting them with mercury, which is used to bleed gold dust from the mud.

A few days later, I hired a taxi to snoop around, wondering what a gold-rush town looked like. I soon found that its two paved streets were lined with competing assay offices, dustless, bright and barred, where wary-looking men behind the counters didn't want their pictures taken. Between them were a surprising number of the cleanest drugstores I have ever seen, lit bright enough to hurt your teeth. Outside a couple of ice-cream carts stood sweating in the heat, and later we passed a lone gynecologist's clinic, a pool hall, a closed bowling alley and a very few food stores. Curious pedestrians watched us pass, one of the few cars on the road. The heat was thick, almost scummy, and we soon stopped at a bar for a drink, picking one with a pinball machine for Gabriel to pass the time.

"Hey! Come see blondie play pinball! Come and see!"

A few children skittered through the doorway.

"Take off," the bartender called, chasing them back out.

"Those are local boys," Gabriel told me. "The man doesn't want them to come in here."

He'd recently taken on the job of deciphering Brazil for me, usually in perfect Portuguese, assuming, often correctly, that I had failed to understand the obvious.

"Felipe and I can't get ourselves a drink," he'd said not long before. "It isn't polite for him to come into my kitchen. Noemi is supposed to bring us some glasses on a tray. Don't worry, I'll tell her."

Another day, he came in after school, holding out his exercise books and saying, "You have to take my schoolbooks to the stationery store and get the covers laminated. It's not hard. Miss says to find the lady behind the counter, not the man. I asked."

"*Tudo bem*," I replied. Okay.

"Please don't speak Portuguese to me," he said. "Your accent is so bad it hurts my ears."

Back in the cab, I thought of my Granny's broken English. Dis dat dose priddie flowers over dare. Suu-ure, she'd say. In a humbling instant, I saw my father's unusual patience with his mother echoed in my young son's usual patience with me. Gabriel sat politely by my side as I peered around with foreign eyes, making a spectacle of myself, taking a child into a bar, rubbernecking, asking the cabby to drive meaningless grids through the watching town.

"What do you think of the Amazon?" I asked Gabriel.

"When are we going home?"

"But isn't it interesting here? Somewhere different?"

He shrugged. I looked back outside, wondering what I might point out. But the sleepy strip of stores gave directly onto housing developments, prefab homes on dusty unpaved streets that lapped off toward the rain forest. I couldn't see any company headquarters, even many tradesmen's signs, and began to feel that he was right, there was nothing much to see. Alta Floresta was like a suburb without a downtown, airy and unanchored, here one day, gone the next, a modern Brigadoon. In one area, the ranch-style houses belonging to mine owners and foremen strained upward from their grassy yards, most with spotless satellite dishes tilting their chins toward the sky. Further from the strip mall were the flyaway shacks where the prospectors left their families, often for months at a time, stick buildings like those in Rio's *favelas*, although a little bigger, with yards large enough for a garden, maybe some chickens, and geraniums sprawling out of painted cans. Knowing what people came from, you could see why they came here, even though "here" was increasingly hard to define.

"It's just normal," Gabriel told me, when I pressed him. "Those are people's houses, that's all."

"Normal for them," I agreed. "But it's not like very many other places."

"Why not?"

Looking over Gabriel's head, it occurred to me that the forest was the real downtown. Business was conducted there, the region's dirty business. Yet gold prices had recently fallen, and the hotel that Edson's family had built to house visiting gold buyers and speculators was now sometimes vacant. That's why they'd pumped it into a small resort and started running nature tours into the bush. It was astonishing, the transition from forest to gold rush to advanced eco-capitalism in just fifteen years, one not erasing the other, but setting up an increasingly complex and mutually destructive synergy.

The unfolding Amazon. Place as process. I wondered what effect the process of expatriation was having on my small son; whether expatriation was a place in itself. Maybe that was the Brigadoon I'd sensed out the cab window, my own reflection looking back in.

"It's a frontier, honey," I said. "There's a gold rush going on. It's the Wild West. Isn't that sort of exciting?"

"Can we go back to the hotel now? I'm hot."

Arriving at the resort, I took Gabriel straight to the pool, ordering drinks and wondering crossly why we thought we needed gold, anyway. I had a gold wedding ring, but with all the street crime in Rio, I hadn't worn it for almost three years. Nevertheless, our marriage had endured. Feeling increasingly irritated, I watched Gabriel splash his way across the pool, tiring himself out and finally pulling himself up to sit on the edge.

"Psssssssst," he hissed at a distant waiter.

"Gabriel, please don't make that noise."

"That's how you call a waiter," he replied. "See? He's coming over."

"*Oi, rapaz*," the waiter said easily. "What can I get you today?"

3 2

 I SEEMED TO HAVE BAD LUCK WITH PLANES. IT WASN'T JUST Brazil. There was also the time in Labrador, years later, when we were heading to the village of Rigolet up the coast from Goose Bay. Once again, I was taking Gabriel—or Gabe, as he now preferred to be called. We'd been back in Canada for several years and flew from our home in Toronto to Halifax, where we got on a smaller plane to fly to St. John's, where we got on a smaller plane to Goose Bay, where we got on a tiny plane, a Twin Otter, bound for Rigolet, so that I kept thinking of those cartoons of big fish swallowing small fish swallowing minnows.

It was April and eight-foot-long icicles hung from the roof of the Happy Valley-Goose Bay airport. Visibility was poor, the windsocks straight out, and most of the flights along the coast had been canceled. But Rigolet was only a forty-five-minute run up the most sheltered part of the coast, and the flight was fully booked with maybe a dozen people heading to an important funeral, a couple of Mounties, an official from the Labrador Inuit Association and us. Eventually we were told to climb on board the Twin Otter, and the copilot walked past us down the aisle, saying, "Can't smoke and fasten yer belts," before disappearing behind a hanging blanket into the cockpit. The pilot revved the engines and we took off.

At first, Gabe thought it was fun, just like a roller coaster. Then a girl vomited nearby and he started looking pale. We rose and thumped back down, gained altitude then thump-thump-

thumped as if we were tumbling downstairs, careening sideways then righting ourselves, plowing our way northeast. Looking out the window, I saw that we were holding a course roughly—very roughly—parallel to the northern shore of Lake Melville, an abrupt white headland swirling with cloud and wind. We were pushed offshore and had to struggle back, then pushed offshore again, the plane buzzing like a toy. As more children puked, I realized why the floor was made of plywood with holes in it. Fortunately, I have a strong stomach and go rigid when I'm terrified, which looks good, anyway. Gabe was leaning against me, almost green and very quiet.

"Is it bad? Comparatively speaking?" I asked the Mounties, who were sitting just behind us, beefy arms crossed, hat flaps down against the cold, taking up the last row of scruffy off-red seats.

"Seen worse."

"Not too bad."

"Not great, but not too bad," the guy from the Labrador Inuit Association put in, leaning over his laptop to hand me a barf bag.

"Seen worse," the first Mountie told him.

"Seen worse," the LIA guy, Tim, agreed.

Bucking and barfing, shuddering in the crosswind, we finally began our descent into Rigolet almost an hour after takeoff. Quite a few of the passengers had vomited by then. After one terrific drop almost to the treetops, we landed and taxied to the end of the airstrip.

"Not *much* worse," the Mountie confided, opening the door.

We were on our way to school that day, an Inuit school on the Canadian frontier. Another frontier: funny the echoes you sometimes hear, the coincidences that can get you thinking. I'd met a teacher who lived in Rigolet, and she'd offered to put us up so I could do a magazine piece about the school where she and her husband both worked.

Gabe was thirteen and still having trouble fitting into Canada, where he'd never lived much until he was eight. It didn't help that after a long search we'd signed him up for precisely the wrong junior high school. It was a small public school where the prevailing style turned out to be cool and hard-driving. His personality was too warm and Brazilian for the other kids, musical when many of them were athletic, happily disorganized when they were perhaps a little over-scheduled. One of the teachers, a caustic, sarcastic type, gave him a particularly hard time. It occurred to me that staying with a couple of sympathetic teachers like Yvonne and Darryl might help, not to mention hanging out with a different group of kids—he'd be going to school while I poked around town and interviewed people. Talk about weighting the trip with an agenda. No wonder the plane kept threatening to fall.

I felt so bloody grateful to get out of that plane. Once the pilot cut his engines, the afternoon was quiet, even muffled. We were all muffled, everyone dressed in thermal clothes, multicolored snowmen rolling wide-legged past the isolated shelter of the airshed. It wasn't really all that cold, just a few degrees below zero, but the ground was under a good five feet of snow, and our boots chumped and thudded as we looked for the people there to meet us. I soon saw Yvonne, a relief, since I hadn't been sure that I'd recognize her. We'd been corresponding by e-mail but had met just once when she was in Toronto a couple of years before, and I remembered her features less clearly than her self-possession, an unusual sort of vivacious stillness she conveyed while sitting in our mutual friend Sandra's garden, telling us about the walk she'd taken through an antiques district the previous day. She'd got into a long conversation with a dealer from Iran, chatting about the way she'd worked her way through university at an Iranian-run restaurant.

"That nice man!" Yvonne told us. "I sang him a song in Persian, sitting there on the counter. We must have talked for half an hour. I think I'll go back and visit him today."

Freckled, I was reminded, hugging her in Rigolet. Fair, fifteen years younger than me, with broad cheekbones I thought must come from the Mi'kmaq grandmother she spoke of.

"People usually want to rest back at the house after that flight," Yvonne said, suggesting Gabe get in the *komatik*, the high-sided sled attached to her Ski-Doo, while I sling up on the machine behind her. She called it a machine; I soon learned that everybody did. Yvonne needs a new machine, they'd say. Got to get a new machine myself. But I'd never ridden a machine before, or anything like it, except maybe a horse. Experimentally, I clutched the padded seat between my knees, wondering what to do with my hands. Then Yvonne flipped a switch and my head jerked back as we roared up the hill. Bouncing, jolting, clutching Yvonne around her waist, I noticed a sign protruding from the snow.

Welcome to Rigolet. Pop. 352, founded 1733.

A former Hudson's Bay trading post. But there was little sign of history as we spilled over the crest of the hill. A scattering of white prefab houses lay to the right and left, tidy with siding, but the storehouses I'd seen in old photographs were gone, and the boardwalk that connected them, although outside several houses we passed firewood being seasoned in the traditional way, spindly tree trunks stripped of branches and leaned upright against each other like tepees, like cones. The land was rolling here, the town tumbling down toward the frozen shores of the inlet, the hills above us treed with dark and stunted spruce. In a very few minutes, we coasted down to Yvonne and Darryl's place and unloaded our gear inside. Then Yvonne roared off for a prenatal appointment—five months pregnant—while Gabe found the TV, *The Simpsons*, and I sat down in a basket chair, wondering what came next.

After we'd left Brazil, I'd tried to keep traveling. In fact, my life wasn't really all that different than it had been in Latin America. Toronto was just another city we'd moved to, although the posting had lasted longer than usual, and people talked to us as if we'd come home. The problem was, I didn't know what "home" meant any more. I was just a traveler, passing through.

But it was getting tiring. Sitting in Rigolet, my muscles only slowly unclenching, research for yet another article ahead, I wondered for the first time whether I was up to it. Maybe it was time to settle down. Settle in, settle for something less challenging—preferably before the next leg of the trip. Yvonne and Darryl had offered to take us to their cabin for the weekend, a two- or three-hour machine ride away, so we could do some ice fishing, maybe see some wildlife. But even the short ride in from the airstrip had left me rubbing my spavined hip, which had ached since a car accident a few months before. Our isolation scared me. Hearing the drone of the Twin Otter taking off, watching the weather closing in, I knew that it would be a long time before we'd see the next plane, and the only other way out of town was a day-long machine ride to Goose Bay, not recommended.

I sat there feeling sorry for Gabe, the misplaced Brazilian, loose and musical, who got such a rough ride in junior high—and now he had to fit in somewhere else? I felt sorry for myself, knowing that I was being absurd, but half-panicked by the windy void out the window, the tiny town giving way to nothingness, frozen water, frozen hills, my thoughts slurry and unfocused until Yvonne got back, and I struggled into my coat to get a tour of the school.

Northern Lights Academy: It looked like a haunted seaside hotel washed up on the side of a hill, all rambling white clapboard with a peaked roof and paned windows breathing in and out in the wind. All the kids in town went there, kindergarten through high school, and it dominated Rigolet, not just the biggest building, but the biggest local employer—a matter of some resentment, I learned later, when so many people were unemployed. I also found that the roof leaked, and electrical cords snaked through the halls to the dangerously few electrical outlets; the building was scheduled to be replaced the following year.

But at least you could find the front door, I thought, following Yvonne up the steep stairs. For the past few years, I'd been writing a great deal about education, visiting a generation of low-slung suburban schools designed without imposing formal entrances, which may have got rid of the Abandon Hope, All Ye Who Enter Here aspect, but often left me circling an unfamiliar building, testing a series of identical locked doors before finding one that finally opened, feeling that it was all a little too symbolic of modern confusion about the proper approach to education. Too many competing agendas, I thought, as we ask our kids to be everything that we can't quite manage to be ourselves.

Then we opened the door on Northern Lights to find a construction paper mural, cutout birds and trees pinned to the main bulletin board: *Save the Rainforest!* Standing beside it was a serious little girl with bottle-bottom glasses, sweet enough to break your heart.

And so I was in school again, still being educated, and forever displaced. Soon Gabe joined me—happily, as it turned out—and the serious little girl took it upon herself to keep me informed of his movements, appearing beside me as I left Darryl's science class or talked with the Inuktitut teacher, Amalia.

"Gabe's in woodworking now."

"Gabe's up to the Science Olympics."

"Gabe and Kristy like each other."

What originally interested me about the school was Yvonne's description of its hybrid program. The kids left the school building once a week for half a day of life-skills courses, learning to hunt seals or trap game, maybe make some moose-skin moccasins, before heading back to the computer lab. But what I hadn't quite understood before was the hybrid nature of the town itself. The factors at the Hudson's Bay post had been the first people to live year-round in Rigoulette more than 250 years before, most of them Scots or French. The Inuit and Innu—whom the factors called Eskimos and Naskapi Indians—led migratory lives, moving from summer to winter camps with the seasonal change of game.

But after Newfoundlanders started to build summer fishing camps on the Labrador coast, people mingled and intermarried, particularly from Rigolet south, and gradually they settled into villages. Many villagers still lived roughly traditional lives well into the twentieth century, but then the kids were removed to one of those heartbreaking residential schools, cut off from their families and their languages, so that traditions cracked like hammered ice. Afterward came television, and city-boy Gabe had no trouble finding common ground with the kids at school.

He had no trouble fitting in at all. Gabe was as tall as I was by then, making him taller than most kids his age anywhere, but with his hair darkening to brown and his eyes the family hazel, he didn't look out of place among the Inuit kids. He spent his days with a few classmates who looked traditionally Inuit, with kids who had dark Inuit eyes and pale skin and brown hair, with dark-skinned, startlingly gray-eyed kids, a couple of blond children with caramel-colored skin and light gray-green eyes, kids with such uniformly European features that their dark skin looked like a tropical tan, hazel-eyed people like himself with fair skin and straight black hair, and a teenage guy in town as a delegate to an Inuit association youth conference, whose father, I was told, had been an airman at the military base in Goose Bay, and who appeared less Inuit than black.

They looked Brazilian. In that dilapidated school among all those beautiful children I often felt as if I was back in Rio. It wasn't the *Save the Rainforest!* mural. You were no more likely to see one of those in Brazil than you were to find a Greenpeace anti-sealing poster in Rigolet. But especially as a group, they looked inter-racial, and in that sense Brazilian, so that watching the kids mingle you could get hopeful about our chances of one day evolving beyond racism.

It was one of those strange coincidences that, when we got home, Gabe's class was assigned to read *The Chrysalids* by John Wyndham, that old school warhorse, a post-nuke fantasy in which some of the few surviving children living far outside the melted cities evolve telepathic powers, communicating mentally between diffuse settlements, and making friends without knowing or caring what the other kids looked like. Gabe came downstairs that night to point out that the book was set in Labrador and that the capital of its known world was Rigo, which the characters understood to be a fragmented remembering of a name from before. I haven't been able to find any connection between Wyndham and Rigolet, and fig-ure he must have picked the name off a map, but his point involved frontiers, it's a frontier story, and I reread it thinking not just about Labrador, but about the Amazon, and the trip I took with Gabe. Children and frontiers, I kept thinking. Children *are* frontiers, that's what Wyndham was saying. And I was glad to see he believed that a few might survive what we do to them in our ignorance.

I also figured that Wyndham haphazardly got one thing right about Rigolet. People told me that the town was as riven by feuds and divisions as his novel, or a soap opera—although that proba-bly just means, as any place else. Most of the teachers came from Newfoundland, including Yvonne and Darryl, and they were regarded as something like rich expats, resented for their union salaries. The local hotel owner wouldn't let them in his bar, and a couple of years after we visited, Yvonne started getting midnight phone calls saying, "Newfie go home," even though she and Darryl felt they'd made their home in Labrador.

A couple of local Newfoundland settlers—they're not all teachers—told me that they sometimes overheard people calling them something like *hublunonuit*, which they interpreted as a not very complimentary way of saying "outsider" in Inuktitut, although an Inuk guy told me later that the word (which no one knew how to spell) is more correctly used by Inuktitut speakers to mean Inuit who are lighter skinned than themselves, sort of like "high yellow" within the black community. According to this guy, it's even less complimentary than the Newfoundlanders think, but it also expresses the same tight-lipped censorious envy as "high yellow," since dark-skinned, Inuktitut-speaking people from the northern coast of Labrador have higher status within the community, they're considered culturally more pure, but they don't tend to get the jobs.

At the same time, the reason I learned all this is that people were uniformly kind, offering us rides on their machines as we slogged through town, or speaking thoughtfully on difficult topics when all I could do in return, at first, was sit in their living rooms and admire the framed photographs of their children, meanwhile ransacking their homes with my eyes: the racks of guns, the big TVs, the animal hides hanging on pegs, crocheted cushions, dog-race trophies, a particularly fetching Elvis clock.

Yet they eventually paid us the compliment of asking for favors, assuming that we were human enough to want to give back, and I found myself contravening all po-faced journalistic principles of noninvolvement by helping teach an English class, and playing both audience and in-house drama critic for a crew of delightful student actors rehearsing their play, *The Story of a Cell*, an educational tale told through dance and gauzy costumes ("There is no life without cells." "Without cells there is no life.") in which a couple of suddenly grown-up-looking girls in suits and heels took the instructional roles, getting a laugh with a reference to Yvonne's elementary-level class, which, counting back,

I realized they must have taken when she first arrived in Rigolet five years before.

"Cells!" the director cried. "I'm going to suggest one or two changes. Could I see the mitochondria, please?"

Yvonne's latest class of seven- and eight-year-olds had been the ones to construct the *Save the Rainforest!* bulletin board, drawing the tropical animals they were studying, and advertising a bake sale to raise money for the World Wildlife Fund. Yvonne wanted me to stop by her class as well, and after a few days, I found myself perched on a tiny molded plastic chair trying to answer questions about the children's favorite rain forest animals.

"Have you ever seen a poison-dart frog?"

No, but I heard tree frogs calling outside my window in Rio, sounding just like doors creaking, tiny frog doors creaking open and shut.

"Howler monkeys?"

Oh yes, in the Amazon, when Gabe was your age, a whole family of monkeys sounding just like they were beating drums.

"A jaguar?"

No, but in the Pantanal, I'd stumbled on a party of hunters who seemed to be going after one. Illegally, I said, since jaguars are endangered. I watched the children hesitate, considering, I think, the thrilling concept of the hunt alongside the distressing problem of scarcity, so many of their fathers having been left unemployed by the closure of the cod fishery.

"Morpho butterflies?" a little boy asked, a safer question. Like this, I said, joining my hands at the wrists and fanning them slowly. As big as my hands, and blue as the sky at sunset.

They raised $129.87 at their bake sale, selling cupcakes and squares to a milling crowd of students and teachers, and sending it off to the World Wildlife Fund to preserve, they hoped, five kilometers of flyway for migratory birds.

33

UP THE AMAZON, WORRIED ABOUT GABRIEL AND HAUNTED by the ghosts of my pregnant grandmothers, I began to think about my Granny's letters home, particularly the one she'd written about her sons settling down after the Second World War. "Things are going well for all three of them," she wrote. "I'm so glad my boys don't have to work as hard as we did."

When I copied it out in Sweden, I thought her letter expressed the fulfillment of the immigrant dream. She'd sacrificed everything for her children, especially for the oldest boy, my rich uncle Walter, whose birth she'd legitimized in Canada.

But I was older in Brazil, twice as old as my Granny had been when she'd arrived in Trochu. It finally occurred to me such young immigrants had no coherent idea of their children's futures. How could they, when most of us never even quite realize that a first pregnancy will result in a baby? No, they'd really come for their own sakes, and only started talking about the kids when life didn't quite work out. The kids justified all of their struggles. They were justification. Self-justification. Which was such a sad weight for the children to bear.

"I don't know the cost, although it must be about 10,000 kroner," Granny wrote home, boasting about my father's house. He worked three jobs to pay the mortgage, but given the expectations placed on an immigrant's child, he probably didn't tell her that, and probably she knew anyway, but chose not to pass it on.

Expatriates struck me as different. They never just settled for bettering their children. They never really settled, taking up new posts, trying a move somewhere else, and traveling, always traveling, either abandoning the children to the maids or taking them along on risky trips that the children never asked for. No wonder so many of the kids grew up to be unsettled, disaffected, even drinkers.

Tito told me, "You're teaching him that there's such a thing as injustice in the world."

He was such a sophisticated man. Years later, as the plane stuttered into Rigolet, I could still picture him sitting there, embedded in irony, and finally saw that self-justification comes in many forms.

3 4

OUR GREGARIOUS TOUR GUIDE STU WASN'T REALLY THE leader of our Amazon group, despite what he seemed to think. The children were, Gabriel and the Brazilian girl, Cleo, since the rest of us tended to do whatever was necessary to keep them happy. Not to mention keep them safe, particularly when we left Alta Floresta for the bush.

The morning after we arrived, we piled into the hotel van on our way to the resort's new river camp, where they promised that we'd see rare and lovely species of birds chased from over-touristed areas further north. Almost a dozen of us were crammed into the van, bumping shoulders as we made our way to a dock on the nearest river, a few hours' dusty ride away. The red ribbon roads that had looked so sinuous from the air turned out to be full of the potholes Paul had described, and we rattled uncomfortably past scrubby forest and poor-looking ranches, bouncing over cattle guards and sweating in the rising humidity. Burn down the Amazon and this was what you got: patchy yards around listing wooden houses, pots of leggy impatiens on the porch. *Maria-sem-vergonha*, they called impatiens here. Shameless Mary. The houses tried to look Alpine, but there was no backdrop beyond the hot and colorless sky, and the fields around them showed rusty through the exhausted grass. Skinny white longhorns, martyred by insects, stood with their humped necks hanging.

"Cows!" Gabriel cried, pointing.

When I was his age, we took Sunday drives through the Fraser Valley outside Vancouver. Look at the cows! I'd cry, pointing to herds of healthy black-and-white Holsteins swishing their tails in the lush green fields, snowcapped mountains rising behind. Those were real cows, at least to me, but as we bumped along, I realized that Gabriel would see things differently. Holsteins would look exotic to him, at least for a while, and the comfort foods he'd always crave would be *flan* and his favorite *linguiça*.

"See the birds!" He pointed to some big clownish toucans cleaning their bills on a hardwood tree, birds I'd grown up seeing only on *National Geographic* specials.

"Don't lean out the window," I told him, holding onto the waistband of his shorts, feeling both pleased and sad.

The van dropped us at a dock on a wide milky river, a southern tributary of the great Rio Tapajós that flows into the Amazon at Santarém. After clambering into an outboard, we got the children into lifejackets and buzzed downstream, cutting a path through the churning current until we reached the mouth of a blackwater river, rich in tannin. We jounced over a brief mixing of dark and light water before turning into the blackwater river, buzzing upstream for an hour as a pleasant breeze riffled our hair. The vegetation was dense on either side and many birds swooped past us—kingfishers and swallows dipping in the river, brilliant macaws and darting green parrots—until we turned a corner to find another dock, and put in at the camp where we'd spend the next few days.

"Cleo!" her mother cried. "Don't get too far ahead! Stop right there and wait for me!"

The camp was built in a grassy clearing, its central dining lodge flanked by bunkhouses hung with hammocks, a series of small private rooms ranked behind them. Some visiting scientists had already claimed the rooms, stacking them with turtle shells, nets and specimen jars, leaving us nothing but the hammocks. Some of the others grumbled, but I wanted to try sleeping in a hammock anyway, and Gabriel wouldn't hear of anything else. As we unloaded our gear, he insisted that we sling his pack into the men's bunkhouse. He wanted to bunk with the guys.

"I'll look out for him," Doug told me. He'd come to know Gabriel well on our previous trip to the Pantanal.

"If you're sure it's okay," I said.

"Don't worry. He can have the hammock next to mine."

And in fact, it was fine. I quickly found that everyone kept an eye on the kids, including Stu, although his idea of supervision left me feeling a little strained. The river was running deep and swift, but he encouraged the children to dive off the dock, fifteen feet high, while he waited for them in the water below.

"It's okay, I'm right here," he called. "Ready? Set?"

"The current's a little fast," I told him, treading water nearby. "I really don't want the kids coming in here without at least two adults."

"Ma'am." He saluted me, disappearing in the water to surface nearby, tireless, the *über*-guide, an indefatigable camp counselor. He was expecting me to laugh, which I did a little weakly, having never been a camper myself. I wasn't sure about the current, either, even though the others shrugged off my fears. The scientists said they'd been swimming off the dock for weeks, and it didn't seem to bother Doug and Stu, who knew the Amazon well. Then Gabriel launched himself toward a point too far out in the river.

"Watch!" I cried, swimming toward him.

"I've got him," Doug called, bobbing to the surface nearby.

In the midst of such dangers, real and imagined, I sometimes had trouble enjoying myself, despite the great beauty of the forest. Enormous blue macaws flapped across the river, a species at risk, a privilege to see. We boated past bitterns fanning their wings and flocks of emerald parrotlets settling into trees. Yet there was also the matter of the current, insects, malaria, snakes, the razor-sharp machetes used to clear paths and, of course, the piranhas, which the cook fished for off the dock after we'd finished swimming. The guide told us that the local species was harmless, but how could he be sure? I wondered if I'd been foolish to bring my son. Probably not. We'd almost certainly be fine. But I watched every move Gabriel made and scrutinized my mothering constantly.

He wasn't bored, was he? Of course not, far too much to do. Bird-watching, canoe rides, singsongs at night around the campfire. He seemed to have an especially good time swimming, a physically fearless child, splashing hard against the fast black current, tiring himself out happily. Maybe he'd remember the waters here as magical, the way I remembered Osoyoos Lake. Maybe he'd agree to come on a nature walk, responding to the forest (his forest) as I once had. *Tudo bem, Mamãe*, of course he'd come, a sunny little boy—and talk a blue streak the entire time about soccer, friends, comic books, TV, everything not immediately in front of him.

"*Puxa*, Gabriel," Daniela said. "Such a talker! So Brazilian!"

"Cleo," her mother cried. "You stay back from that machete!"

Together we padded down the narrow trails, rustling through the thickly fallen leaves, peace descending like autumn. A screaming piha shrieked. Motmots chuckled. A hoot of hidden monkeys. High above, the canopy swayed, and I canted my head toward the stirring green sky. Surely Gabriel would remember this, the way I would always remember the wet cedar smell of the BC rain forest. He'd remember the buttressed roots of an immense brazil-nut tree twisting along the leafy ground like the raised veins on an old woman's hands. My poor old Granny's hands. If I lived to be old, I hoped that Gabriel would look on my hands as fondly as I'd looked on hers.

"Botafogo, Botafogo," he sang out sweetly. Ahead, the guide picked up what looked like a coconut, hacking it open to show brazil nuts curled like fingers inside. When we caught up, he offered us nutmeat on the point of his machete, the meat a creamy white, much denser than the skim-milk hearts of palm he'd cut down earlier. Gabriel would never eat anything new, but he ran his finger along the cool side of the blade as I watched tensely. Further along the path, Doug and Stu told the manager, Edson, that he'd have to widen the trails for their tour groups. Otherwise, they'd get ticks.

Ticks? Cleo cried at the sight of the busy little specks on her wrists. But the guide taught us to dive into the river, where the ticks lost their grip in the cold. It wasn't so bad, especially when we boated upstream, so deep in the jungle that flowering trees erupted through the canopy like fireworks. We were heading for the stretch of the river where scientists had recently discovered an odd species of bird, the hoatzin, which showed vestigial signs of its reptilian origin, making it closer to a living dinosaur than almost anything known. Their roost proved vacant that day, but the guide got the children fishing amid the nearby bloom of water lilies. Cleo caught a piranha, its needle teeth flashing as she pulled it over the side of the boat. Surely they'd remember this: the time I went fishing for piranha.

But there was a problem. Gabriel was too young to master the quick tug you needed to give your line the moment you felt a bite, and time after time, he lost his bait.

"I'm feeding the fish," he cried in despair. "I'm feeding the fish their dinner."

"Dinner" being a piranha the guide had caught and cut into bait-sized strips.

"Cannibals!" he cried suddenly, looking horrified.

I pushed back his sun-bleached hair, wishing that I could make everything perfect. It sometimes seemed as if parenthood was one long fight to push back failure and danger as they encroached on your child, the darkest of swaddling forests. Arriving back at the isolated camp, I understood the frontiersman's drive to conquer nature, to pacify the wild, to make it useful and predictable and safe.

In a way, the frontier was what I came from, and what I'd brought my son to. I was infinitely more privileged, of course. I pictured my Granny riding the mailman's team and democrat to the isolated farmhouse near Trochu. She had no idea when she'd leave, or how, while I was expecting our rich posting in Brazil to end soon, as we'd always known it would. Yet as I looked out at the Amazon rain forest, I felt that I shared far more with my Granny than eyes, hips, lips, shoulders, blood.

Mother, my father called her, playing rummy in her Edmonton kitchen.

Mor, they said in Swedish, a word I'd heard for the first time after she was dead.

"*Mamãe*, I need a costume of cowboy for São João Day, or maybe the spaceman. You can *costurar* me one, okay?"

I had never dreamed that this would happen again, either to myself or my son.

3 5

WE LEFT RIGOLET AFTER SCHOOL ON FRIDAY TO SPEND THE weekend at Darryl and Yvonne's cabin. Gabe was behind Darryl on his machine while I rode with Yvonne, and we were joined by their friend Ray, another teacher, who had built the cabin with them. It was a beautiful afternoon, the first sunny day we'd had since arriving. The blue sky, scudding with clouds, brightened the white and gray townscape, which was otherwise varied only by the smartly painted doors on the houses we soon rumbled past, and softened by woodsmoke drifting out the metal chimneys.

The cabin wasn't far from Rigolet as the crow flies, just across Hamilton Inlet. In summer, they got there fairly quickly by boat. But in winter, the inlet didn't completely freeze up, and we had to take a U-shaped route, heading west out of Rigolet to the point where the inlet narrowed and reliably froze. There we'd turn south, crossing deep wind-scoured ice toward the nub of further shore. Once safely across, we'd double back, heading roughly southeast on the homestretch to the cabin.

It was warm as we left the last of the houses behind us, four degrees above freezing, and Darryl was surprised that the snow remained in such ideal condition. He led the way, having the better machine, an outdoorsman who kept his gun and fishing gear stashed in the *komatik* he towed. Darryl was as dark as Yvonne was fair, decisive in a way that you could read physically, and quiet, I'd found, except when he felt talkative. A month before, he'd joined the town hunt for the fourth straight year, traveling fifteen hours by machine up the coast to locate the George River caribou herd. In two days' hunting, each man got an animal for his family, and they took a couple more for the old folks. It wasn't rocket science, Darryl claimed. "They're not too bright, caribou. Tend to stand there looking at you."

That day, he pushed on hard, making it difficult for Yvonne and me to keep up.

"All the men in Darryl's family die at forty," she said later.

"Got to get it all in beforehand," he agreed.

We were following the coast, where rocks encased in ice erupted from the frozen shoreline, humped things, turquoise at their compressed depths. "Balleycaters," people called them. An old word. Economical people, they preserved vocabulary around here. Mushy nasty ice was called slob; you could see where the modern usage came from. "'Twere slobby down to the balley-caters," one man said. I found the turquoise thrilling, waves of crested color rising like icebergs above a crystal sea. Yet it was jarring to ride along the rough coast, bouncing and hanging on with clenched knees, and I was glad when Darryl called a rest to point out a landmark.

"Mealy Mountains," he said, gesturing toward a low range just coming visible, folding into the distance, worn white mountains beaten smooth by time. Then we were off again, passing the occasional cabin on the coast, door open, looking abandoned, although Yvonne explained over her shoulder that some of them were fishing cabins used by people from Goose Bay in the summer. Sometimes we even saw a cairn of piled stones, an Inukshuk—reminder, memorial, directional sign, all of these things, of half-forgotten significance, carefully maintained. More often the markers we passed were Coke cans tied to trees.

Darryl didn't seem to need signs, anyway. At places that looked to me like no place at all, he'd turn inland, leading us up and down hills on what Yvonne called portages, trails through the trees. Spruce, mainly. When we stopped once at the crest of a steep hill, the ground was covered with tiny black snow fleas, hopping dust. Yvonne said that we were lucky, the trail sometimes thawed into a river, but the ideal conditions improbably continued on an unusually warm day. We rode smoothly up a steep bluff, Carwallow Head, pausing again to look over at the Mealy Mountains. There were no cabins now, no signs of human habitation anywhere in sight, just low mountains and frozen water and one treeless oblong island caught between two hilly shores. It seemed desolate even before Ray told the story. Innu had massacred Inuit there, or maybe whalers had massacred the Inuit. In any case, many people died, mainly women and children, and human skulls stood weathering on sticks for long years before they were finally decently buried.

Down from Carwallow Head, we crossed the frozen strait, bucking and roaring along the rough snow cover, belching gasoline fumes as we made the far shore, following more coast and more portages toward the distant cabin.

"You're probably wondering why we don't wear helmets," Yvonne said, as we rested. "People do in Goose Bay and on the south coast, but here we don't."

We finally pulled up outside the cabin after a two-hour ride, cutting motors on the sound of a rising wind. While the others leapt off their machines, unloading the *komatik* and lighting the woodstove, I could barely haul myself off the seat, and when I did, I found I was walking like a cowboy, my legs absurdly bowed. Stretching, shaking out the cramps, I tramped back and forth along a hump of rock that in summer would be shoreline, watching my uncertain step and only glancing up briefly—to be transfixed, awed at how quickly the clouds blew in, the blue sky shredding, the sun paling, the horizon quickly smudging into fog. The brisk wind chilled my upturned face, and as it blew, the world turned gray—the sky ghostly, the hills smeared, all color leached from the landscape. Any sense of perspective was lost. Or gained: The log cabin behind me looked so tiny that I shivered. Once again, I didn't know what I was doing there or even where I was.

I couldn't get my bearings after that. The whole weekend, I fought dread at our remoteness, wondering if my Granny had felt so lost in Trochu. In the huge sweep of icy bay and hills on every side, I could see nothing human, nothing made, nor see how humanity could last here. The desolation was immense. We were pinpricks in a huge wash of foggy, formless gray, hopping little snow fleas. You had to laugh at our insignificance, except that for once I couldn't. I felt rubbed so raw that everything took me deeply, and I was helplessly touched by the way Darryl and Ray got Gabe driving a machine as soon as we arrived, something he'd been longing to do. They took him with them to get water from the spring, then casually trusted him, sending him back on his own to get more.

Just as helplessly, I watched Gabe recede into the distant fog and disappear, more aware of our isolation than ever until I saw a dot returning, saw Darryl clap Gabe on the shoulder as he unloaded jugs of water. Gabe beamed, and I felt close to melting. Maybe this trip would boost his self-confidence, teach him to be proud of his experiences, make him feel more fully Canadian—fully *something*—after all.

"Hey, Mom," he said, coming into the cabin. "You need a hand with anything?"

The next morning we went ice fishing, heading out through the fog and a gritty rain that streaked my cheeks like feeble tears. "Not far," Yvonne promised. A freezing hour later, we pulled up at the bottom of Back Bay, where people were already fishing. I've never been so glad to see anybody in my life. They were Rigolet people, the game warden, the school secretary, a nurse from the clinic, and they'd already drilled several holes through five feet of ice to reach the shallow water beneath. Some of them had fished enough and kindly gave us their stations, while Darryl handed around rods—bamboo sticks with hooked lines tied to one end.

Gabe quickly pulled up a trout, then I did, and Yvonne. A cheering start, and we got a few more before the others left. But they took our luck with them, and Darryl had to drill a couple more holes with his power auger before he and Ray started catching anything worthwhile. I marveled to hear that Inuit women once hacked out these holes by hand. Also stamped my feet to try to get warm, hoped that I'd get one final trout, lost all interest in fishing, thought fondly of our neighborhood supermarket, concluded that my nose was about to freeze off and jumped on board Yvonne's machine as soon as it was time to warm up at the game warden's cabin, invisible, but apparently nearby.

Such lovely people. They welcomed us with hot drinks and Tupperware tubs full of sweets, rumballs and cherry squares neatly layered between sheets of waxed paper. The conversation was pleasant, idle, quiet, kind. We talked about the Sears catalogue. I have never been so interested in the Sears catalogue. I didn't want to leave but eventually we had to, heading out into sleet that was like needles on our skin, the snow on the ground increasingly wet and slobby, our return slow. I began to think about how satisfying it would be to go crazy and jabber at the malign nullity around us. Also worked up a theory about hell being cold and white and empty, if hell, as the Jesuits say, is an absence. I'd always felt heat as a presence in Rio, something that you wore, a weight that slowed you down, while this landscape froze something off. Self-confidence, I think.

Wind and sleet whipping my face, the ride loud and rough, my hip aching, I knew less than ever what I was doing there, particularly since I'd been struggling ever since we'd returned to Canada to write the novel that I'd researched in Brazil. It suddenly struck me as insane to keep sending myself out after material when I couldn't seem to shape it into anything worthwhile, a coherent narrative, a feeling description—justification for all of the trouble I caused people. Self-justification, too.

It rained for the rest of the weekend, and we stayed inside reading, cooking trout and caribou stew, mashed potatoes, corn kernels heated in their open can on the stovetop. I made my feckless notes, not wanting to leave the cabin, where the windows both framed and limited the outdoors. But Sunday afternoon came soon enough, and when we went outside to load the *komatik*, we found that snow conditions had deteriorated badly. Frowning at the slush, Yvonne admitted to being worried that her old machine would get tippy, turn over, and I kicked myself for putting her to all this trouble when she was pregnant. It would have been best for her to ride with Darryl, as she usually did, but neither Gabe nor I could handle her machine under conditions like these. Ray had already left, planning to meet his wife at a second cabin they'd built on the other side of Rigolet.

"Not far," he'd said, a statement I'd come to distrust. It wasn't far to Rigolet, either, but as we headed off into the fog—me behind Yvonne, Gabe behind Darryl—the trip ahead seemed endless.

Five hours, as it turned out, with stops both scheduled and not. A few minutes into the trip, we made a quick detour to check up on the Inuit trapper, Hubbard, who had let Darryl and Yvonne build on his land. Pulling up, we found piles of animal entrails and fat laid out on the snow, along with a couple of sealskins stretched on circular frames. Behind them was a log cabin, smoke curling out the chimney, a postcard sight. My father's uncle had been a trapper in the Northwest Territories for several years during the 1920s and 1930s, and I had pictures of him standing outside just such a cabin, solemnly holding some furs toward the camera. This was Uncle Klas, my grandmother's oldest brother. My father told us that he'd been shot and wounded by the Mad Trapper of Rat River. A tall man, Uncle Klas looked rather morose in the snapshots, but who wouldn't under the circumstances?

Hubbard, I found. He greeted us happily: a tiny, agile, hospitable man. He was one of the few people around Rigolet who still spoke Inuktitut, and he'd been giving lessons to Darryl and Yvonne, although they spoke English now.

"Be coming in soon myself," Hubbard said. He must have been at least seventy, but he was still trapping and hunting, riding his machine all over the coast. My hyperventilated adventure wasn't anything special to people here, although there was another side to the story. One woman I interviewed told me that she hoped her children would make it off the coast. She described herself as unadventurous because she'd never left

Labrador. Going to university was the adventure that she wanted for her daughters, even though she knew that if they left, they'd probably never come back.

"Better go," Darryl said, clapping his thighs.

"My tippy old machine," Yvonne added cheerfully.

"You got to get a new machine," Hubbard told her.

"I do," she answered just as cheerfully, and we left.

Actually, our first spill wasn't so bad. Not long after leaving Hubbard's place, we fell over when trying to make a steep corner around a headland, a slow-motion concave turn in which we both leaned in but the machine tipped gently outward, allowing Yvonne to hop off quickly but pinning my right leg underneath. It was such soft snow that my leg just kept sinking harmlessly under the weight of the machine, a painless pressure ending when Darryl lifted the tippy thing off. The only problem was, I'd gone down so far by then, I'd hit the ice beneath the snow and ended up with my foot wedged into a very cold-looking crack. It took three of us to pull out my leg, a minor thing, not difficult so much as awkward, except that I thought again of Ray heading off on his own, and of Hubbard out on the trapline. The depth of their experience struck me, compared to the shallow breadth of my own.

"That's an otter slide," Darryl told Gabe, pointing to a streak in the snow. Then we were off, skimming over the wet snow, spinning sometimes, Darryl wanting to go fast to keep up a momentum, keep his control, with Yvonne and I continually falling behind. We tipped harmlessly a couple more times, righting ourselves quickly, but I was getting cold and sore, and worried about Yvonne and the baby. Everyday life for people here, I tried to tell myself. But Yvonne looked grim and the weather wasn't clearing.

A distraction in the distance, some sort of activity. Lifting myself up in the seat, I tried to see what was moving toward us, a line scrawled in the snow. Then I slumped back, feeling relieved. It was the fishermen we'd met the day before, seven of them traveling in a convoy we angled to meet, our two lines drawing toward each other across a blank white slate. I was usually such a loner, someone who fled company and hid in crowds. Now, leaning toward the others, my arm around Yvonne's waist, I began to see how this had kept me from belonging anywhere. I seemed to have a problem with trust. This was hardly surprising when I'd been brought up on stories that often proved to be untrue. What was true? Was Tito justified in saying that you should expose children to injustice? Maybe I was wrong to trust sweeping judgments like that. But as we rode toward the fishermen, I understood that not trusting people was another form of mistake.

Without much fanfare, our two groups met, and by silent agreement we fell in line behind the game warden, Derreck, who was the best hunter and woodsman in town. From then on, Derreck led us forward at a stately pace.

"He's always taken it slowly," his wife said, "even when he was younger." Despite the deteriorating conditions, I felt reassured and looked up to see a view that was purely gorgeous: white mountains scored with black trees, a gray sky above us and a pool of turquoise water at our feet.

Derreck spotted a seal on the ice, a distant comma. Hunting season had opened the previous day, but he decided to press forward, and we crossed the inlet skimming over meltwater, passing finally to the Rigolet side, where it was warmer, and even worse. The portages were like rivers, as Yvonne had warned, and she and I kept toppling, heading fast into scrub once before flipping, my leg again pinned, more painfully this time. On the final portage, even Darryl went over, running helplessly off the trail in our well-pressed tracks. I began to think that we'd never get back. Finally, after Yvonne and I had flipped for the fifth or sixth time, Derreck wagged his finger and told us, "You don't do that again." Joking. But we didn't, and I soon saw Rigolet over the hill ahead. Civilization! Where we thawed Gabe's frostbitten toes in our hands.

He didn't complain about the frostbite during our last couple of days in town, attending classes, joking with Darryl and Yvonne. Gabe was always pretty stoic about what we asked of him, and I guess he had a dramatic story to tell, a frontier story, maybe this time with a conclusion about himself and who he was. Myself, I saw that I'd been traveling a long slow arc, out to the fringes of settlement, deep into my family's past. But the boomerang was turning a corner, and a few days later, as we flew—smoothly— out of Rigolet, I felt as if I was finally on my way back home.

3 6

ON OUR LAST NIGHT UP THE BLACKWATER RIVER, I HEARD Edson talking to Doug and Stu outside the men's bunkhouse.

"Do you think you could bring your tours to our camp?" Edson asked, having apparently taken this long to get up his nerve. "Once we make the changes you suggest."

"Actually," Stu told him, "I won't be taking any more tours myself. This is my last trip. I've had it with traveling. Time to try something else, frankly. No offense."

"What you got in mind?" Doug asked.

"Summer off. Stay home. Then I've got a new job—going to teach. Private school near where I live."

"Teaching," Doug said, sounding surprised.

"I like kids," Stu told him. "Never had any of my own, that's probably why. But the time comes to put something back. In a manner of speaking, invest."

I hadn't taken to Stu, but this time I didn't think he was wrong. He was probably letting himself in for more than he bargained for, but he wasn't wrong.

"And what about my camp?" Edson asked anxiously.

"Do the stuff we talked about, I don't see any problem," Stu said. "Keep in mind, it's a question of limiting your potential damage."

Despite the request from Paul's editor, we decided not to stay any longer in Brazil, having turned over in our minds the question of potential damage. Maybe I was being selfish, too. I wanted to speak the same language as my son. I didn't want things turning out the way they had for either of my grandmothers, and although that sounds harsh, by the time we left Brazil, I had an idea that they would agree.

A PLOT .

OF LAND

37

WE MOVED BACK TO TORONTO THREE MONTHS AFTER THAT trip to the Amazon.

"We're going home!" we told Gabriel.

"Home!" we said. "Your first day of school at home!"

"*Mamãe*," he said, a month later, "I can't find my coat or my *mochila*."

"You can't find your backpack?"

"I want one like Carson's. It's awesome."

Faced with constant shifts like that, I ended up embracing the famous qualification, you can never go home again. You can't go back. For a long time, I really did feel that Toronto was just another place we'd moved to. It had changed, I had changed. I wasn't going back to quite the same place, especially since "I" was a somewhat different person. So how, precisely, did you define "home"?

On the surveyor's plan, it was simple. We'd moved back into our detached brick house located on a long thin lot in the east end of Toronto, not far from downtown. Walking in the front door, we could glance to the left and see the small living room opening onto a larger dining room, both trimmed with plenty of dark wood—plate rails, moldings, baseboards almost a foot deep—and curved plaster ceilings the color and texture of whipped cream turning to butter. We'd walk down a narrow hall to the large box of a kitchen, which still had its original porcelain sink. There weren't any counters or cupboards, but someone had built a large pantry into an uninsulated Insulbrick shed tacked onto the back of the house, along with a closet-sized sun porch.

Upstairs, the house was just as antique, the three bedrooms trimmed with a more modest amount of dark wood and the bathroom almost filled by a claw-footed tub. We could reach the unfinished attic through a trapdoor in the middle bedroom closet. The basement was unfinished too, with a cold room for preserves, a rough workshop and a laundry. Out back was a tin-covered garage leading onto a scruffy laneway.

When we'd first lived there, I'd thought that the house was perfect—radiantly *ours*—even though it was really nothing more than a worker's cottage and the bank owned most of it, anyway. I guess we'll be going home now, I would say, forgetting that I'd always told people that I'd be moving home to Vancouver soon. Vancouver remained "home" for several years after I'd left, a concept unattached to an address. But then we bought an address in Toronto and started life as a family there. We're going home, I whispered to my baby, leaving the hospital where he'd been born, awestruck and terrified to be holding a newborn, the first one I'd ever held, and itching to be safe within my own four walls.

Years later, after moving back from Brazil, I stood in the front hallway feeling that the place had become dimmer and vaguer and somehow hunching after all the blowsy brilliance of the tropics. Home was *too* safe. These were the same walls, but they'd turned claustrophobic. I didn't understand how the place could feel so changed when it looked unchanged, although I began to see that the stability of home was what I'd always defined myself against. It stayed here and I often didn't. But now that home had changed, I wasn't sure where that left me.

It was the sort of thing I could get curious about, trying to figure out what kind of place I'd washed up in. *Moving back*, I thought, and started doing it.

38

WE'D ORIGINALLY BOUGHT THE HOUSE IN 1982 FROM AN old Czech-born couple named John and Anna Piskura. They seemed to have second sight into our finances, draining every last penny, which we didn't mind so much knowing that it was their retirement fund.

At the time, the street was heavily European. A woman from Poland lived two doors to the north, Pauline, and we had many Italian neighbors. Many others were Greek, just like the steam-table restaurants on Danforth Avenue to the south.

Yet the neighborhood was changing, and most of the people who'd moved in just before we did were often better educated than the earlier immigrants, and originally from Asia, places like Hong Kong and Korea. Also Ceylon—Sri Lanka; Michael Ondaatje lived up the street for a couple of books, including *The English Patient*. This new wave of immigration bothered a neighbor from Italy named Joe, a retired construction worker whose hobby was advising his neighbors on the best way to clean out their gutters and trim their shrubs.

"I don't know what the government's doing," he told me once, "letting in all these people. What's going on? We had to have x-rays, that's what we did."

I think that's what he said. Joe's accent was very heavy. But people mostly got along, nodding to each other and patting Freddy, Pauline's cat, a friendly tabby with a high mew who was everybody's favorite, running up when you got home from work and rubbing against your legs. Late one summer night, as a vicious raccoon fight broke out in the Norway maples overhead, half the neighborhood came outside in dressing gowns, walking the hot dark street in garments so long and shimmering they looked ghostly. Where's Freddy? people asked. Is Freddy okay? They haven't got him, have they?

A man who did some work on our house told me that he'd grown up on the street during the fifties and sixties when Joe and the Piskuras were just arriving. There were only low post-and-wire fences then, so kids ran through everybody's yards, wearing paths in the grass like animal tracks. People didn't drive around so much, he said. It was quiet except for kids yelling and wind in the maples and chickens clucking in the occasional backyard. "It was a great place to grow up," he told me. "The afternoons were longer here. The summers, the winters."

His name was English, just like the neighborhood before the European immigration. I'd read somewhere that it was "a flat suburb of English, Irish and Scotch cops, TTC motormen and T. Eaton Company tie clerks." Our friend Lorne knew it from when he was a kid riding out on his father's truck to deliver meat to local restaurants. Anti-Semitic white-bread working class was how he put it. Elsie, who lived on the nearest corner with a number of arthritic-looking matted cats, was one of the few people left from that era. She was a dandelion-haired old lady by the time we talked, or she did, since Elsie was quite deaf and mainly you listened to her monologues. Standing in her brightly painted garden, the air rich with the scent of carnations and pesticide, she told me that she'd been born in that house, never married out of it and had become a vegetarian. "It started with pork," she told me. "I cannot tolerate pork. It repeats on me, pork will do that." Then, leaning forward, "They eat cats, you know. The Chi-*nee*."

That's where we were living, in a place of eddies, a backwater of bigger issues, small-scale racism, the local reverberations of migration and acculturation. Yet on the whole, it was a pretty good place for Gabriel to move back to. With kids from a couple of dozen countries in his elementary school, no one made fun of his English, and he found friends who understood all his traveling. But to move back beyond our experiences, beyond memory, even beyond the secondhand memories of neighbors, I had to do some real research, and one day I headed off to the land registry office.

There I found that the Piskuras had bought the house in 1958 from a woman named Hazel Slade. The Piskuras had told us that we were only the third owners, and the registry book showed that Hazel and Gordon Slade had bought the place in 1917.

Later, in the library, I found the house on a map from 1919. Toronto was suffering through a smallpox epidemic, one of the last, and someone in the health department had stuck milliner's pins in the map to mark reported cases. One pin was stuck here. I knew it might have been placed a little wrong, but I still imagined walking up our front path, quailing to see the cardboard quarantine sign newly nailed to the front door. I open the door, entering the wallpapered hallway, the leafy brown and silver paper glimmering in gaslight. It's cold outside, the coal furnace burning, the big black stove in the kitchen firing, steaming up the windows. I run up the stairs two at a time, then slow outside the bedroom door, opening it quietly to see a form in bed, the green walls, the white sheets, candlelight low and wavering at the draft from the door.

A loud whistle blows, the 6 P.M. whistle at the nearby glue-works. A face turns in bed, feverish, the pox red and crusting, scarring in a way that soon becomes antique. Blue eyes open sight-lessly and lips form words from dreams.

Closing the map book, I thought about the types of faces we no longer see now that smallpox has been eradicated, faces like glaciated earth. If I was ever to write about this period, I would have to remember to put in people with badly pockmarked faces who were shorter than we are now, put in the stench of the glue-works I read about, its noon and quitting-time whistles precise enough to set your watch by, put in the boom of dynamite at the brickworks just to the south, where the good blue clay was blown out of the hillside. I'd have to remember the leafy wallpaper and green paint—we found it under almost everything—and the gaslight—there were pipes in the walls—and the coal furnace and stove that vented into a kitchen chimney. Also that people thought they were as modern as we think we are. It's so easy to be condescending toward the past, but Hazel and Gordon Slade had moved into a neighborhood that bustled every bit as much as the traffic-packed Danforth does now, just in a different way.

Yet the Slades weren't really the first owners of the house. I found that Hazel and Gordon had bought the place from a couple named Hawthorne, Albert Hawthorne having been a builder who constructed the house in 1914 and 1915. The new Toronto Civic Railway Line was just opening along the Danforth and the latest in macadamized surfaces was being rolled on top of the famous local mud. Albert Hawthorne was a player in a small civic revolution, and the Piskuras half-knew this. They told us that the house had been built by the owner before them, a contractor who had put up many of the houses on the street and designed this one for himself.

The air must have been loud with Albert's crews as the First World War began. It was easy to imagine two lengthening rows of houses across from each other on the new scar of street, a dirt street running north off the Danforth, which was itself a rough dirt road in 1914. Our new street was one of Toronto's furthest suburbs, a garden suburb surrounded by farmland. Buyers would have had to step carefully after rain, the women raising their long skirts, the men kicking aside stray shingles as they tipped their hats to Albert in his shirtsleeves. I picture Albert as broad and red-faced and hearty, talking loudly above the shout of working voices, male voices, older voices once the war began, most of them English or Scottish or Irish, like the renters and buyers themselves, slum dwellers who had come to Canada during the last great wave of immigration before the war.

It must have smelled so strongly of activity and hope. No power tools, few motorcars and little exhaust, but sawdust and churning chalky cement and new bricks like loaves of warm bread brought directly from the brickyard. You'd get the adhesive reek of paint and the sweaty wool of the workmen's clothes, the milky smell of plaster and of horsehair stirred into it and the workhorses themselves, their clean damp dung, the bales of hay, and everywhere the sound of hand tools, hammers pounding and saws pulling back and forth, zizz and zaw as horses whickered.

Albert had bought his lots from a speculator, who'd bought the land only three months earlier from the original developers and flipped it at a good profit. At the time, the east end was frantic with speculation. On May 12, 1911, an advertisement in the *Toronto Daily Star* for land very near ours trumpeted,

> Here is your last opportunity to invest your money in a SUB-DIVISION within the CITY LIMITS, where property will more than double in value when the Ontario Railway Board approves of the plans for the CIVIC CAR LINES on DANFORTH AVENUE. There is no need of going out of the city to make an investment, as Toronto is the fastest-growing city in Canada and will have a population THREE-QUARTERS of a MILLION within a very short time. This SUB-DIVISION is located in the heart of a district which has made more building progress than any other portion of the city.
>
> PRICES FOR OPENING DAY
> $18.00 TO $22.00 PER FOOT

The original plan to develop our street was filed six months before this, on December 23, 1910, when a family named Warwick sought permission to subdivide the pair of five-acre lots that became our street. The land had been annexed by the City of

Toronto only a year before, and despite the CAPITALS of newspaper ads, it was still farmland, mainly market gardens, part of a swath of flat sandy fertile soil generally called The Plains.

Reading about The Plains took me back to the summers when my family picked fruit in the market gardens of Lulu Island outside Vancouver, a peaceful place that smelled powerfully of cow dung and stagnant weedy ditches. I remembered picking strawberries, moving along my raised row in the watery West Coast sun, squatting until my thighs hurt. One time, when I was seven or eight, the foreman went over my row to check under the fuzzy leaves. He nodded and told me, "You done real good, sweetheart," which became a family saying, something my parents would repeat later, half-joke, half-praise.

Smiling, I read one Danforth historian's memories of riding his bicycle down poplar-lined trails of The Plains, passing miles of gardens cut like green checkerboard into the damp soil. A coke path let him fly toward a beekeeper's cottage, and sometimes he stopped to cadge radishes, the first crop in spring. Another local historian remembered the mud.

"My parents used to allow me to go in my bare feet from the 24th of May till the beginning of September, and it was a pleasure to me to get out in my bare feet and run in the muddy road along Danforth Avenue. It was a mud hole—that was what made it so nice to run in, in your bare feet. The mud squeezing between your toes was nice and soft."

The Danforth was so muddy, a teamster told the *Toronto Daily Star* in 1911, that seven teams of horses had got stuck along the roadway the previous Sunday. "It's safe to say that more broken brick has been put on the Danforth avenue roadbed than on any other road east of the Don, but there's no bottom to that road, the bricks must go clear through to China, for they are all swallowed up in about a week after they are put down."

I told myself to remember how different people's diction was in the past. "Clear through to China." "There's no bottom." "There's no shame in clean dirt," my mother would say, washing my face with a rough washcloth after Lulu Island. "I believe I will," my Nannie said, having come from a time in which people still believed, they didn't just think so, much less guess so.

I told myself to remember how little childhood changes, what running feels like on grass, that kids can always find mud.

I told myself to remember how many different meanings there are for the word "moving."

3 9

IT TURNED OUT THAT THE HOUSE WHICH IS NOW NUMBER eight on our street was once the market gardening farmhouse. The first of the Warwicks who subdivided our land moved into the house in 1899, but John Warwick wasn't a farmer. He was a cabinetmaker taking advantage of cheap prices during a recession to buy the land, probably renting it to his farmer-neighbors before subdividing it. The real farmers were the Somers, Hugh Somers having lived in the old farmhouse before 1896, at a time when only twelve houses were listed along the whole sleepy length of the Don and Danforth Roadway. A map from 1878 shows even fewer, although Hugh's father Bernard Somers was living in the old farmhouse and farming a total of four five-acre parcels, including our land.

The enormous decaying poplar in our alleyway would have been a young tree in Bernard's time, just eleven years after Confederation. I could imagine standing beneath it, stroking the papery new bark. A squirrel chatters above, a sight rare enough to get me craning, squirrels and raccoons being uncommon visitors to this part of York County. I see birds through the brush of branches, scattered outriders of a flock that must be flying up from the south. I swivel on the rich brown earth and find them— passenger pigeons darkening the sky, their wings beating the air in a purring whirr that's growing quickly louder.

It is evening, the sky is rosy to the west. As the great flock begins to spiral down, I hear the inrush of a door opening nearby, the Somers' door, Bernard's voice lilting in the accents of County Cavan. Mrs. Mary Caffray Somers calls from inside, something that makes Bernard laugh. Holding his shotgun, he strides through the farmyard and into the fields. The pigeons wheel, settling in poplars, cooing, ruffling their feathers. Bernard steps over rows of early beans, early peas, maturing radishes. Scarcely breaking stride, he raises his shotgun and blasts the tree. Pigeons rise in wheeling confusion, battering together as he blasts and blasts, many falling—reloading—dozens falling, until Bernard lowers his gun, looking pleased. He stoops to get the nearest birds, wringing the necks of the ones still living, gathering them together like a bouquet in his big red hands before walking around to the back of his house, where he's planted a silver maple tree. Wounded birds push themselves along by their wings, trying to rise. The rest of the flock settles back in the trees. I see smoke rise from the chimney, watch the sunset fade. Bernard returns and wrings more necks. The next day, Mary Somers will bake pigeon pie.

Reading through the land registry books, I came to understand that our house is built on waves of immigrant labor, from the Czech Piskuras back to the Irish Somers, who might have been the first to fully clear our land. It was also built on speculation, one hunger feeding the other to the point where I found it hard to trace land ownership during the market garden period, not just because the typewritten pages in the record books were browning and crumbling off at the bottom, but because the hyperactive flips and sales made it difficult to note all the buyers and tease out precisely what they'd bought. People were desperate for property. Owners are recorded as selling the same acreage several times, the flat notations in the musty books hinting at stories of hopeful buyers registering a mortgage and defaulting on it, of speculators buying lots and reselling them days later, of failure, rapacity—so much rapacity—and tearful pleas against foreclosure, until I began to see a rich new meaning in the phrase "a plot of land."

The confusion cleared once I moved back to 1859. In December of that year, the wealthy dry-goods merchant John McMurrich carved out the five-acre plots that would define our neighborhood and embrace our undifferentiated land, filing a plan to subdivide a 200-acre family farm that he had bought earlier that year. It was a well-known farm that appeared often in historical records, and he used the name to impressive effect on his subdivision plan, headed:

PLAN

OF

BUILDING AND PARK LOTS

FOR SALE

UPON THE BANKS OF THE RIVER DON

NEAR THE CITY OF TORONTO

KNOWN AS

THE PLAYTER FARM

I already knew the Playter name. West of us, there were a couple of streets called Playter, and people said that the substantial houses around there were part of The Playter Estates. Finding out that the Playters had owned our land, too, turned me into an amateur version of the genealogists-for-hire, the delvers into other peoples' family secrets who kindly helped me find maps in the White Print Room at the registry office and microfilm at the reference library.

I'd researched things before, of course. But my formal research was usually haphazard, things like taking off to the Amazon and the Pantanal on the off chance that I'd learn something useful. Moving back seemed to have made me want to do a better job, maybe feeling more self-confident in my home setting, or maybe just self-conscious, aware that after years abroad I didn't fit in anywhere, and beginning to examine everything I did, wondering why not.

It proved simple to research the Playters, retreating into the past through their well-documented begets: the John and Emmanuel Playter who seemed to have been the last family members to work the 200-acre farm, appearing as farmers on the site in the 1850–51 Toronto directory; the Richard Playter who came before them; the Captain John Playter who came before Richard, granting him the farm in 1839, value £5,000.

It wasn't hard to imagine Captain John walking east from the Don River on a sunny autumn day, planning to survey his property before turning it over to his son. The captain was born a Quaker in the American colonies and grew into a United Empire Loyalist, coming north from the newly hewn United States of America after the Revolution, in which his father, George, was a British spy. John has the confident gait of a successful man, having achieved high rank in the British militia during the War of 1812, when American soldiers ascended the Don Valley and ransacked his farm, seizing Upper Canada's archives, which he'd secreted there, not far from the river meadow he now crosses.

The Don Valley is a wide floodplain, pleasantly treed with butternuts so great and old that it takes three men to link arms around one. Wild strawberries cover the ground and gooseberries grow in thickets. It's a fertile place. Fishermen pull big salmon from the river and potters take clay from the slick bank that the captain scrambles up, looking toward his farmhouse on the crest of the hill. They also have good brick clay around here, and the Playters are making respectable money from a brickworks. John has been ambitious of improving his family, just as he improved this land. He trained his son, Richard, to be a lawyer in the Town of York—or Toronto, as it's been called for a year now. But just as York reverted to its old Indian name, Richard reverted to the farm, illness coming on. The captain shakes his head, passing the farmyard, the horses and oxen, and stepping into the fields.

His crops are mixed, hay, oats and spring wheat, all harvested now, the heavy soil clodding on his boots. To his left is an old grove of butternut, ahead the orchard, where he pulls a Spy apple from a tree, biting the white flesh. It's pleasant to walk here once the insects have passed. The air is fresh, the ague that struck York—Toronto—so badly this summer has been chilled away. John pastures cattle in the grassy orchard, watering them in a small creek near the eastern end of his property. Pine still stands here, in the east, a remnant of the great pine forest that once covered this land. His boots hush on the fallen needles, and he remembers finding swaths of the great trees overturned by tornados, pulled up by their shallow roots to lie strewn like pick-up-sticks on the soft dry ground. John cleared much of the farm himself, managing teams of men and oxen in hard labor he isn't sure that his disappointing son could have directed, with Richard's nervous inability to navigate even the tiny society of York, where he. . . .

I reminded myself that the records were ambiguous. Some documents suggested that Richard had a smudged-over breakdown, yet even so, I didn't know what might have caused it any more than early settlers knew that their frequent attacks of ague were malaria, spread by mosquitoes breeding at the muddy mouth of the Don. I reminded myself that people then were not only smaller and sometimes pockmarked, but they examined different aspects of their lives than we do and found themselves wanting in different ways. I reminded myself that thinking people often had bad teeth, greasy hair, no questions about their relationship to other species and agonizing qualms about their worthiness before God. Also before successful fathers, just as Esau did before Abraham, just as sons do now.

The Playters took possession of the 200 acres embracing our small plot of land less than twenty years before Captain John's war. They were granted lot number 11, Second Concession from the Bay, by Crown Patent on August 24, 1796. George Playter's service to the British Crown meant that the family's land grants were among the first issued by the Lieutenant-Governor, John Graves Simcoe.

It was, of course, Governor Simcoe who opened up York to European settlement, moving the capital of Upper Canada to the mouth of the Don River in 1793. Until 1788, it was Indian land, bought from the Mississauga band for 149 barrels of goods and a bit of cash, total value £1,700.

40

GROWING UP OUT WEST, GOING TO HIGH SCHOOL WITH Indian kids from both the local reservation and the coast, I learned early on about the nasty, unfinished history of European colonialism in the Americas—on which, of course, my life is built, and on top of which my refugee friends from all over the world are rebuilding theirs. We're implicated. We're here, on what was once Indian land. As I moved further back in history, I spent more and more time thinking about land as the key, how it's always been the key. What I'd been thinking of as our small plot was really a big plot, *the* human plot. Getting land, using it, being forced off it: The story of humanity was the story of frontiers, always newly defined.

In Toronto, you have to move back a couple of hundred years to see this fully. Then it appears, the Toronto Purchase, which seems to have been about as cheap and lousy as these things usually were, especially where it touched on our little local area. When surveyor Alexander Aitkins set out to map the purchase in September 1788, the unnamed Mississauga chief with him protested that the tribe had not sold the land east of the Nichingguakakonk, the Don River. In his survey report, Aitkins says, "that to prevent disputes I had to put him off some days longer . . . when Mr. Lines settled with them." So our land entered written history as either a fast one or a mistake, and it's made worse by Mississauga complaints that they weren't even paid the full £1,700.

Early European explorers and diarists, many of them French Jesuits and *coureurs-de-bois*, wrote about finding primeval forest on the northern shore of Lake Ontario. The age-old haunt of the Indian, they said. That's true, but I found it even truer to say that many First Nations peoples lived here in succession. The Mississauga people originally came from the north shore of Georgian Bay. They only moved south a hundred years before Governor Simcoe arrived, after they'd fought the Iroquois Confederacy out of southern Ontario. Before then, it was the Iroquois who lived and trapped on the north shore of the lake. At least, they'd lived here for about thirty years, having been pushed out of their traditional homes to the south and east by their enemies, both tribal and European.

Picturing the temporary Iroquois settlements, it struck me that this land has been a waystation for refugees for a very long time. I recently met a refugee from Serbia, a dissident journalist who happily repeated something she'd learned in the resettlement center: that Toronto means "meeting place" in the Ojibway language. She said that she hoped she could make a place for herself here too. Yet around Toronto, no one seems to stay in one place for very long. More than 300 years ago, this land was an unfenced camp at the center of no one's territory, a land of shifting wars and boundaries like the journalist's former country, or maybe like some ancient corner of Central Asia, where many languages were spoken and many battles fought.

Locally, the Nichingguakakonk was known but unimportant, although trappers must have walked its banks, or taken fox and wolverine in the pine forest above—trappers like my Uncle Klas, or agile Hubbard in Labrador. Hunters must have come through, too, not to mention warriors. The arriving English and French had unsettled so many old alliances that they convulsed the land with wars: wars against Europeans, wars between Europeans, and wars between their jockeying First Nation allies, who were trying to salvage the life that they'd known. Much of what we call Danforth Avenue is really the memory of a trail leading to a good fording place on the Don River. One summer, an armed posse might well have slipped past here, right *here*, making their way to the ford. They would have been Iroquois, and this would have been sometime during the 1640s, when warriors from the eastern Iroquois Confederacy moved west summer after summer in repeated waves, wiping out their old enemies, the Huron, who had lived on Lake Ontario for many hundreds of years. How strange to think that for a decade, this land was a war zone, gaudy with fear and blood.

The Huron culture was exterminated in this war, the people dispersed: killed, fleeing south or east, disappearing into other tribes. At least, that's what happened to the remaining Huron, the ones who hadn't died in massive epidemics of measles and influenza introduced by the Europeans less than a decade earlier. Half the Huron people died in those plagues, mainly the children and the old, the Hurons' future and their memory. I hate to think of it, but it's possible that a child sickened on this land as her family fled contagion. I think of bringing her water from the creek, of bending over her as she lies feverish and coughing in a hasty shelter of pine boughs, her small body spotted with crusty eruptions, measles so vicious that if she lives, her face will be like glaciated land—a type of face that is becoming far too common these days—and if she does not, she will become the land herself.

Yet there was a more settled time before all this war and pestilence, a time that made me think of my peasant ancestors, crofters in Scotland and subsistence farmers in Sweden who lived off both their stores and stories during the dark cold of winter. Centuries before the Playters came, and the Iroquois came, for many years before the pines grew back, this was farmland. The Huron were farmers, and sometime before 1530, they built a village not half a mile away; Gabe's junior high school was built on the site. Their village was surrounded by palisades and the families shared longhouses within. The tribe chose a place that was good for hunting as well as farming, overlooking the Nichingguakakonk, if that was their word for it—or perhaps the Wonscateonack, the name recorded by another early surveyor, who said that it meant "coming from the black, burnt lands."

The surveyor, Augustus Jones, was married to a Mississauga woman, so perhaps his version is more accurate. It would also be appropriate, since the Huron burned patches of forest to plant their crops. The men did the burning, while the women and the elderly tended the fields, working each one for twelve years until the soil was exhausted and another site chosen. Given all the years that they lived in the area, there's a very good chance that they farmed here, so that I can close my eyes and see the women camping out in summer, cooking bannock, wiping the faces of the happy, muddy children (such clean dirt!), gossiping, laughing, crooking their arms behind their necks to listen to the elders' stories, the drum of words, until they finally fall asleep under a sky milky with stars.

I read that if I decided to search in our back garden for traces of the Huron, I'd have to dig down through more than three feet of soil deposited since their time. After all that work, maybe I'd find an arrowhead or a shard of pottery missed by the early European settlers. But I wouldn't have the education to recognize the important signs, the subtle changes in the color of the soil showing the ashes from the fire set to clear the land, much less the traces of pollen from the crops. They grew tobacco and sunflowers, although their main crops were corn, beans and squash.

How strange—these were Mexican crops, identical to the ones I'd seen so often in *milpas*. But the archeologists told me this was natural enough, since when the Hurons or their ancestors learned to farm corn sometime around 1,500 years ago, both the seeds and the knowledge of how to farm had been passed on from tribes immediately to the south, who learned agriculture from tribes to the south of them, who learned it from people south of *them* all the way back to Mexico, where crops were first domesticated in this continent. The fact is, corn arrived here from the same place that I arrived back from, part of the dance of time and coincidence that makes up human history.

Before then, hunter-gatherers lived here for thousands of years. Archeologists believe that the first group moved into the Great Lakes area about 10,500 years before the present. No one knows what they called themselves, so when I surfaced from my books, I just thought of people: a group of people chancing onto our patch of forest; of a child jumping down from a fallen log, squishing mud between her toes; of friends telling lies over a campfire as they cook deer stew, or a leg of caribou, the rich dense smell drifting on the wind. I watch a woman giving birth, old people dreaming, feel the muskeg soft underfoot, the winds hard, smell a woolly mammoth gutted and steaming nearby—all this continuity and change receding toward the last Ice Age.

If I wanted to get a true idea of our small plot moving this far back in time, the scientists told me that I should picture the soil getting thinner, picture trees getting shorter, stunting into a boreal forest of spruce and fir, picture the forest growing scantier until there weren't any trees at all, just tundra growing over land scoured by the retreating glaciers: land gouged and runneled as a pockmarked face. The climate was very different, too. It was warmer, a hot summer sun beating down on the peat, the tenuous flowers of the white dryas and blueberry often shredded by gale-force winds coming off the retreating glaciers. Katabatic winds: The name made me hear them throw boulders.

Such endless alteration! The paleoecologist E.C. Pielou writes, "One of the most interesting aspects of this never ending change from the ecological point of view is that, over the time interval we are considering (and probably for the whole of the earth's history), physical conditions on this continent (and everywhere else) have never repeated themselves."

That was probably true of the mix of animals as well, particularly before the last great extinction, the Holocene extinction of the huge mammals that once lived here. This was once the land of saber-toothed tigers and giant short-faced bear and of dire wolves stalking caribou, which were plentiful even then, even this far south. Judging by the tooth marks found on human skulls, the great mammals hunted people too, while people hunted the woolly mammoth, perhaps to extinction, each beast so cumbersome, so huge, that its tusks would have touched one side of our small plot of land while its small tail whisked the plentiful flies at the other.

And then they wouldn't have been here, because our land was under water, beneath the cold surface of Glacial Lake Iroquois. Move back further in time and you'd see on its northern shore a wall of ice calving icebergs the same thrilling turquoise as balleycaters into the frigid waters. Then the lake was frozen and the glaciers were here, thicker and thicker as you receded into prehistory, two miles thick at their dome during the height of the cold, 20,000 years ago, their white weight making the land groan.

Before the last Ice Age, glaciers retreated and advanced across the earth in a mammoth dance for perhaps a billion years. Long periods of glaciation were followed by much shorter and warmer interglacial periods, like the one that's maybe ending. Whether people lived here before the current interglacial period, beginning 10,500 years ago, is a matter of scientific dispute. Maybe they arrived 13,000 years ago, maybe much earlier. It all depends on a complex reading of disputed archeological evidence.

Elders from the First Nations put it much more simply. As I understand it, they believe they've always been here. They've been here since time began. I am not of their religion, nor of any particular religion, but while reading what they say, I began to realize that time is a human construct. It's one of the measurements that we use to make sense of the ceaseless movement of life and space, which means that our small plot of land existed outside time until one of the ancestors arrived and said, "Why don't we sleep here tonight?" So I ended up feeling, myself, that people have always been here, and that the preglacial bedrock that lies far beneath me was here before that, and that there is no contradiction.

Except, of course, that the bedrock has never been exactly *here* before. Tectonic forces have been moving the continents over the molten core of the earth since deep into pretime, so that even before the start of the last Ice Age, our small piece of bedrock was not quite in its current position: *Here* was somewhere else. And somewhere else before that, as the continents drifted together and apart over aeons, a waltz of rock and water. The land around here once lay south of the equator, and for long periods of pretime it disappeared beneath shallow tropical seas. Maritime animals swam here and died here (when it wasn't anywhere near *here*) so their skeletons settled into the warm sediment on the floor of the sea. The maps told me that if I dug up this land halfway to China—maybe they didn't quite say that, but something like it—I would find maritime fossils from the Ordovician period, 450 million years old, branching corals and bivalves that once lived (approximately) where I do now.

And before that? Moving back, further and further, there was warmth and simple one-celled creatures, then a sulfurous age of belching volcanoes, of life that was forming and land that was melting, ambiguity retreating toward dissolution, molten, shapeless, the earth itself a heaving globe coalescing out of cosmic debris, until it was not, and the movement back became a movement out, the earth exploding into space, the moment of creation become destruction, so that *here* turned into nowhere and time moved beyond irrelevance, and all was glittering dust.

All of which is to say that we moved back home, and I spent a long time trying to figure out what that meant. What bothered me most was my unexpected sense of claustrophobia, my feeling that the walls were closing in. I didn't like to think that my travels might be over, but I couldn't help wondering whether you eventually reached a point where you'd learned what you had it in you to learn. You were trapped inside yourself. Your personality was set.

Not yet, I decided. Home now struck me as a very deep place. You could burrow into it, further and further. You could research, create a history for your home just as I created a history for the characters I wrote about. Your home might be utterly ordinary, completely typical. But what was typical was also dramatic, nuanced and essential. I wanted to embrace it, to let go of being a foreigner and finally belong.

And so we did what everyone else was doing. We renovated.

BLACK

CROW

FLYING

THE FIRST CROW I SAW IN JAPAN, I SAW FROM ABOVE. I'D flown into Tokyo the night before and was sitting by the window in my sixteenth-floor hotel room. It was so early, nobody else seemed to be awake. A gray dawn was limping in after a typhoon, and the streets in the business district of Shinjuku were wet and empty. Moving home didn't mean that I wanted to give up traveling, and I'd been looking forward to this trip for weeks. Yet now I felt bleary with jet lag. Couldn't sleep, couldn't wake up. Then I glimpsed a dart of movement outside, a big crow spreading its wings to land on the sidewalk across the street.

At that hour, Shinjuku looked like an architect's model, the buildings dormant, the wavelike mosaics on the sidewalks so perfect they looked painted. Drenched trees stood as still as moss in concrete planters. And here was a crow, strutting toward a staircase that zigzagged up the outside wall of a low building, a white plaster wall with just this one corrugated break. The crow hopped onto the first step, then the second—hopped up the whole first flight, never missing a step, blue-black, big as a raven, and glaringly armless as it did this human thing of walking upstairs. When it reached a landing, it turned and hopped up the second flight to another landing, where there was a door.

I expected someone to open it; they had an appointment. But the crow just kept hopping upstairs, turning every corner. I watched it go up four double flights, five, then six. It was almost up the seventh, hop, hop, hop, and finally reached a narrow top-floor patio that ran the width of the building. The bird never paused, never rested, and never stretched its wings. It hopped along the tiled patio before turning, three-quarters of the way down, and leaping up on a planter of low greenery. Two quick hops took it across, and it reached a tenuous concrete ledge that gave onto nothing. A plaza lay far below, the puffball trees. The crow stopped there, angling its head from side to side. Then it flew.

I thought, It's worth traveling halfway around the world to see a crow walk up fourteen flights of stairs. I was drinking green tea, wearing a hotel robe, a *yukata*. I'd jumped on an offer to go to Japan, hoping to stretch myself, to see new things, but I'd never pictured anything like the crow. How could you?

Depressing, though, to consider the limits of imagination at the start of a new trip, especially when I didn't speak the language and already knew that I'd need to use everything I had to understand what was going on. It was a working trip, I had to play journalist, but mostly I was thinking about the Second World War. My prisoner-of-war uncle. My father. I'd be joining other reporters on a tour of Japanese schools, but at the same time, I hoped to learn something about reconciliation, and it occurred to me now that imagination was maybe the biggest part of that.

As it turned out, I learned a great deal about the uses of imagination on that trip. I also kept seeing crows, hearing stories about crows. People told me that they'd only appeared in Tokyo a few years before, refugees from the overcrowded countryside, a talking point, scavengers, a nuisance. The crows, the crows, everybody said. Their huge pendulous hooked-down beaks made them look like toucans after a bar brawl, like Raven on a totem pole, the Trickster of West Coast Indian mythology, the unreliable messenger of the gods. Appropriately enough, on a tour of journalists.

That first morning, time had turned to syrup. I kept looking at my watch and it kept not being time to meet the others downstairs. Finally the minute hand clicked onto five-minutes-to, and I got up, unsteady on my feet, wondering if there was an earthquake, if the hotel was swaying, but knowing that this time it was jet lag, it was me.

THE GERMAN REPORTER WAS LATE. WE MILLED AROUND IN the lobby, ten of the eleven journalists on tour, a translator, the tour guide and an official from the Japan Foundation, which had brought us over to study the school system. It was hard to sort everybody out at first, especially when people insisted on subverting their national stereotypes. Both Australians were gentle and reserved. You had to strain to hear the woman's voice, and it turned out that she was always the first to leave the bar. Stephanie, the Parisian, was even shyer, self-effacing, unpretentious, sweet-tempered and mild.

And German Angela was always late, finally breezing in that first day, crying, "Shite, shite, shite, here I am, holding everybody up. Look at me, a terrible person, I apologize to all of you and promise that I will do better the next time." Which she didn't, distressing our Japanese hosts, although her frequent shite-ing and irreverent comments became a safety valve on the heavily scheduled tour.

I hate tours, but I could never have afforded to go to Japan otherwise, and this one turned out to have its advantages, considering what I was up to. As we trooped on board the first of many buses, I realized that everyone but the guy from neutral Ireland came from countries that had fought in the Second World War. On the Allied side, you had two Canadians, the pair of Aussies, a New Zealander, three Brits and Stephanie from France (if we ignore the Vichy government), with the Axis countries represented by Angela and our Japanese hosts. I wasn't the only one to notice.

"Germany and France seem to have formed an alliance," one Brit said later, as Angela and Stephanie became friends. "Of course, they have a nasty little history of that."

"Let's remember who won the war," he said another time, so that the Australian woman and I exchanged glances.

In fact, it was the Brits who mentioned the war most often, especially this man, who was our one flaming national stereotype. Geoffrey was an overage lad, a tall, beefy, rosy-cheeked man with an Oxbridge accent, heavy black eyebrows, a store of dim-bulb questions trotted out during interviews and a complacent sense of superiority that often tumbled into foul schoolboy racism. In one hotel, he was tickled to find an electronic toilet-bidet in his bathroom with instructions on the wall for "rectal washing."

"Lectal washing," he told us, in a cartoon Japanese accent. "Ah so, lectal washing. I wash your lectum. Prease to pless button. Ha!"

He was also claustrophobic and loathed elevators, which can be a problem in Tokyo. The rest of us would crowd on board, ready to ride up to the twenty-seventh floor, when he'd glance inside to cry, "That's a bugger of a lift!" before running upstairs, a puzzled Japanese escort pumping legs behind him.

Yet it all fit together neatly, especially when it turned out that our hosts wanted to talk about internationalization. Our first stop was at the headquarters of the Japan Foundation, a liberal cultural-affairs institute run at arm's length from the government. Foundation officials said when inviting us over that the tour was simply for background, an attempt to broaden our picture of the Japanese education system. But of course they hoped to impress us, and they especially hoped to impress us with the idea of Japan's increasing internationalism, of attempts both inside and outside the government to defeat xenophobia, to open up the country to foreign ideas, and even to risk doing this in the schools, where students were now required to study foreign languages and culture, often with the help of imported teachers.

This being the case, it was inevitable that on the way to the foundation we were blocked by a political cavalcade, one van blaring unmistakably right-wing oompah brass-band songs through a loudspeaker on its roof.

"These are the nationalist parties," said our guide, Hiroko. "They want to take us back to the days of World War Two." Apologetically, she added, "We don't like them."

The memory of Hiroko's pained face stayed with me far longer than any of the speeches we heard. That ended up being true of all our guides' moments of hesitation, surprise, nerves, sudden laughter and enjoyment. I thought that they were brave to open themselves up to this degree of scrutiny from journalists with such excellent credentials and occluded motives. *The Times* of London, *Le Monde*, *The Age* of Australia. I was an also-ran, a free-lancer, asked along because Canadian media didn't allow staff reporters to take free trips. Eleven pairs of eyes followed our hosts' every move (one pair, it's true, rather dim). The war, the war, I thought, we thought, watching them closely.

Although I wondered later how hard our hosts needed to apologize for xenophobia when few news outlets in Canada—or, I learned, Germany or France—proved interested in running stories about Japan.

At foundation headquarters, we sat around a board table in a sleek conference room as the officials handed out copies of the first part of our itinerary. After giving us ample time to study it, a foundation official read it aloud, point by point, while we squirmed. I thought of my friend Derek in high school, a guy from the Kwakiutl band. "You know, Lesley, it's an insult to Indian people to say, 'It's such a nice day!' because you're imply-ing that we're too stupid to notice." I got his point immediately, but only in Tokyo did I understand how irritated he must have felt to say it, his chafing resentment at my babbling. Keep quiet! I know that!

Different cultural definitions of how much you need to say. Cultural chafing. The day passed in speeches, internationalization, statistics and envelopes of yen handed out to pay for the meals that wouldn't be provided at group events, a pleasant but embarrassing surprise. Many of us tried to put the money away discreetly.

"Count it, please," the official asked.

Almost a thousand bucks. Multiply that by eleven around the table, and consider that the official was concerned with accuracy, not theft—it was quite astonishing, especially when all that cash walked out of the foundation later that day and climbed back onto a bus that was quickly pinned in downtown traffic. In Brazil, we would have been relieved of our envelopes within three blocks. Armed men expecting us, ramming the bus, tipped off. Here we purred unmolested through the neon city. Later, I saw an improbable legend stenciled on another tour bus: "Happiness wrapped in a sense of superiority, riding around the country on a dream."

We were greatly privileged people.

4 3

I'VE NEVER HAD SUCH TERRIBLE JET LAG AS I DID IN JAPAN, waking up at two in the morning, unable to get back to sleep. By nine at night I was often staggering, caught in that thick sense of time not passing as the ground rode by beneath my feet. My visual memories come back plasticized, elongated, stretched, and Tokyo is so vertical anyway, no core detectable, just endless repeated skyscrapers, metal and glass, concrete and glass scrolling by our slow-moving bus, making the city seem as if it was cloning itself into two, four, sixteen Tokyos pulsing out to every horizon, so that we'd never see the end of it, just crawl along forever on the elevated expressways, ten stories up.

At night, on foot, we were lit by blinking neon signs, hot pink and yellow. Signs flushed green on our search for a restaurant, blue-lighting the menus posted outside with their lurid photos of arranged food. Pachinko parlors chicked and crackled behind us as crowds surged by, so many drunken businessmen leaning on each other and laughing. We found brightly lit vending machines standing full and untended in the darkest alleys, each offering cigarettes or instant cameras, bottles of Pocari Sweat sports drinks or the soiled underpants of school-age girls. Prostitutes taped business cards inside the telephone booths, pink cards with Hello Kitty-style drawings. We sidestepped ranks of homeless men camping out in cardboard boxes, disturbed squadrons of crows breaking open bags of garbage, got carried along by rivers of shoppers, squeezing through commercial streets like canyons, jostling and rushing and knocking bags together, human white water. I soon came to think of the spare flower arrangements of *ikebana*, which I'd always admired, as gaunt weeds struggling through cracks in the sidewalks. Not that there were any cracks in the sidewalks to speak of.

It was overwhelming and compelling to catch all these glimpses, to sail over a surface that never stayed still. But the school visits were different, a break and a treat. I love going into schools—have ever since I stopped being a student—since visiting schools is such an excellent way to try to tease out what's really going on in society. And so in Japan, where I was hoping to learn something about reconciliation, I know it's ironic, but I was happy to have a chance to visit schools filled with children who'd had nothing to do with the Second World War.

Plus, I just enjoy being around kids. Driving up to a sprawling brick low-rise school outside Tokyo, passing long sheds full of bicycles crammed together, pulling up to the imposing front door—no confusion about finding the entrance here—I felt pleased at the prospect of mixing with adolescents Gabe's age, a reminder of home.

I was also glad to get off the bus, sloughing off the rude presence of Geoffrey. It sometimes seemed as if the only time Geoffrey stopped making fun of our Japanese hosts was when he went after Stephanie, trying to get her attention with a fake Parisian *zank hay-ben for leetle gulls*-style accent before asking the other men, in a thrilled whisper, who wanted to shag her. Either that, or he'd lean forward and talk through his nose, a supposed Kiwi drawl designed to irritate Megan from Auckland. Megan was the youngest reporter, mid-twenties and a little vulnerable, telling me once that she felt inexperienced and sometimes got upset at how much Japanese she'd forgotten; she'd worked as an English teacher in the west of the country a couple of years before. Megan could survive Geoffrey's fake Kiwi accent, but her face reddened at his *Ah so*-ing and the constant *l* for *r* shifts, especially when he got another English guy going, a milder type who as Stephanie observed looked rather like Tintin.

"Ah, they're just little shites, talking out of their bums," Angela said. "That's where their brains are. Let's ignore them."

Inside the school, classes were changing, the halls crowded with uniformed students talking and laughing, many of the boys with their pants slung low and their navy jackets unbuttoned, all of the girls wearing fashionable white slouch socks, making the ones with fat little calves look like they had fetlocks. Could it really be true that they kept the socks up with glue? This was Inagakuen high school in Saitama prefecture, a model school, the largest and most modern in Japan, with 3,000 students and a program that stressed foreign languages and international studies.

"Good morning," a few students cried, as we walked past. "Good morning. Good morning."

Some of them looked as if they'd called out on a dare, proud of themselves, pursing their lips, staring straight at us. Others seemed more curious, waiting to hear what we'd answer. I figured there had to be several proto-Geoffreys pushing past us, pausing only to torment a large cadre of pre-Megans. But these Geoffreys weren't lost yet, congealed into permanent adolescence. The promise of growth surged past us in robust red-cheeked faces and winter-pale ones, in giggles and curiosity and abstraction—one sweet befuddled boy walked right into me—while teachers took a quick sharp look as they hurried on to class.

Like all the schools we visited, Inagakuen was architecturally modern, with familiar-looking desks in familiar-looking class-rooms, the buildings notable mainly for being spacious in a coun-try where people generally lived in tiny apartments. Inagakuen employed eight foreign teachers, many of them English speakers from the Japan Exchange and Teaching program, and almost all of them just out of university. JETs provided our entry into the Japanese school system. They were young, often lonely, eager to talk about Japan, and no match for a group of sympathetic jour-nalists. I hope that none of them got in trouble for talking to us, but they had the goods, anecdotes about entrenched resistance to the government's internationalization program.

I heard a kaleidoscope of stories: how a great many tradition-alist parents refused to send their kids to schools with foreign teachers; how even more parents didn't have much use for school at all, expecting their sons to follow them into their busi-ness or factory or shop and their daughters to marry; how some local teachers undermined foreign colleagues by making snide comments about them in class; how most teachers complained that loosening up the system meant that students weren't as well-prepared as they were five years ago, how language text-books were inadequate. One JET pulled out an old Jesuit primer, a pronunciation workbook full of impossible sentences. "Deafening the ear with its thundering, the gleaming river plunges along."

I'd hate to live in a place where government policy, even the most benign, was carried out seamlessly. Yet I found it interesting to hear how few people complained that the country was opening up too slowly and realized that I'd been making a mistake, unconsciously equating peoples' wish to modernize with a desire to westernize. They weren't the same. Perfectly modern-looking history textbooks described a very different Second World War than the one I'd studied in school. JETs confirmed stories I'd heard that history texts ignored Japanese atrocities in Manchuria and glossed over the army's brutal treatment of Allied prisoners of war.

If reconciliation required us to use our imaginations, to put ourselves in the shoes of others, I wondered what it meant to try to keep students from knowing about their country's most disgraceful actions during the war. Sitting in the corner of a classroom at Inagakuen, I also found myself thinking once again about growing up in a house where the most important things weren't talked about openly. If it had helped make me curious, turning me into an observer and a writer, if it had taught me to pick up clues from information adults dropped and to build them into stories— then for some students, at least at model schools like this, it might not be so important what the textbooks said. They could observe foreigners and reach their own conclusions. But I found myself worrying about the ones whose parents tried to shield them from foreign contact, what their imaginations fed on and what grievances they might incubate.

Fascinating, especially in light of my conversation with a local teacher. The Japanese teachers usually avoided us, and the prospect of any trouble, but I managed to get permission to visit the music department at Inagakuen for a story I was doing, and an English-speaking teacher was assigned to be my interpreter. He watched me as closely as I watched the students, and in the end, he had a question. How did his school compare with ones abroad? I told him that it was equivalent to model schools everywhere, that if he toured Canada, he would see others like it. The man took my point and smiled slightly.

"The problem is creativity," he said, as we walked downstairs. "The government worries that students in our system are competent, but not creative. Our society suffers from a lack of creativity. There is a difficulty in developing new products, for instance. Societies like the United States are more successful. We are attempting to correct this, through modern policies." He looked wry. "To instill creativity."

"And I understand that teachers have been complaining that students aren't as obedient as they used to be."

He was smiling as we rejoined the other reporters, and I would have liked to keep talking, but Geoffrey bustled up and inserted himself between us. "What's he saying?"

I looked apologetically at the teacher. "We were about to discuss how much I admire Japanese literature," I replied.

"Yes, you would, wouldn't you?" Geoffrey asked, shouldering me aside to do an interview. The flash of dislike in Geoffrey's eye shocked me, and I stayed there only long enough to thank the teacher for his courtesy, wondering why it was always so surprising to find that someone you disliked also disliked you.

Back on the bus, we passed crows flying from the telephone poles, scavenging in the narrow yards of nearby houses and a few scattered fields. I ended up sitting with Angela, always a relief. She could be counted on for her frisky observations—a tall, cracklingly slender, quick-moving woman—although I was beginning to notice that she volunteered little about herself. Only eventually did I learn that she'd trained as a veterinarian; journalism was a second thought. Her husband was a Venezuelan whom she'd met at veterinary college. "He treats big nervous animals like horses," she said. "Like horses and like me."

That afternoon, we talked about a meeting a couple of days earlier at an association that brought foreign students to Japan. During one interview, I'd asked an official about the unintended consequences of internationalization, telling him that I'd never seen a road that didn't run both ways. If Japan was going to open itself up to foreigners, might it not get more than it bargained for, importing ideas that could challenge its intricately calibrated social system?

"You'd better ask the politicians," the official said, before pausing and apparently deciding to reply.

"Japanese people like to have a cause, whether it's local, national or international," he said. "They want to help people and bring over foreign students who should help their countries in turn. Yet I've observed that many foreign students come here just to get the type of education that will help them earn a lot of money and be individually successful afterward. So yes, that's a problem."

Now Angela and I were speaking about the same thing in her country—call it the unanticipated effects of globalization—as I wondered whether there was a connection between the increasing number of Turkish refugees in Germany and the rise of neo-Naziism. She didn't like my question.

"The Nazis are always there," she replied. "Maybe this brings some more of them out of the woodwork, but that can't stop us from doing the right thing for the refugees. If we stop, the Nazis win. They're the final winners." She paused. "The war isn't really over, you know. It doesn't end."

We both looked at Geoffrey, and I thought that Angela was going to say something more, but she didn't. The official at the foreign exchange institute had gone on, though, to tell us about problems that they'd faced trying to bring foreign students to one of the southern islands. His group had proposed building a residence for foreigners at the local university, and the farmers had been outraged. They demanded that a three-yard-high perimeter fence be built around the residence compound, complete with night lighting. But the university sponsored meetings between the farmers and foreign students, and the farmers withdrew their opposition. Three years later, popular friendship clubs continued to bring foreigners and locals together.

A success story. Except that what the official actually said was, "We told them that these were university students, future professionals, not refugees who were going to steal their vegetables."

That night I had a dream. My friends Goran and Amela from Sarajevo were trying to get into a lineup with their children. They had to be in a lineup outside a concrete structure that was something like a university, and they finally succeeded in getting a place. But their son, Darije, wandered into a forest and Amela had to go after him. It didn't seem wrong or dangerous. This was a natural thing for a child to do. But suddenly there was a farmer after them, chasing Darije and Amela through the forest. They ran between big cedar trees, Douglas firs like the ones I grew up with, holding hands until they weren't Darije and Amela any more but one person, and that person was also me. Together we were running, leaping over gaping holes between the trees, mantraps in the forest floor. The dream had become a nightmare. I was terrified and sweating, gasping for air, my heart pounding. Suddenly a huge mantrap loomed and I tried to jump over it and I couldn't and was falling, falling, falling, falling. . . .

Jarred awake, sweating and trembling, I thought of my uncle, the prisoner of war, whose real story I had heard only months before, the story of his incredible four-day journey to escape imprisonment by the Japanese army in Thailand. As it turned out, he did.

44

I'D ONLY MET MY UNCLE DAVID A HANDFUL OF TIMES ON family vacations when I was little. A tall, thin, sandy presence, that's as much as I can recall, although I vividly remember the day that I arrived home to find my mother crying at the kitchen table, her back to the door. It was terrifying, the way she sat doubled over in a white short-sleeved blouse that dug into her upper arms. My father was back from work early, too, and I'd brought my brother home from wherever we'd been. I was nine and he was six. We stood holding hands.

"You're going to be sad," my father told us. "Your Uncle David died of a heart attack. Your mother's feeling very sorry."

Obediently, my brother and I began to cry.

"He was only fifty-two," my mother wailed, and we wailed, although it seemed very old to me. I would tell the neighborhood kids importantly, my uncle died and he was only fifty-two. We would be solemn for a moment. I would have something over them, a dead uncle. In a few days we'd play funeral, feeling over-excited and strange, especially when I saw my father standing by the living-room window, watching us as if we were ships coming into harbor.

Years later, I realized that my uncle's early death probably had something to do with having been a prisoner of war, and possibly with all the muffled talk about his drinking. Knowing that he'd been imprisoned in Thailand, I made the connection with Japanese attempts to build a rail connection between Burma and Bangkok, the real-life version of *The Bridge on the River Kwai*. He must have been in a Japanese prisoner-of-war camp near the Thai-Burmese border, I decided. I never really asked. Building up a story in my imagination was enough.

Then my younger uncle, Douglas, grew interested in family history, and I found myself sitting at a patio table at his house in Barbados reading through file folders of information about his much older brother, whom he hadn't known very well, either. It was a treat to go snorkeling during the day and return, salty and sandy and tired, to sit at the table on the covered terrace and drink something icy, chatting and sorting through army records in a gossipy attempt to tease out a personality. The air was clammy with a slight breeze that felt like the wake of the earth turning, a cool lapping into night. Waves crashed and retreated, crashed and retreated; the edge of my aunt and uncle's yard fell off at a ridge above a marsh and a beach. Walking to the ridge, facing south and looking up at the starry sky, we could watch the comet Hyakutake—a puffball, indistinct, with a very faint tail—carry the name of a Japanese stargazer in a slow arc a few degrees above the horizon. I had not yet been invited to go to Japan. All was serendipity.

Reading through the files, I found that my Uncle David had joined up in 1942. He didn't have to. He was thirty years old and married with a five-year-old daughter, but he joined the air force and was chosen as a candidate for officer's training school. As a young man, he'd drifted a little, disappointing his parents by quitting high school and working at odd jobs, eventually settling into life as an accountant in northern Ontario. The timing of his decision to sign up had something to do with problems faced by the lumber company where he worked, although he'd also been waiting for the air force to open up recruitment rather than jumping into the army or the navy.

He was six feet tall, a good weight, blue-eyed and starting to bald. His service record shows that he topped his classes on the ground and they pegged him as a pilot, which he didn't want to be. He said that he wanted to be an observer or a navigator, but since the air force wanted him to be a pilot, he had to give it a try.

It didn't work. In the records, the instructors' comments on his training flights grow more impatient daily. Disoriented on cloudy days, evening flights, loses the horizon. Landings dangerous, too steep, he was spooked, he brought the plane down too hard, instructor had to take the controls to avoid crashing. The instructors' comments look mean and dismissive on the page ("nervous flier!"), but with everything at stake, they probably had to be. My uncle flunked out as a pilot but got his wish to become an observer. Runs in the family, I guess.

He seems to have excelled as both observer and navigator, and was posted around Canada before going to Bermuda, where he flew submarine-spotting missions and otherwise had a grand old time. Rum punch and palm trees, the tropics—he was only the second one in our family to make it to the tropics, his seafaring grandfather having been the first. Then he was posted to India, a lieutenant seconded to the Royal Air Force to fly bombing missions against Japanese positions in Burma and Thailand. On one flight, enemy antiaircraft fire shot their gunner dead, damaging the plane so badly that it smoked and wobbled, flying low over enemy-held territory, an easy target. But the pilot managed to muscle the plane back to base and crash-land it on the runway, bringing it to a stop against a brick wall—all this described in a newspaper article. Hero Crew Escapes.

The next time they didn't. They were flying a mission over northern Thailand to bomb a railway bridge at Utteradit when the plane was badly hit. My uncle later said that as they dropped, roaring, toward the earth, he watched a flight gauge fall, marking a lower and lower altitude. The moment they were low enough, he ran to the open bay and jumped, parachuting into a field where he was immediately surrounded by Thai peasant farmers. Three other crew members floated down beside him. The plane plunged nose first into the ground, exploding and killing four other members of the crew, including the pilot. The Thais buried them where they fell and turned the survivors over to the local police.

Of course, Thailand was officially allied with Japan and Germany, and at the beginning of the war in the Far East, most Thais had celebrated the arrival of a Japanese army that promised to throw European colonial powers out of Asia. But Thailand had never been occupied in its 700-year history, much less conquered, and although the Japanese were not technically an occupying power, some Thais began to feel that they behaved like one, and the alliance grew unpopular. People also disliked the way that Allied prisoners of war were treated as they slaved on the railway. Many Thais smuggled food to the POWs, often throwing it from passing trains. Not all of them, of course. Some stole from the prisoners, as well. But eventually a Thai resistance arose; it turned out after the war that it had been run by the Thai government. Canny Thais, no wonder they'd never been conquered.

All of which is to say that the Thai police didn't turn the surviving fliers over to the Japanese army. Instead, they did an extraordinary thing. They decided to take my uncle all the way from Utteradit to Bangkok, planning to turn him over to their Thai superiors and receive instructions about what to do with the other fliers. The only vehicle they had for this four-day journey was a railway handcar. And so they set out from Utteradit on an adventure I can only imagine, so elemental that my uncle could never say much about it, maybe didn't understand very much about it at the time. Obviously not the way it would end.

But I've built up a picture of what he went through, imagination overlying a few stray words and the coincidental fact that I took the same ride once in reverse, catching an express from Bangkok through Utteradit on my first backpacking journey, scattering the ghosts on the line.

And I see my uncle as a ghost, a tall, pale, balding man, half out of uniform in the heat and pumping the handcar through the night. His two captors ride beside him. It's a flat ride, there are rice paddies on either side that he can see by moonlight. The heat is thick, mosquitoes are thick, but if he keeps pumping, pumping, they will not be able to settle.

Burning, off in the distance, he sees the campfires of an army. He knows that the army must be Japanese and wonders if he will be turned over to them. But there were Japanese in Utteradit and he was hidden by his captors, given food and kept quiet, none of it gently. He doesn't understand why. He doesn't understand their language, and he finds their behavior and motives impenetrable. They give him water that gives him dysentery and food that keeps him alive, never taking a turn pumping, pumping, at the handcar themselves, but in this way saving him from the bites of the malarial mosquitoes. If they're taking him to prison, he won't arrive ill, unable to work, whether to their benefit or his, he can't decide. Wouldn't he wish to die quickly under torture? He doesn't know what information they might want, might not have, what he might know. His two captors sit on the handcar, their knees pulled up, drawing on unlit cigarettes as the vectored fires smoke and burn.

Beneath them, the rails begin to buzz. His captors grow alert, gesturing for him to stop, and jumping off as the handcar slows to halt it, lift it off the rails. No place to hide it, they set it on the embankment before pulling him toward the flooded paddy, sliding him down the bank like a snake, all of them snakes coiling into the paddy, warm as urine.

The ooze of mud. His jaw chatters on the skin of the water until he holds it closed, battening his face in the crook of an arm. With his head held down, he can't see the train approach, but it's all he can hear. Screech of metal on metal, a slow chuff, male voices, male laughter entering the night. Troop train. A repeated slant of barred light passing. He crouches, soaking, taut with listening, until the screeching train recedes north and all is quiet under the moon. They slither quickly up the bank and lift the handcar back on the tracks.

Pumping again, he holds his face and body low. He gleams in the moonlight, pale and wet, but understands that if his captors try to blacken him, their intentions grow all too clear. A Japanese soldier might cry out, They're hiding him! He knows that he would understand the cry; also what would happen next. He feels grateful for the risk his captors are taking, but not just that, never just that when he's half collapsing from exhaustion and fear. Can't they take just one turn pumping? One turn pumping, one turn pumping, one turn pumping through the night.

He can smell the smoke of the campfires now, the fires on the far side of the village that they're about to pass. Clumsy with dread he pushes along, breathing ashes and waiting for a challenge, some watchman, a sentry, a trainman who knows that no one is scheduled to pass. The feel of a sleeping village fills him, the spaciousness of dreams, the innocence of a child's mouth falling open, the hectic terror of nightmares, heart pounding, the sweat. He pumps, pumps, all staccato, until they finally pass the town, the fires, all behind him, thank Christ, to the north. He slumps. Keep moving! He feels a slap.

This is all my uncle tells people later: that the Thais saved his life, that they made him pump the handcar on his own. He can't ever talk about it and can't forget.

Can't sleep, either, trying to dream through the glaring tropical day, hiding in fields or brief stands of trees where villagers feed them and don't see them pass. Once he hears planes far above and knows that bombs will soon drop on the railway line. He sees himself from a great distance up, crouching in a patch of forest, maggot body curled between the trees. How tempting to burst it—but the bombs don't drop, nothing ends, days revolve into night and he's pumping through the sweaty air, meat evaporating from his bones. Two nights, three nights pass, and trains become more frequent, towns more frequent, Japanese more frequent. He scurries into pipes, into burrows to escape. He is a ghost. No one sees him. He's died, won't die, doesn't want to die. Pumping, pumping, down the line going God knows where.

One morning, he's dozing, a captor jumps up. There's a Thai army convoy on a road nearby. The captor waves them down and a Thai officer strolls over, leans over him, four days after his plane crashed. Four days? He sees a shadowed face, he blinks and is formally taken prisoner, saying his ambivalent farewells to his ambivalent captors before he's driven the final few miles to Bangkok. The jittery city is cackling at him, and he understands that some of this cackle is English. They're saying that the military prison is still under construction, that he is to be placed in a civilian camp. He's driven there, low louvered buildings behind barbed wire. The sign says university. He's driven inside and assigned a bed in a barracks. He laughs in nervous exhaustion. This was once a classroom in the faculty of political science, imagine that.

International protocol now clicks in. First an official from the Red Cross visits, checking his papers and reporting his presence to the Allies, who telegraph his family that he is no longer missing in action but safe somewhere in Thailand. Afterward, the Swiss Consul visits and files a report that he is healthy. Finally, the Japanese army learns that he's there, a downed Allied flier held by the Thais in the middle of Bangkok. An officer wants to interview him, and a date is set. My uncle understands that the Japanese are trying to seize him from the Thais, who have been treating him well, and he doesn't know how to resist. He wishes to be subtle and elusive, but when he enters the interview room, he learns that his attempts at subtlety will have to pass through a Thai translator, who speaks both Japanese and English. He sits down unhappily on the schoolroom chair.

The first questions are routine, establishing his name and rank. Then the Japanese officer asks about Utteradit, the shot-down plane. This we know for a fact, since my uncle also told one story of his captivity. After the officer finished speaking, the translator said, "Which side of the river did the shots come from that hit your plane you don't know."

"I don't know," my uncle answered. A Thai friend he made in the camp later told him that the Japanese were trying to prove that their guns had shot him down, not the Thai guns on the other side of the river, and that he should be their prisoner. But when they couldn't prove that the shots were theirs, the Thais refused to let him go, and he spent the remainder of the war in their custody.

It wasn't easy. There was never enough food and he lost forty pounds, suffering from jungle rot on his feet and running sores on his calves, from malnutrition and beriberi, repeated terror at the incessant Japanese attempts to seize him and, between those, boredom. But when the war ended, he was met at the camp gateway by his Thai friend, who had been released a little earlier. His friend ushered him into a Rolls-Royce and took him on a tour of Bangkok, the mirrored temples and the Buddhas, the finest restaurants. It turned out that this friend came from a very influential family and my uncle was the first Allied prisoner of war to be repatriated from the eastern theater. When his photograph appeared in *The Globe and Mail*, he looked like a boy wearing his father's uniform. You could have put two fingers between his collar and his neck, and his hat looked as big as a mortarboard.

When I was small, I somehow got the idea that the people in his hometown held a parade to welcome him back, but Douglas told me in Barbados that this wasn't true. It was true, though, that they made him sheriff, and his picture appeared often in the local paper on ceremonial occasions. He handed out trophies to Boy Scouts and served on a number of charitable boards, reaching a high rank as a Mason. I asked Douglas what his brother felt afterward about Thai and Japanese people, and Douglas laughed.

"Where would he see them?" He never left northern Ontario again. There was one Japanese-Canadian family in town, and they got along very well. But what did the Omuras have to do with the war? My surviving uncle shrugged.

So much of my own life has to do with the war, which was over a decade before I was born. My mother finally told me that she'd moved to Vancouver not just because she'd grown tired of delivering other women's babies. After we got back from Barbados, she said that her decision was also tied up in the restlessness she felt at the time of her brother's imprisonment, a helpless wish for movement, for change and escape. And Vancouver, of course, was where she met my father.

As far as that goes, we were vacationing in Barbados because of the war, or a distant ripple from it. Such a huge boulder dropped in the water, you still felt these ripples. Douglas had decided to take early retirement because he grew conscious, as he approached fifty-two, that both his brother and father had died at that age. He stepped down from a corporate vice-presidency to start work on international aid projects, moving to Barbados so he could oversee the accounting for foreign aid in the Caribbean. And we only went there because Douglas was there, and his wife, Margaret, a very dear aunt who was ill with cancer, wanting to laugh with her on the terrace over icy drinks that she wouldn't hear of anyone else pouring, as blackbirds chattered from the ridge nearby and Hyakutake arched above.

A few months later, a friend was invited by the Japan Foundation to join their tour, but she was a staff reporter and her editors wouldn't let her go. Generously, she suggested that I might want to take her place, and I did.

4 5

"BUT SOME PEASANTS FOUND ME, SO I GOT A PROPER BEATING. I hadn't pinched a single potato. They treat us like rats."

A year after leaving Japan, I was reading a translation of Kenzaburo Oe's novel, *Nip the Buds, Shoot the Kids*. Stealing vegetables,

I thought. The book is about reformatory boys herded into the central Japanese mountains during the Second World War. They're not foreigners, they're internal refugees—Oe calls them prisoners of war—and they're treated with dreadful brutality by the peasant farmers. Childhood, the future, becomes not just frontier but a battlefield; it happens so often. And in this case, I closed the book wondering how rural Japanese traditionalism could be reconciled with the future. Also whether the survivors of war can be reconciled to their splintered selves, whether any of us can.

I thought of my uncle, his drinking. I also thought about our tour of Japan, the parts that didn't give rise to either solemn educational insights or funny stories. Watching Geoffrey bait the women, I'd seen an increasing amount of sexual game-playing. If you didn't bother listening, just sat back and watched, his working eyebrows and wet lips made Geoffrey look testosterone-fueled, horny as hell, desire dripping off him. If anyone had showed any signs of taking him up on it, I'm sure he would have run for the hills. No one was going to, but I began to think that one woman was responding, surprised by seeing her surreptitious glances and angry petulant mouth-biting blush—angry at herself, I thought, for feeling such a physical pull, unwilled and unwilling, the undertow.

For a while in high school, I'd had a crush on a good-looking boy who was very full of himself and confident of his opinions. It wasn't a cover for teenage insecurity. He thought he was great. One day, when he was holding court in the cafeteria, I saw that my friend Derek was seething in his chair, barely able to contain himself.

I kept thinking about Derek in Japan, a tall guy with a raven profile straight off a totem pole and beautifully thick black hair falling halfway down his back, an eagle feather holding it. He was usually quiet, but after the boy had left, Derek burst out, "That guy is such an asshole."

I knew that. He didn't need to tell me, I knew that I was stupid. I wanted to like a sweet boy who hung around my locker with puppy-dog eyes, a shy boy, quiet as Derek, but I couldn't and I loathed myself. I had a crush on the asshole.

When I believed I saw someone feel that way in Japan, I took a good hard look at Geoffrey and thought, Well, in a certain light, I guess he's not bad. God knows, he's in good enough shape after running up all those stairs. But I knew very well how hard it is to reconcile helpless instinct with a functioning brain and thought, Poor woman, splintered like that.

I won't name her, it's unfair. I might have been mistaken, after all.

4 6

I THINK I GOT MY IMAGINATION FROM MY FATHER. THAT story he'd told about his uncle having been shot by the Mad Trapper of Rat River? Not quite. When I started looking into family history myself, I found that Uncle Klas had come over from Sweden in 1923 to join my grandmother and her brother in Alberta. Klas worked as a farmhand for six years before taking off for the Northwest Territories. He and a partner laid a trapline and built a cabin at each end, walking the line every day and always finding someplace dry to stay at night.

I sought out Klas the time I backpacked through Sweden. He'd returned home when his father died in 1933, called back, as the oldest son, to take over the family farm. By the time we met, Klas was well into his eighties and the farm long sold. The train deposited me in a small town in south-central Sweden, and I walked over to the old folks' home where he was staying temporarily to recover from an operation. Many people in wheelchairs watched as we sat and talked, the room heavily scented by forced spring flowers, the

way Mexican funeral homes often reek of tuberoses. Since then, whenever I smell hyacinths, I think of Uncle Klas.

He was tall, of course, and stooped, rather courtly, with a long face and pale eyes. He'd been married twice but never had any children, and while he didn't strike me as lonely, exactly, he seemed pleased to have a visitor, a young person to talk with. The problem was, he'd forgotten most of his English, understanding more than he could say, and when I asked about the trapline, he ended up walking me over to his nearby flat to show me the photographs of himself outside a cabin, holding up pelts. Yes, he'd trapped near the Rat River. Yes, he was shot in the leg by people stealing furs. People? Person, he said, correcting himself, making the word sound like the Swedish surname Persson. The Mad Trapper? I asked. He looked confused. Yes? he answered.

My father always said that he learned about Klas being shot from the newspaper, and my mother remembers other relatives talking about opening up the paper and seeing the story. Klas was in the hospital, they read. His partner had shot him. The Mad Trapper of Rat River: It has such a satisfying ring, half-mythic, half-tabloid. The trapper was probably a Norwegian named Albert Johnson; no one was ever sure of his identity. They just knew that he shot a Mountie before leading the police and their Métis guides on a mad dash across the territories in winter, temperatures falling to fifty below, plains as windy as Jupiter. Reporters were able to telegraph bulletins home; it made headlines for weeks. A Mountie finally shot Johnson dead, but not before Johnson had shot a few more people himself. Reading the history books recently, I found that none of these people was my great-uncle. Klas probably thought that I was asking if the fur thief who shot him was angry. Sure, and Klas had probably been angry too, especially if the thief had been his partner.

"You take," he said, handing me the pictures and a large bank-note. "Such a long time ago. No one cares."

I'm afraid that many of my father's yarns wouldn't bear looking into. There was the one he used to tell about his old chum Grant McConachie, a pilot who had great respect for my father's mechanical abilities, wanting to form a partnership to buy an old plane or two. My father and his brothers were running a delivery business and he said no. The delivery service went bust. Grant McConachie started up what became Canadian Airlines. "Shoulda listened to Grant," my father told me, shaking his head.

I don't think so, but it's a good story. Or at least, it was a good story at first, when my father was happy casting himself as the underdog, the good-humored chump. But gradually he became the jerk, the failure, the put-upon, the loser. He started complaining about how badly he was treated at work, the constant slights from his former friends. They were all doing better than he was when he was a damn sight better at the job. He banged around the house, yelling that he was going to leave, he couldn't take it any more. We'd all starve, he'd rather starve, we'd be better off if he was dead. I took my little brother down to the basement rec room and turned up the television, making caves out of the chesterfield cushions, trains that chugged loudly across the floor.

As the years passed, my father grew solitary and remote. He wouldn't go out socially, especially once his job disappeared as part of the technological change in newspapers. The old Linotypes he'd fixed for so many years were retired with the introduction of cold-type technology. Afterward, he worked until his own retirement putting newspaper plates into a machine and taking them out, putting them in and taking them out. His lower lip hung open in such painful disappointment and chagrin that I hate to even picture it. At home, he sat at the kitchen table playing solitaire for hours.

I didn't see much of him by then. It had never been easy to be his daughter, and I wasn't exactly an easygoing girl. If anyone had thought to use big words, they might have said that we grew estranged. I moved out when I was seventeen to take a summer job in Toronto and never moved back, although I saw him fairly often after starting work as a reporter in the same building in Vancouver where he put plates into a machine and took them out, wearing his green work clothes while I wore girl-reporter suits and earned as much at twenty-one as he did after working there for almost thirty years. The injustice enraged me. I hated the way they treated him and once lashed out at a union meeting, my jaw chattering so hard that I could barely speak, after a sports-writer whose column my father read every day talked about "the green-suited growlies in the back shop." Why did they treat him like that? Why did he let them treat him like that? I could barely stand it. I could barely stand him and had to stay away. Then I got older and knew a little more, felt a little guilty, a little helpless, and tried to stay in touch. I didn't think in terms of reconcilia-tion, exactly. We didn't use big words any more than we talked about the important things, and what happened, or didn't, was never clearly defined.

The call came through after we'd moved to Mexico. My father had gone into hospital for a routine operation and something went wrong. When my mother phoned the first time, no one knew what had happened, just that he'd woken up abnormally weak and confused. One doctor thought he might be having a bad reaction to the anesthetic. Another thought that it was a traumatic worsen-ing of a preexisting condition: his shamble, a growing clumsiness in his hands. He might also have had a stroke during surgery. My mother, the nurse, didn't think it looked like a stroke. But she didn't know what it did look like and started weeping on the phone.

When I flew up to Vancouver, I found my father as weak as she'd said, lying in the hospital bed attached to tubes. But he made perfect sense as we talked, asking about Mexico, what Paul was doing, and I grew puzzled.

"I think you're getting tired," I said finally. "Haven't you been sleeping well?"

My father looked troubled. "I don't like to complain," he said, "but for some reason, they put me down on the B.C. Rail tracks last night, and I couldn't sleep for all the noise of the trains."

He was never able to walk again and spent the rest of his life in the wheelchair. Something complicated had happened, some higher ability to coordinate both movement and thought had gone awry. Simple gestures he could manage, and at the start, he usually spoke coherently about what was in front of him, although he already had trouble with abstract thought. A motor neuropathy of unknown origin, the specialists finally decided, which was a complicated way of saying they didn't know what the hell was going on. This was about the time one neurologist said that he thought that my father might be suffering from lead poisoning, or poisoning from another heavy metal at work. There was nothing measurable in his bloodstream, but there wouldn't be by then. In any case, the treatment was the same, rehabilitation and physiotherapy, although he couldn't manage the exercises, or quite perceive that he didn't.

"I want to go home," he kept saying, but he was too tall and unwieldy and helpless to care for outside hospital, and he had to go into extended care.

It was terrifically hard on my mother, who felt guilty about being unable to bring him home, and who went in to visit and feed him every day. I felt confused myself, mourning someone who was still alive. How did you manage to reconcile when the person you'd been estranged from wasn't around any more? He'd always been so difficult to get along with, and now he wasn't. The deep lines on his forehead and cheeks gradually relaxed so that his face became as smooth as paper. At the same time, the perturbations and knots in his character disappeared, so that some essential childlike sweetness shone through. Sitting in his wheelchair, he had a kind word for everyone passing, unimaginable as the brooding and difficult man I'd known.

"You look pretty," he'd tell my mother, before turning to me.

"Hi, sweetie. So here you are," he'd say happily, although I soon understood that he had little idea how long it was since I'd last been to visit. "What you been up to?"

"Well, I live in Mexico, you know."

At first we talked about life there, usually the same things each time, several times over. But as the years and visits went by, he slowly lost track, and one day I saw that he didn't know what Mexico was any more, looking confused and unhappy when I mentioned it, apparently aware that something was missing, but unsure what.

"Don't the mountains look beautiful?" I asked, nodding out the window.

Happy now: "Snow."

It was a slow decline, six years, encompassing most of our time in Latin America. On my last visit he didn't recognize me, bedridden, skeletal, his mouth pulled permanently open, suffering from a compendium of awful awful ailments. We were getting ready to leave Brazil when my mother phoned to say that he'd developed pneumonia.

My friend Estela greeted me at the door of her Rio apartment that afternoon. "Your father has fluid on his lungs. Be careful!"

Careful that they didn't try heroic measures to save the poor soul, my poor father, and they didn't.

After the funeral, just family left, we went through old photograph albums and papers. I finally asked my mother if she'd ever seen the documents I'd found so long ago in my father's footlocker, and she hadn't, although they'd released some military papers at a Veterans' Affairs hearing into her request that he be granted a pension. I thought that they might be the same ones, but they weren't, they were meaner, and they didn't have to be. One was a psychiatrist's report, and I recoiled from the words. "A life-long personality disorder. . . ."

He was twenty-four and fighting a war. He died at seventy-four, having lost it. I'd brought along Ernest Hemingway to read on the plane, *A Farewell to Arms*:

"I was always embarrassed by the words sacred, glorious, and sacrifice and the expression in vain. We had heard them, some-times standing in the rain almost out of earshot, so that only the shouted words came through . . . and I had seen nothing sacred, and the things that were glorious had no glory and the sacrifices were like the stockyards in Chicago if nothing was done with the meat except to bury it. There were many words that you could not stand to hear and finally only the names of the places had dignity."

"Sicily," my father would say, shaking his head.

"North Africa," he'd nod, watching another documentary.

Of course, I supported the war against fascism, but I couldn't reconcile myself to war itself. And reconciling with people now struck me as a different question, if only you could figure out how to phrase it. Something about how you caught ripples of water in your hands.

4 7

WHAT FINALLY TRIGGERED THE CONFRONTATION WITH THE British journalists was their attitude toward a man from the Japan Foundation, Takahashi, who was in charge of organizing our tour. We all liked Takahashi, but the Brits refused to get his name right. On our final night, after saying good-bye to our Japanese hosts, we foreigners had dinner together in a Tokyo restaurant. Geoffrey was needling people, background noise, except that it was going on a little too long, and his sidekick, Tintin, insisted on chiming in. They kept referring to Takahashi as Yakabushi or Mitsubishi or Nintendo, with a red-faced Megan correcting them each time and the rest of us taking Angela's line, ignore them and maybe they'll drop through a manhole.

Finally Tintin said, "Taka-shitty. Ah so, Nippon Foundation toul olganized by Taka-shitty. Velly good toul. Thank you, Taka-shitty."

"It's Takahashi," I told him. "Ta-ka-ha-shi. It's not really very difficult. Give it a try."

Tintin looked at me blankly, then blushed.

"Taka-shitty," Geoffrey said, raising his chin.

"Ta-ka-ha-shi," Stephanie repeated. "Can you say it? It's actually a very easy name. I think you might be able to do this."

"Meaning what?" Geoffrey asked belligerently.

"That you're vile and racist," Megan burst out. "Making fun of everything Japanese."

Outraged, Geoffrey answered, "But I make fun of everybody."

He looked wounded, pouting while Megan analyzed his shortcomings, starting at accurate and getting worse. The Australian woman, Jane, laughed quietly in the corner.

"John Bull seems to be losing the war," she said. "Should we tell him who really won?"

"Fifty years later, I think women," Angela replied. "Not men, I'm afraid."

4 8

THE CROWS, THE CROWS. OUTSIDE THE IMPERIAL PALACE, they squawked and cawed, scavengers ignoring the moat to fly between the trees on each side, craning their necks to watch us as we watched them. I asked our guide, Hiroko, about them.

"Actually, you know, we never saw crows in Tokyo before five years ago," she said. "For some reason, they came down from the mountains, and now they're a problem. I hear that sometimes they attack babies in parks, trying to take them away, and there's a government commission meeting to decide what to do about them."

So now I had my Japanese baby-snatching myth, too. We're all so concerned with our children, we all make their education a battlefield, we all need to be more imaginative, being so marked by the war. By the end of the tour, I finally felt I had some idea where I was.

Anywhere.

BRINGING

IT ALL

BACK HOME

49

"CHARACTERS," I REPEAT, WRITING ON THE CHALKBOARD. "What are some of the other components of fiction?"

"Setting," a student calls out.

"Plot."

"Imagination."

What would my father say? I'm not a professor, just a night school teacher, a creative writing instructor in the faculty of continuing education at Ryerson Polytechnic University. I've taught before, but never for a university, so being here makes me think of him. This is as good as it gets, Dad. Adult students here by choice. A tiny windowless seminar room that we call the bunker.

"There's also the question of obsession," I say, and underline the word twice on the board.

50

THE ROAD DIPS SOUTH AS IT HEADS OUT OF TROCHU, ALBERTA, into the rich farmland that my great-grandparents cleared almost a hundred years ago. My grandmother and her brother, Johan, slogged down this slope in 1912 in the mailman's team and democrat, huddled against the driving rain. When I drove the dip myself, Gabe was about the same age as they'd been at the time. He'd just turned fifteen. My grandmother had been sixteen, Johan seventeen. Jumble black-and-white photographs together and Gabe could be their younger brother, they look so much alike. The nose, the shoulders, the coloring. They had long legs and watchful eyes: tall kids who'd lived on two continents and spoke a couple of languages.

I was driving around old family sites in Alberta, searching for the ends to stories that I'd heard half-told at kitchen tables. I'd already started writing down whatever I remembered, inspired not only by the research Douglas was doing into the Scottish side of the family, but by what my friend had said not long before on the Danforth about learning from your travels. I felt that I was making a final reckoning of my family's travels, maybe with traveling itself. Primarily, I was looking for the Swedes, making a long looping journey into the past as I pressed relatives for their memories and revisited places that I'd known as a child.

My cousin Charlotte was helping me, organizing day trips from her home in Airdrie, north of Calgary. Actually, she was my second cousin, granddaughter of Johan-turned-John. But you'd pick us as related, even though Charlotte's eyes are pale and her face rounder than mine with a dimple on her chin. Both of us are tall enough that we were crammed for headroom in the rental car, her short haircut practically brushing the ceiling, my long impractical hair whipping whenever we opened the windows, both of us starting to gray. We'd met as kids when my family drove out to Alberta for summer vacations. Her parents farmed back then and we stayed with them sometimes, Charlotte a bit more than a year older than me and taking charge, showing me around in her cowboy boots, while I wore the wrong shoes and did city-kid things like give names to the barn kittens.

We wrote back and forth as pen pals in the winter, and when Charlotte got married, at nineteen, I came out to be one of her bridesmaids. After the big Catholic wedding—she converted— we'd driven around, laying grids through Drumheller and honking our horns cheerfully, the cars decorated with yellow and white tissue-paper carnations, Charlotte and her husband Lyle in the same car now, both of them as pale as her gown. We bridesmaids and the flower girl drove behind them, wearing our long dresses with green velvet bodices and yellow chiffon skirts and sleeves. The reception was in the community hall in Rumsey, the town where my father had been born. I danced the two-step and the polka with Uncle John, who was clapping his hands to the music and having a great old time, whirling Charlotte and the bridesmaids under colored lights (I think they were colored), the ushers all drinking from flasks of rye, Uncle John chuckling and ducking, teaching me the steps. I was not quite eighteen, he was seventy-eight. After half a dozen polkas, he tired me out.

Charlotte and I lost touch after that, our lives diverging. She stayed home and had three kids while Lyle worked for NOVA, on the gas trunk line. But twenty-five years later, they wanted to get the wedding party back together for their silver anniversary, and I flew out for a November celebration. Now it was August and I was back, this time for the wedding of their eighteen-year-old daughter, Cheryl, who was maintaining a family tradition by converting when she married, in her case to Mormonism, the Church of Jesus Christ of Latter-day Saints. Amazing how most of the truly important decisions in people's lives are still made before they're twenty.

The prairie sky seemed low as we drove down the highway, a deep blue rolling with fat cumulus clouds. In August, the grain was high and golden, the coulees dry as we sloped down and up on the fast black road. I was following a route mapped in Charlotte's head, heading eventually for her parents' new home in the town of Munson where, she said, her mother might have something to tell me about my grandmother. But first we stopped in Trochu for breakfast and a look at the Swedish Lutheran Church, the outskirts of town a blur of car dealerships and grain elevators and eggs over easy, hash browns on the side. What struck me most was the dip out of town, the feeling that my grandmother must have had as the mailman's democrat slipped down the muddy slope, the gut sense of descending, her muscles tensed, pulling back. What am I doing here? Oh, I want to go home.

As we headed out of town, I told Charlotte some of the other stories I'd run across. In my backpacking journals, I'd recently re-read Edit's tale of our great-great-grandfather Johannes, born about 1829, who took the surname "Sten," which means stone, when he became a soldier. Also the story about one of my grandmother's cousins, who died when he fell from the dome of the great church in Lund during its reconstruction.

There was also my father's divorce. By now, my mother had told me that he and his first wife, Queenie, had married very young, and that their daughter was born soon afterward. Then my father went to war for five years, and his wife began living with a man she later married. I guess this wasn't really surprising when my father was gone all that time, with no home leave that I've ever heard of. But he had a shock when he got back. His wife handed him a second daughter, a child no one had mentioned in letters. He thought she looked too young to be his. The divorce was bitter, and his ex-wife wouldn't let him see my half-sister afterward. For years, he had no idea where she was.

I remember the day she turned up in North Vancouver. I'd started university by then, and my mother called me to come over and meet her. I found a woman almost twice my age sitting in my parents' living room in what she couldn't have known was my father's chair. I'll call her Hazel. She was slighter than me, but we looked a great deal alike, even though I saw her as being over the hill, coming up to forty. Well-preserved, I thought, checking out her good skin with practical-minded selfishness. But Hazel was dressed like a member of a different generation—everything matched, and she wore a scarf—and I couldn't seem to connect with her. Maybe if she'd been introduced as a newly discovered aunt? She said that she and her husband had five children, the oldest not much younger than me. Three girls, two boys, but she wasn't very forthcoming about them. Poor woman, she was probably rigid with nerves. What this must have cost her. I was eighteen, nineteen. I had no idea.

I didn't stay long; there didn't seem to be much point. My mother told me later that my father and Hazel went out for a drive after I left, and that my father returned devastated. Hazel had told him that she and her mother never got along, and that Queenie had put her in a home when she was eleven years old. She'd been kept there for two years, and the experience had been searing. Where was my father all that time?

He hadn't known, no one had told him. He said he would have taken her in, but Hazel didn't seem to believe him. I picture her keeping her eyes on the road, her jawline tight, her good skin radiant with anger. She left after that drive, and that was the last we saw of her. My father had never talked about Hazel before and wouldn't speak of her afterward. Nor did she show any interest when he died.

Some stories have no ending, although I could probably find out more about my half-sister if I wanted to. Working in journalism means that I can get to people. As it turns out, that's why Hazel can too. She works for a newspaper. I heard fifth-hand that her first grandchild was born not many years after our visit, and Charlotte and I calculated that she must be coming up to retirement age. We agreed that we hoped that the visit had helped her, but neither of us could see how.

"It's funny the way Dad found out about the second daughter's birth date," my mother told me in Vancouver, a few days later. "For the divorce, you know. He went into the hospital pretending to be a doctor and just pulled the files. He managed to write everything down before they sent him packing."

Her smile faded.

"The poor girl died at seventeen. She had cancer, it's so sad. Queenie told someone that she saw it as a judgment, but I don't understand that way of thinking. Why was it the girl's fault, poor thing?"

We crossed the river after leaving Trochu and drove into Rumsey, passing the community hall where Charlotte's reception had been held. The town was smaller than I remembered, just a few straggling blocks of little square houses on big square lots, many of them planted with well-tended vegetable gardens larger than the houses. I had no idea where my father might have been born, although we drove past the house where Uncle John had spent his last years: deserted now, and overgrown with weeds. Earlier, Charlotte had pulled out a local history that said my grandfather Rune first homesteaded northeast of Rumsey in 1910. When John came over from Sweden, he worked for a couple of years as a farmhand, earning $20 a month, then claimed the homestead next to my grandfather's in 1914. They roomed together in Rune's place while John hired out to break land, opening 250 to 300 acres with his plow and five horses—two horses in the lead, the book said, and three next to the plow.

Rune sold his land four years later, when my father was just a year old, buying half a section of land near Edburg, then selling his half-section to buy a store back in Rumsey, starting his restless travels, his unending quest. More practical-minded John traded his homestead for fifteen horses in 1918, trailing the horses over to Rune's place in Edburg the following year. But with automobiles coming in, the bottom fell out of the horse market in 1920. John had to sell, keeping just a saddle pony and a team. He worked a team well into the Depression, hauling ice from the river for $1.50 a ton, picking rocks for a dollar a day, breaking horses in the spring. John managed to buy back some land near Rumsey and worked his farm into the seventies. Charlotte and I drove past it, the house hidden by a thicket of trees, before turning down a gravel road onto the spread where she'd grown up.

No one in my family farms now. Charlotte's father and brother left their farm and John's during the eighties. They started driving truck afterward, and recently her father had been in charge of gravel crews for the local roads department. As we spun through the golden wheat fields, my small car uneasy on the ruts, Charlotte grew silent and I concentrated on driving, making the corners at the edge of a great coulee that fell down into the Badlands, the moonscape surrounding Red Deer River.

"A team from the museum found a complete dinosaur skeleton right over there," Charlotte said, pointing to a small ravine encircled by wheat. "I'd moved out by then, but my parents were still here. The farmers own the top land here, the government owns the bottoms."

We parked on a grassy verge, planning to scramble down into the Badlands. I was trying to remember the times we'd come here as kids, although as we hiked down the first steep bank, I came up dry as the grass. Still, it was dazzling to leave the farmed plains and walk down into the Badlands, far above the river here and maybe a mile distant, yet on a level with the top line of hoodoos eroded from the cliffs, like endless ranks of castle keeps guarding antiquity.

We scrambled down a slope to the base of the hoodoos, the ground a white-gray color, powdery and frost-heaved, with hummocks of gray-green sage and the occasional cactus. Charlotte told me that in the spring, the coulees turned brilliant with purple, blue and yellow flowers. A while later, the cactus bloomed orange and red. We might see garter snakes, she told me, and fox, deer, coyotes. Cattle wandered down here sometimes. We might find bones.

We did find bones, fossils, fragments of dinosaur skeletons scattered across the hillside. The slopes were covered with washouts of coppery and black-colored rocks fanning down from the hoodoos. Stooping, Charlotte taught me to recognize the blue-black sheen of fossils in the washouts, their textured surface and pocked interior. They were everywhere, mixed with clear quartz crystals that I would later see in the Royal Tyrrell Museum lining the interior of fossils. Some were just fragments, some were clearly the remnants of porous bones.

Albertosaurus, Tyrannosaurus rex. Both were commonly found around here. I picked up one smooth curved fossil that might once have been part of a bone the size of my femur. It was only a few inches long but surprisingly heavy. I'd never held a dinosaur fossil before, having only seen them in museums. It made me remember childhood fantasies about becoming a pale-ontologist or archeologist, which largely grew out of reading about the Leakeys in *National Geographic* and which dissipated when I realized how much time paleontologists spent crawling around on their knees with toothbrushes. I couldn't have found fossils so easily with Charlotte as a kid, or I might never have given up the fantasy.

Illegal to take them. But I rattled some fossils together in my palm, rattling dice that might have fallen differently.

It was a warm day and almost noon, but there was a pleasant breeze blowing, so we decided to scramble further down into the Badlands. Jumping a crevice, we landed on the shady side of the coulee, flushing a white-tailed deer that seemed to leap up the hill-side on springs. We walked downhill on ground-hugging juniper, raising a pungent evergreen scent. Alberta rose grew by the path, wild strawberries underfoot. Moss was everywhere. It was odd to see such a difference in vegetation across such a small gully. But the green soon gave way to heaved white ground again, and we walked between the hoodoos, jumping over dried-up streambeds that Charlotte said were torrents in spring. I recalled some of it now, the moonscape strangeness, the sense of being somewhere challenging, ungiving and closed. It was as if I was remembering childhood itself, and I asked myself if I really wanted to go back.

The breeze trailed off, and the midday sun drilled down as sharp as needles. Charlotte's mother was expecting us for lunch, and we decided to turn back, hiking up slopes that seemed far steeper than they had coming down, especially since I'd left my water bottle in the car and didn't want to drink from Charlotte's. She needed it; she was recovering from pneumonia and probably shouldn't have been out there. But Charlotte was doing far better than I was. I grew parched and had to rest more and more often, the sun baking the back of my hair, my thigh muscles protesting, my eyes aching behind my sunglasses, until we finally reached the car and I poured half the water over my head, drinking the rest down quickly. Yet I still pulled into the town of Munson feeling bleary and unfocused, and found myself unprepared for a couple of things that Charlotte's mother, Irene, had to say.

"What I always heard," she told me, "was that he took the name Sten when he moved onto a new farm. It was the name of the previous owner. That was the way they did it then, the name stayed with the farm."

Irene was Uncle John's daughter, white-haired and stylish in the same matched pastel outfits that my mother favored. She and her husband, Colin, had recently moved to Munson, planting a new double-wide trailer on a lot not far from their son, Ron, and his family. The trailer was still settling and they'd sown potatoes in what would be the front yard, digging a rich vegetable garden out back. Inside, all was spacious and forward-looking, done up in shades of pink and gray. I'd never been in a double-wide before and was impressed by the amount of space, which struck me as truly suburban. Irene encouraged me, ever nosy, to look in all three bedrooms. Yet despite her courtesy, I could tell that she wasn't happy to dredge up the past, finding it unseemly to pick over fossils, to rattle old bones.

"You were going to tell Lesley something about her grandmother," Charlotte finally prompted. "Something about Walter."

Irene crossed her arms, a distressed smile on her face. "It was a Carlson that did it," she said. "It happened after they got here. Auntie Ida was working in the hotel. My father told me, it was a Carlson at the hotel who was responsible."

"What I always heard," my mother insisted, "is that Dad's grandmother brought Granny over because it had already happened. She was being kind. She wanted to help. And you know, I didn't think anyone else knew the story, but in Uncle Walter's obituary, Ann put in that he was born in Sweden. I was so surprised to see it. Here, I'll show you."

She went to look in her bedroom chest but came back empty-handed.

"Do you think I can find it?"

In the local history, the sites of my grandfather's homesteads are given precisely, but his marriage date is serenely fudged. That seems to be true in many of the potted biographies in the book, if you look closely. But the history confirms two suggestive details. Ida worked in the Trochu hotel after arriving in Canada. Uncle John worked in the Vislanda Hotel before leaving Sweden. My mother said she'd always heard Ida had worked there, too.

"The only other thing my Dad ever said was that the Kruegers worked them hard," Irene told me. "He didn't like talking about the past, but he said that when they first got here, the Kruegers worked them hard so they could pay back their passage. They wanted to go home, but they could never get the money together."

The road south of Trochu falls into rich farmland. But in the rain, they wouldn't have seen that. Rolling through the wet and mud, they came seasick to a new country, leaving everything behind. One day that would include us.

5 1

"I DON'T KNOW WHY YOU WANT TO KNOW," MY MOTHER said. "All this old *stuff*."

I'd flown out to Vancouver to see her a few days after the drive. She was eighty but keeping in good health, getting around in a twenty-year-old boat of a car and living most happily in a condo with an excellent view of the mountains and harbor. She'd been traveling quite a bit since my father died, making her first trip to Scotland and England, taking a cruise up the BC coast, going to Barbados, out to the Maritimes—she'd always wanted to see Cape Breton in the autumn—and making repeated visits to Toronto. My brother and his family lived just three blocks away from us, all three grandchildren within easy walking distance. I'd never quite expected my mother to be collecting frequent-flier points; she'd never seemed to like traveling. But I guess her own preferences had been subsumed in my father's driving trips to the Interior.

Sitting on hassocks in her living room, we leafed through the family albums. I'd persuaded her to pull them out again, and she told me all the family birth dates, including my grandfather's in North Dakota. She even remembered that great-grandmother Mary Krueger had died in 1947. Like Uncle John, Mary lived well into her late eighties, dying only a few years before my grand-father Rune, her only son.

As we looked at old photos of the square-faced, square-shouldered Rune, my mother told me a different story about his restlessness. It wasn't just the spiritualism, she said. He was always encountering problems at work, thinking that he'd been slighted. My father said they had to move so often, he never had friends at school like other kids. And they were so poor. Only once, for a happy two-year period, was there enough money for the kids to get some spare change, not quite an allowance, but a reliable event. Another time, they stayed in one place long enough for my grandmother to plant, harvest and sell a crop of potatoes. She earned $176. It was the only money of her own she ever had.

My mother said she had no idea what made Rune that way. His stepfather had been good to him, taking him on a trip to Germany when he was a child, staying long enough that Rune learned German; he spoke it all his life. Mike Krueger probably worked Rune hard, too. But people worked hard then, and fathers routinely beat their children, if that was part of what Uncle John meant. My mother said that Rune beat my father and his brothers, whaled them with his belt, but that my father adored his Pops. One time, not long after my parents got married, my father paid for Granny and Pops to come from Edmonton out to Vancouver for a two-week holiday, but Pops insisted on leaving after a week. My mother said that she'd never seen my father so upset. He came back from the train station almost in tears. There didn't seem to be any particular reason why they left, either. Pops just had to be going. No wonder my father worked at Pacific Press for thirty-five years. While Pops and Granny were in town, they couldn't even afford to buy a loaf of bread.

We looked critically at the oldest pictures, one a wallet-sized black-and-white snapshot of Granny standing in a scrabbly field beside a shorthorn steer, her four children kicking clods nearby.

In another, the children are ranged across the porch of a clapboard house in the city. Walter was supposed to be only seventeen months older than his next brother, Michael, but in both pictures, he's almost a head taller than well-grown Michael and his face looks much more mature. How much older was he? More than four years, if the obituary was right and he was born in Sweden. More than three, if Granny had been pregnant when she rode the mailman's democrat. More than two, according to the story Irene had always heard.

My mother and I brought out the magnifying glass, deciding that more than four years was pushing it, and wondering why Ann had said that he'd been born in Sweden. Because it suggested his looks, his allure, their story? Perhaps, but looking at the pictures, we were unable to agree whether young Walter looked more than two or three years older than Michael. I remembered my father saying that Walter had spent his early years on the Krueger farm, brought up quietly by Mary before joining the rest of the family on their travels. I thought of my Scottish grandmother. Maybe there was another reason Rune kept moving his family around, not just beyond memory, but forgetting.

Walter had been dead for several years by the time we looked at the snapshots, puttering into his eighties before fading; we're a long-lived family, by and large. But Ann had outlasted him, living well into her nineties before dying suddenly of an aneurysm. It turned out that she was a decade older than Walter. My mother had never suspected a thing until Ann's daughter, Pat, invited her to Ann's ninetieth birthday party. Ninety! She'd claimed she was in her seventies! And looked it, her face soft and surprisingly unlined, her hair always coifed, face powdered, neck hidden, her petite frame swathed in designer clothes and furs. When I was a kid, she often sent us boxes of her old clothes, outdated evening gowns and beaded cocktail dresses that my parents usually gave me for dress-up. One time a box arrived when my father was on strike, and we opened it to find Walter's old tuxedo.

"I'm supposed to wear this on the picket line?" my father asked.

My cousin, Pat, laughed when I told her the story. My mother and I had given up on trying to figure out Walter's age on our own and decided to ask Pat about a birth certificate, meeting for tea and cakes in the local mall. Pat was Ann's daughter from her first marriage in England, just a child when they came out to Canada after the war. Meeting again after several years, I thought Pat was starting to look like her mother as I first remembered her, although she was unpretentious and direct in her manner, a tennis player, athletic and tanned, who spent part of each winter at her condo in Hawaii. She had little to say about Walter, who may have been amusing as an uncle, but not as a stepfather. Yet Pat said that she'd be happy to look for his birth certificate among Ann's papers if I thought it would help—which she doubted.

"She shaved a dozen years off her age on their marriage certificate. An official document." Pat shook her head, smiling and confounded. "That was my mother."

"I loved one particular coat she sent," I said. "I wore it for years, all through my teens. Retro by then—a mustard-colored car coat with brown velvet trim and buttons. I haven't got a clue what happened to it. Whatever happens to clothes you don't mean to lose?"

"It sounds like something she would have had. She had such great taste in clothes." The baffled smile. "When we scattered her ashes off the boat, no one knew what to say."

Back home in Toronto, I wrote to the North Dakota Department of Health requesting a copy of my grandfather's birth certificate, giving the date that my mother remembered.

"We have thoroughly searched our state wide alphabetical index under variations of the surname," came the reply, "as well as the Williams County records on and around October 12 for the years 1889, 1890 and 1891. We did not find a birth certificate registered for Rune Haughlund or Krueger."

Shortly afterward, Walter's birth certificate arrived—or at least a photocopy of a copy issued in 1947, before he and Ann got married. It gave the birth date from the official family story, 1914, which would have made Walter a little more than a year older than Michael. His place of birth is given as Trochu, his father as Rune Krueger, born in Wisconsin.

"Fake," my mother said.

"So many people of that generation found out later they were a year older than they thought," Charlotte said.

A family of strong women, I thought, and wacky fictions.

"You're not going to write about this, are you?" my mother asked.

5 2

MY CREATIVE WRITING STUDENTS ARE DISCUSSING A STORY that one of their classmates has written about a woman who makes a radical change in her life.

"My only problem with the story is that your character seems so self-aware," one woman says. "Usually when I'm doing something, I'm flailing around, I don't know what I'm trying to accomplish. Then, three years later, I'm standing on a street corner and I'm like, 'Omigod, *that's* what I was up to. I had no idea.'"

"That's been my experience precisely," a man agrees. "There was a time, a city boy, when I moved to the country for five and a half years without ever realizing what a mistake I was making. Then I got back. I was standing on the corner of Bloor and Yonge and it hit me. What the hell had I been doing?"

The question of intentions, Dad. I never intended to be a teacher. I never intended to rebel against you by not becoming a teacher. I've simply tried to live a full life by taking advantage of opportunities as they arose, and only started looking for things like intention, pattern and meaning very recently. Now I pick them out in retrospect, just like my students. Tell me one thing, Dad. Were they there before I looked?

5 3

THE NIGHT BEFORE HER DAUGHTER'S WEDDING, CHARLOTTE and I sat upstairs in the kitchen, staid matrons now, while Cheryl and her bridesmaids took over the rec room in the basement. Hilarious giggles rippled upstairs, the electronic cluck and chitter of Nintendo, the smell of nail polish and of nail-polish remover. The groomsmen had taken the groom, Wayne, out for his stag—a game of paintball. They were all clean-cut kids, almost all of them Mormons who'd recently graduated from high school, the girls notably coltish and feisty, beautiful young women with clear eyes and glowing skin, the boys somehow calmer, the type of self-contained young men who come to the door in dark pants and white shirts holding out pamphlets about the Church of Jesus Christ of Latter-day Saints.

Knowing that I'd be attending a Mormon wedding, at least the civil ceremony, I'd been reading up on the church. Meaning no disrespect to the people I met, who were genial, industrious and good-living, I found the theology impossible, with its insistence on the subordination of women, and a long-standing doctrine of white supremacy that was rescinded only recently, and as far as Indian people are concerned, only in part. Still, it was fascinating to read about the emergence of a homegrown church on the American frontier, with Mormon prophet Joseph Smith spending his youth digging up the burial mounds of ancient native corn-growing peoples to the south of the Great Lakes, later creating his own religious doctrine out of early-nineteenth-century archeological theories, appropriating the formerly wide-spread belief that American Indians are actually descendants of a lost tribe of Israel to write his Book of Mormon—some critics call it a novel—about the tribe sailing out of the Red Sea to populate the Americas, a light-skinned people whose skins turned dark when evil triumphed among them, and whom Mormons feel they must convert back to righteousness to ensure the Second Coming of Christ.

So that's why they try to adopt Indian kids, I thought. The books called it the first truly American religion, not least for its emphasis on upward mobility and self-improvement. Mormons could even improve after death, ruling over more and more of their own planets until the most enlightened among them—at least among the men—achieved equal status with God. Meanwhile, their wives bore children unto Eternity, sealed into polygamous postmortem marriages.

I think the good people sensed that I wasn't a potential convert. But I'd gone with them to the ward house that afternoon for the wedding rehearsal, their local church, pulling up to the low-slung building on a curving main street of Airdrie, just across from the creek. It was a new structure and cleanly designed, with little ornamentation. Inside the front door was a single framed painting of a pensive brown-haired Jesus, an airbrushed hippie just like the Christ figure that I'd grown up with in the United Church, his picture spotlit by a halogen bulb so radiant his pink cheeks shimmered.

Behind the portrait was the hall where Cheryl and Wayne would be married. A folding barrier closed off the back half of the room, which would be thrown open for the wedding and filled with chairs, its basketball hoops tucked up toward the ceiling. The front part was neat with pale wood, carpeting and pews, the main body of the room commanded by a raised altar—I don't know if that's the right word—like a stage receding in ranked platforms away from the congregation, windowless and backed by teal- and maroon-colored laminate. Guarding the front of the altar were a series of simple wooden panels depicting stylized human figures, rows of little round heads on top of long rectangular bodies that looked rather like hoodoos, but which I thought from their number must represent the Eleven, the governing council of the church. The only other decorations were a few cloth plants. No art, but plenty of money. The room reminded me of a lecture hall in a modern American university with a substantial endowment.

My job was to do some modest decorating, helping the bridesmaids tape ribbons to the pews. Kneeling in the aisle, I remembered spelling out "Charlotte and Lyle" in tissue-paper carnations on a banner for their reception almost twenty-six years before. This time, the work was quickly completed, and I sat down with a hymnal as the bishop bounded in to direct the rehearsal—an energetic balding blond man elected as minister by the congregation. Thumbing through the book, I found many of the hymns and Christmas carols familiar, but others must have expressed Mormon theology and were designated for either men or women to sing. Each was accompanied by a one-word exhortation: vigorously, joyously, peacefully, earnestly.

I thought of my father's vigorous question as my mother brought us back from church: "You planning on letting them fool you?" I remembered the peaceful Buddhist monks, wondering again if the teacher had cured me, pictured Geraldo, the *pai-de-santo*, and my earnest friend Estela with her tarot cards, even Charlotte's wedding mass, a resonating ceremony so long that one bridesmaid fainted. It occurred to me that all my life, in searching out travelers and seekers and outsiders, I'd also been meeting believers, people who said yes, there is a pattern to life before you start to look for it, an underlying purpose to be revealed. I loved many of the old Christian hymns myself but still felt that my own private hymnal would be marked with words like doubtingly, hesitantly, ambiguously, skeptically. Despite all my travels, I still hadn't arrived at any conclusion, and wondered if I'd learned anything at all.

The wedding was the next afternoon, family and friends filling the hall for the brief civil ceremony. The religious service would be held later at a temple, a closed gathering in which Cheryl and Wayne would be sealed into marriage for eternity, cleansed and dressed by church elders in the type of sacred underclothing sewn with symbols of fertility and silence that they would wear throughout their lives. I picked up the hymnal again as we waited for the wedding party to enter the hall, opening it this time on a Mormon hymn, "Arise Ye Saints and Temples Enter," reading it absentmindedly until I reached the last lines of the first verse: "Seal in everlasting circles, all our loved ones quick and dead."

I shivered with claustrophobia as the bridesmaids entered the hall, knowing that the hymn was the expression of a Mormon belief that church members could baptize their ancestors, bringing their souls from a lower circle of heaven to the highest, but feeling repelled by the idea of circles and sealing and entrapment. As the lovely girls formed a line before the altar, their green dresses subtle in the indirect light, I watched the groomsmen shifting shyly into place and wanted nothing more than to leave, hit the road, push off, my gut clenching as if I were slipping down a muddy slope.

I put away the hymnal and clasped my hands tightly, only looking up as Cheryl walked down the aisle in her full white gown, veiled and carrying flowers, reaching the altar just as Wayne stepped up beside her with such a look of hope on his young face that my gut unclenched, and I found myself silly with tears.

Behind her veil, Cheryl looked so much like her mother, smaller, but with the same soft round face and dimple in her chin, light eyes that glimmered as she looked up at Wayne. I remembered Charlotte at the altar with the same expression of trust on her face and thought not of closed circles but of the complex double helix of genes and memory that bound us into family, the circle that never closes.

Caught in everlasting spirals, I thought, able to accept that much.

The ceremony was short, a homespun prayer offered by a woman congregant, a homily from a friend of Wayne's family, the bishop's quick blessing. Afterward, in the receiving line, I clasped Cheryl lightly in her stiff dress, her hopeful new role, as behind us, the strong women of our family wept their congratulations and sent her off on her life's journey.

5 4

AT NIGHT, AFTER TEACHING, I CAN'T SLEEP AND END UP thinking about the criticisms that Europeans make of creative writing programs. It's part of a North American obsession with self-improvement, they say, an expression of the myth of perfectibility, the idea that you can be anything you want to be, even, God help you, a writer.

Rubbish, they say. You can't learn talent. Either you have it or you don't.

It's true that some of my students are far more talented than others. Some will go on to be published writers, most won't. But I don't think that very many of them are fooled about their abilities, any more than most people who take skiing lessons believe that they'll compete in the Olympics. They enjoy it, they hope to learn something, why not? I figure that I can probably show them a few shortcuts to effective writing, save them some of the time it's taken me to get this far myself.

Imagination. Setting. Plot, I write, wondering why the Europeans dismiss our obsessive self-improving culture. I find it riveting, myself, to ask why so many people feel compelled to write, why they feel compelled to travel, why I've felt compelled to both write and travel.

We're all writing our lives, I think. That's what traveling is, and what writing is: an act of self-creation. I think that when we travel, we're creating ourselves, calling ourselves into being out of a confusing mass of impulses and impressions, just as the Ancestors created Time and Space by stopping one day in their ceaseless journey to ask, Why don't we sleep here tonight?

Are you sleeping, Dad? I've been thinking lately about those Sunday drives that you used to take us on when we were kids. You chain-smoked as I tried to breathe through a crack in the window, developing a lifelong aversion to smoking as you drove us through the Fraser Valley, or out to the airport to watch the planes taking off and landing. A couple of times in the past few years, I've smelled cigarette smoke in the car when I've been driving some-where late at night on my own. Both times, I've known that if I turned my head, I would see you sitting beside me, and the thought has been so alarming that I've jolted upright in my seat. Until then I'd been falling asleep at the wheel.

I wonder if any of this is connected to something my brother told me, something that you told him. After the war, when you were getting divorced, you locked yourself in your father's garage and turned on the car engine, sitting in the driver's seat and breathing carbon monoxide until you slumped. Pops found you and pulled you out, slapped you awake, took you to the hospital.

Was that when you had the idea about going back and looking for the second daughter's birth record? Or when you crossed out "honorable" on your discharge papers?

There are so many faked papers in our family, so much rewriting, so much fiction. Or maybe that's just the way I see it, the patterns that I read into things, and other people see it all differently. I'm sure they see it very differently, which is what makes life such a brilliant spiral.

I never intended to write about any of this. It's just what happened.

ACKNOWLEDGEMENTS

FOUR YEARS AGO, I RECEIVED A SURPRISING REQUEST. LINDA Spalding, editor of *Brick* magazine, asked me to write anything I wanted to about Mexico—a dream assignment that eventually led to this book.

My thanks go out to Linda for her inspiration and encouragement, as well as to my agent, Jan Whitford, and editor, Susan Renouf, for shepherding the book into print. Along the way, my friend Cynthia Holz gave the manuscript an incisive and invaluable reading.

I also owe a great debt to my traveling companions over the years, as well as to my family and the many fascinating people I met in distant cities. I have used pseudonyms for some to protect their privacy and for others because we've lost touch, but I hope that the people mentioned here don't mind being named with enormous gratitude for their friendship, insight and forbearance. Any mistakes in the manuscript are, of course, my responsibility and not theirs.

My great thanks go to Sherry Brydson, Ann Ireland, Laura and Carlos López, Frances Lowndes, Paul Macrae, Paul Mylrea, Rod Mickleburgh, P.K. Page, Darryl and Yvonne Pevie, Adriana Ramos, Carminha Stalker, Danny Stoffman, Doug Trent and Sue Vohanka.

In my family, my enormous thanks and any necessary apologies go to my mother, Isabel Krueger, my uncle, Douglas Bruce, my aunt, Marg Richardson, and cousins Charlotte and Lyle Heck, Kirsten Jonsson, Pat Macleod and Colin and Irene Storch. While this book was being written, we lost my most dear aunt, Margaret Bruce, to cancer, along with Sandra Gwyn, mentor and friend, who introduced me to Yvonne and Labrador. Yvonne and Darryl's daughter, Sarah Pevie, and Charlotte's granddaughter, Emma Stephenson, were born.

I'd like to thank The Japan Foundation for the fellowship that took me to Tokyo, Kyoto and Aomori. My trip to Labrador was underwritten by *Today's Parent* magazine, where editors Fran Fearnley and Linda Lewis showed a lively interest in a part of the country seldom visited by journalists. I would also like to thank the Ontario Arts Council for invaluable funding provided during the writing of this book.

Part three, *Faultlines*, originally appeared in *Brick* in a slightly different form.

My greatest thanks, as always, go to my dear husband, Paul Knox, and to my son, Gabe Knox, for their constant support.